D1484003

Toward Rediscovering The Old Testament

Other books by the same author:

Classical Evangelical Essays in Old Testament Interpretation (editor)

The Old Testament in Contemporary Preaching

Toward an Old Testament Theology

Ecclesiastes: Total Life

Toward an Exegetical Theology: Biblical Exegesis for Preaching and Teaching

A Biblical Approach to Personal Suffering: On Lamentations

Toward Old Testament Ethics

Malachi: God's Unchanging Love

The Uses of the Old Testament in the New

Quest for Renewal: Personal Revival in the Old Testament

Quality Living: Bible Studies in Ecclesiastes

A Tribute to Gleason Archer: Essays in Old Testament Studies (co-editor with Ronald Youngblood)

Have You Seen the Power of God Lately? Studies in the Life of Elijah

Exodus in The Expositor's Bible Commentary

Toward Rediscovering The Old Testament

Walter C. Kaiser, Jr.

Academie
Books
Grand Rapids,
Michigan
Zondervan Publishing House

TOWARD REDISCOVERING THE OLD TESTAMENT
Copyright © 1987 by Walter C. Kaiser, Jr.

ACADEMIE BOOKS
is an imprint of
Zondervan Publishing House
1415 Lake Drive S.E.
Grand Rapids, Michigan 49506

Library of Congress Cataloging in Publication Data
Kaiser, Walter C.
  Toward rediscovering the Old Testament.

  Bibliography: p.
  1. Bible. O.T.—Theology. 2. Bible. O.T.—Evidences, authority, etc.
3. Bible. O.T.—Canon. 4. Bible. N.T.—Relation to the Old Testament.
I. Title.
BS1192.5.K33 1987   220.1   86-32420
ISBN 0-310-37120-1

Edited by Lyman Rand Tucker, Jr.

Printed in the United States of America

87 88 89 90 91 92 93 94 95 / AF / 10 9 8 7 6 5 4 3 2 1

To my colleagues
in the Department of
Old Testament and Semitic Studies

Gleason L. Archer, Jr.
Barry J. Beitzel
Thomas E. McComiskey
Dennis R. Magary
Samir B. Massouh (part-time)
John N. Oswalt
John H. Sailhamer

לְךָ יְהוָה
הַגְּדֻלָּה
וְהַגְּבוּרָה
וְהַתִּפְאֶרֶת
וְהַנֵּצַח
וְהַהוֹד
כִּי־כֹל בַּשָּׁמַיִם וּבָאָרֶץ

לְךָ יְהוָה
הַמַּמְלָכָה
וְהַמִּתְנַשֵּׂא
לְכֹל לְרֹאשׁ

1 Chronicles 29:11

Contents

Preface

How should the Christian church in the midst of the modern world understand and appropriate the significance of the Old Testament? It is no exaggeration to claim that this question outranks every other problem in biblical interpretation; it is *the* problem in Christian theology. The manner in which this question is solved affects every other area of theology in one way or another. Therefore, we can pose no more fundamental question in all of theology: the answer to this problem will leave its mark in every realm where we formulate and act out our theology.

This book belongs to a specific, emerging genre of books. It is not an introduction to the Old Testament in the sense that it takes up the questions of higher and lower criticism—date, authorship, purpose, canonicity, etc.—although it does touch on the general question of canonicity. Likewise, it is not a survey of the contents and characters, nor is it a biblical theology, attempting to record the historical development of doctrines in each of their continuing epochs. It cannot, moreover, be classified as a hermeneutics book that discusses the general theory of understanding and then applies that theory to special literary forms found in the Old Testament.

Our task is a different one. There is a new corpus of theological writing represented by works such as *Sens chrétien de l'ancien Testament* (by Pierre Grelot in 1962), *L'Actualité chrétienne de l'ancien Testament* (by C. Larcher in 1962), *The Old Testament and Christian Faith* (ed. Bernhard W. Anderson in 1963), *Understanding the Old Testament* (by A. H. J. Gunneweg in 1978), *Approaches to Old Testament Interpretation* (by John Goldingay in 1981) or *The Relevance of the Old Testament for the*

9

Christian Faith (by S. M. Mayo in 1982). Like them, we have set out to describe how Christians may once again find meaning, relevance, and direction from that part of the canon that all too many believers all too frequently have summarily rejected as a source of any Christian guidance for faith or life. This mental and literary block is not limited to the laity; it probably exists in more massive proportions among the clergy, many of whom would do almost anything—yea, would rather die—than attempt to teach or preach from an Old Testament passage! Meanwhile, over three-fourths (someone has said it is about 77.2 percent) of the biblical canon, which many espouse as the source of their authority for addressing Christ's church, is left begging for exposition and proclamation.

Our concern is first of all historical: how has the church up to the modern era handled the problem of the relevance of the Old Testament? Will we not be doomed to repeat the errors of the past if we do not learn from history?

Second, we are enthusiastic about the hermeneutical questions that bring the Old Testament and Christians into closer alignment with one another. All too frequently the Old Testament receives short shrift because the text has not been exegeted with enough patience in its own right before the interpreter flees to the sanctuary of the New Testament text that presumably (or actually) parallels the idea expressed in the older Testament. Therefore, we have tried patiently to weed out much that was ephemeral, trite, or just plain incorrect. Among the texts that belong to this class are Genesis 15:6 and Zechariah 12:10. But we have not neglected to raise the same issues in the New Testament; therefore, we have treated in detail such great texts as John 14:16–17 and Romans 11:11–12, 26.

Our third concern is theological. It is one thing to affirm that the Old Testament has authority over us as Christians, but it is a totally different question to spell out *how* we shall recognize that authority and *what* the contents of that authority are for us today. The second, that is, the "material question," is far more difficult than the first, the "formal question," but the history of the Christian church is replete with examples of how central the solution of this problem of the Old Testament is to building a proper theology.

We have dared to ask some of the most difficult theological questions that a Christian can put to the Old Testament. Each bristles with potentiality for bitter dispute among equally sincere believers. Nevertheless, our confidence in the Reformation principle of *sola Scriptura* forces us to "keep our finger on the text of

10

Scripture" as we consider such questions as: What was the exact object of Abraham's faith? Was it just God in general or did he also believe in the only name under heaven by which men and women can be saved? How effective were the sacrifices and the forgiveness of the Old Testament? Were the sins of those forgiven merely relegated to a cover-up (in the Watergate sense of "cover-up")? Or did the believers of olden days truly experience forgiveness and the removal of their guilt and of their sins? What was the believer's experience of the Holy Spirit in Old Testament days if Jesus held Nicodemus accountable for knowing about the new birth and the work of the Holy Spirit? What was the prospect of life after death for those who lived then? Were there any Jews who really understood the teaching about the person, work of redemption, and two comings of the Messiah prior to Jesus's life, work, and explanation in the New Testament? Can the Christian honestly believe that the promise of the land of Israel to the Jew is still part of the everlasting covenant still in effect today without being thought of as having a weird cultic or unorthodox mind-set? How relevant, if at all, are the various Old Testament laws to our situation today? By what method, or dint of reason, dare we presume that any of us can sort out what is normative and what is culturally contextualized among such a plethora of laws? These are just a sample of the types of theological questions we have set before ourselves in this work.

For all its selectivity, this volume should be more than just a nudge in the right direction for Christians who have puzzled over one or more of these issues. We have attempted to address not only scholars but also the whole church. Thus, the topics range from the practical issues of personal application and relevance to more complicated theoretical and academic concerns, such as the history of methodologies of historical criticism. But neither laypeople nor the clergy should overlook the practical importance of even such remote and complicated matters as critical methodologies. Given the history of the success of many of these methods in their unexpurgated forms, they pose as much a threat to the church as does our general neglect of the Old Testament. Therefore, we plead for the genuine involvement of all people of the church in the critical questions, no matter how difficult the going, for on the answers to these questions hangs the future of the church in the West!

Therefore, with great joy we commend to you, our readers, this new genre on the Old Testament. It is our prayer that the volume may not fall stillborn on the church, but that it may result in a holy and vigorous response that leads to the restoration of the Old Testament to its proper place in the hearts and lives of Christ's followers.

All that remains is for me to thank my wife, Margaret Ruth, for her faithful labor of love with me as she translated my strange script onto the more readable computer discs. I am also deeply grateful to my President, Dr. Kenneth Meyer, and to the Board of Directors of Trinity Evangelical School of Deerfield, Illinois, who graciously granted me an administrative sabbatical so I could begin research and writing on this project. I also appreciate the additional duties that were assumed by Dr. Warren Benson (my associate vice president), Mrs. Lois Armstrong (my secretary and administrative assistant), and David Sullivan (my graduate assistant). Without these friends, and the help of our Lord, this work would never have been completed. I remain in their debt and now in your debt, my reader.

Soli Deo gloria!

Chapter 1

The Old Testament
as *the* Christian Problem

"The Old Testament problem . . . is not just one of many. It is the master problem of theology," according to Emil G. Kraeling.[1] For when the question is put in its most elementary form, the real problem of the Old Testament (hereafter OT) for the Christian is this: should the OT have any authority in the Christian church, and, if so, how is that authority to be defined?

The centrality of this question for the Christian cannot be avoided. The fact is that "Once one has awakened to the commanding importance of this question one will be able to see that it runs through the whole of Christian history like a scarlet thread. Yea, more: one can see that much of the difference in theologies springs from the extent to which they build Old Testament ideas or impulses into the primitive Christian patterns."[2]

A. H. J. Gunneweg echoed a similar assessment and declared that this problem is the most central issue in all of Christian theology. In his judgment, " . . . it would be no exaggeration to understand the hermeneutical problem of the Old Testament as *the*

[1] Emil G. Kraeling, *The Old Testament Since the Reformation* (New York: Harper, 1955), 8.
[2] Ibid., 7.

13

problem of Christian theology, and not just one problem among others, seeing that all other questions of theology are affected in one way or another by its resolution. . . . No more fundamental question can be posed in all theology; providing an answer for it defines the realm in which theology has to be done."[3]

No less adamant in expressing this same view was Bernhard W. Anderson: "No problem more urgently needs to be brought to a focus . . . . It is a question which confronts every Christian in the Church, whether he [or she] be a professional theologian, a pastor of a congregation, or a lay[person]. It is no exaggeration to say that on this question hangs the meaning of the Christian faith."[4]

THE SIGNIFICANCE OF THE OT
AS *THE* CHRISTIAN PROBLEM

Christians must face two issues in this problem of the OT: (1) the formal question: does the OT have authority for us as Christians? and (2) the material question: *how* shall we recognize that authority, and what are the *contents* of that authority for us today? The first question of the Scripture principle is relatively easy compared with the more difficult practical and substantive questions as to how the OT will yield the mind and will of God for the twentieth-century Christian.

So demanding have these questions been that some have been led to adopt the oft-quoted thesis of Adolf Harnack (1851–1930):

> To reject the Old Testament in the second century was a mistake the church rightly resisted; to retain it in the sixteenth century was a fate from which the Reformation could not escape; but still to preserve it in the nineteenth century as one of the canonical documents of Protestantism is the result of religious and ecclesiastical paralysis.[5]

Harnack's solution was summarily to reject the OT. But it was that view (assisted by the racial anti-Semitism of Gobineau and Chamberlain, the anti-supernaturalism of the scientific criticism of

---

[3]A. H. J. Gunneweg, *Understanding the Old Testament* (Philadelphia: Westminster, 1978), 2.

[4]Bernhard W. Anderson, *The Old Testament and Christian Faith* (New York: Harper and Row, 1963), 1.

[5]Adolf Harnack, *Marcion, Das Evangelium vom fremden Gott* (Leipzig: 1921), 248f. (Eng. trans. mainly from Geoffrey W. Bromiley in Arnold A. van Ruler, *The Christian Church and the Old Testament* (Grand Rapids: Eerdmans, 1971), 10.

the OT by Friederick Delitzsch, and the anti-Christian cultural criticism of F. Nietzsche) that led to the infamous Sport Palace demonstration of Berlin German Christians on November 13, 1933. There the district chairman, R. Krause, demanded "the liberation from the Old Testament with its Jewish money morality, [and] from the stories of livestock handlers and pimps."[6]

With these words the battle against the OT was launched anew in pre-World War II Germany and eventually led to the atrocities against the Jews and to silencing of the OT message in the German church.

But few Christians have opted for such a total disparagement of the OT as did the second century A.D. heretic Marcion or the twentieth century spokesman Adolf Harnack. Surely Harnack was involved in special pleading when he opined that the OT had to be rejected because "the largest number of objections which people raise against Christianity and the truthfulness of the Church stem from the authority which the Church still gives to the Old Testament."[7]

Nor had the view of Friedrich Schleiermacher (1768–1834) been any less disparaging:

> The Old Testament Scriptures owe their place in our Bible partly to the appeals the New Testament Scriptures make to them, partly to the historical connection of Christian worship with the Jewish synagogue; but the Old Testament Scriptures do not on that account share the normative dignity or the inspiration of the New.[8]

The easy reductionism exhibited in Schleiermacher failed to face either the formal or material question; it simply relegated the OT to an appendix behind the new standard of the later twenty-seven books of Scripture.

But the view of Marcion, Schleiermacher, and Harnack were not those that had been embraced by the church since apostolic days. Beginning with the NT, the permanent value of the OT was repeatedly affirmed with explicit statements. Some of the summary statements declared:

---

[6]Reported from J. Gauger, *Chronik der Kirchenwirren*, 1935, 109, in Martin Kuske, *The Old Testament as the Book of Christ: An Appraisal of Bonhoeffer's Interpretation*, trans. S. T. Kimbrough, Jr. (Philadelphia: Westminster, 1976), 7–8.

[7]Harnack, *Marcion*, 254; trans. S. T. Kimbrough, Jr., in Kuske, *The Old Testament*, 11.

[8]Friedrich Schleiermacher, *The Christian Faith* ([Ger. ed. 1830²] E.T., Edinburgh: 1928), sec. 132.

> Do not think [apparently, some had thought so] that I have come to abolish the Law or the Prophets; I have not come to abolish them but to fulfill them. I tell you the truth, until heaven and earth disappear, not the smallest letter, not the least stroke of a pen, will by any means disappear from the Law until everything is accomplished (Matt 5:17–18).

Again:

> For everything that was written in the past was written to teach us, so that through endurance and the encouragement of the Scriptures we might have hope (Rom 15:4).

And:

> These things happened to them as examples and were written down as warnings for us, on whom the fulfillment of the ages has come (1 Cor 10:11).

Or:

> ... continue in what you have learned and have become convinced of, because you know those from whom you learned it. And how from infancy you have known the holy Scriptures [i.e. the OT], which are able to make you wise for salvation through faith in Christ Jesus. All Scripture is God-breathed and is useful for teaching, rebuking, correcting and training in righteousness, so that the man of God may be thoroughly equipped for every good work (2 Tim 3:14–17).

These positive assessments of the OT continued in the various Protestant creeds and confessions at the time of the Reformation. For example, Article VII of *The Thirty-nine Articles of the Church of England* (1563) read:

> The olde Testament is not contrary to the newe, for both in the olde and newe Testament everlasting lyfe is offered to mankynde by Christe, who is the onlye mediator between God and man. Wherefore they are not to be hearde which faigne that the olde fathers dyd look only for transitorie promises ...

Likewise the *Scots Confession* (1560) in section IV confessed:

> ... all the faithfull from Adam to Noe [Noah], from Noe to Abraham, from Abraham to David and so furth to the incarnation of Christ Jesus, all (we meane the faithfull Fathers under the Law) did see the joyful daie of Christ Jesus, and did rejoice.

16

No less specific was chapter VII of *The Westminster Confession of Faith* (1647), which said that OT believers "had full remission of sins and eternal salvation" by faith in the promises of Messiah.

No matter how great the uniformity of opinion has been from the NT writers down to the Reformation, and no matter how great the difficulties in answering the formal and material questions posed here, the OT remains the most central and decisive problem for Christian theology. How we respond to this problem will automatically set much of our Christian theology—whether we do so in a deliberate or in an unreflective fashion.

The implications of this move in theological construction are massive. Arnold van Ruler warns that our answers to this problem will decide:

> ... how we understand Jesus Christ in his historical character, his Jewish context, and his divine validation. It decides the church's view of itself as the church of God, as an element in the *mystērion* of God's saving action in history. It decides our interpretation of the salvation given us in Jesus Christ, ... our estimate of earthly and temporal life. ... It concerns ... the relation of the church of Jesus Christ to the chosen people of Israel. Our whole understanding of the Kingdom of God—and therefore also of the catholicity of the Christian faith, the Christian church, and Christianity—is determined by what we think of the Old Testament and how we handle it.[9]

Thus, it is difficult to think of very many areas of Christian theology that are not affected in a major way, either by the inclusion or the deliberate omission of the OT data from its systematization. Moreover, when it is recalled that *over* three-fourths of the total Bible is found in the OT, it is enough to make one pause before cavalierly bypassing this most extensive record of God's revelation to mankind.

By any fair reckoning, it is impossible to teach the "whole counsel of God" (Acts 20:27 KJV) without deeply involving oneself in the details of OT life and thought. Those who choose to describe or teach the Christian life and doctrine without ever drinking deeply of the teaching in the OT usually commit one of two prominent mistakes some Christians have perpetuated down through the centuries: (1) the mistake of omission, whereby seedbeds for future deviation from Christian teachings are left open

---

[9] Van Ruler, *The Christian Church*, 10.

by the vacuum created in neglecting to teach those parts of the OT that are not repeated or explicated as fully in the NT, and (2) the mistake of imbalance, whereby the holistic emphasis on temporal and spiritual becomes lopsided because only the last one-fourth of God's revelation is made the whole yardstick by which we measure norms. This last error in its more exaggerated forms has led at times to either a Christoexclusivism or a spiritual monism that fails to develop such things as a full doctrine of God, a theology of culture, or a theology of the Kingdom—which is both realized and future, terrestrial and supraterrestrial.

THE REASON THE OT IS *THE* CHRISTIAN PROBLEM

While every age in the Christian era has faced the problem of the OT, the reasons for the existence of the problem have not always been the same. For example, a clash developed early in the life of the young church. Some brethren from Antioch came down to Judea with this teaching: "Unless you are circumcised according to the custom taught by Moses, you cannot be saved" (Acts 15:1).

All at once the problem of the relevance of the OT was thrust on the new group of believers. But it is to the credit of the church's leadership that James was able to bring an authoritative basis for deciding on the relevance of such teaching to the church's contemporary needs in the first century A.D. For after noting that the relational and experiential theologies of Peter and Paul (based on their testimony of their experiences) failed to persuade the hopelessly divided and bitterly distraught audience, James boldly pointed to the OT word found in Amos 9:11–12. This passage clearly indicated that the salvation of the Gentiles, indeed this inclusion in the very "house" of David (tottering and dilapidated as it was in danger of becoming in the days of Amos—"David's falling tent"), was part of God's eternal plan.[10] James's conclusion was, "It is my judgment, therefore, that we should not make it difficult for the Gentiles who are turning to God. Instead we should write to them, telling them to abstain from food polluted by idols, from sexual immorality, from the meat of strangled animals and from blood. For Moses has been preached in every city from the earliest times and is read in the synagogues on every Sabbath" (Acts 15:19–21). Thus the problem of legalism was met and solved.

---

[10]Walter C. Kaiser, Jr., "Including the Gentiles in the Plan of God," in *The Uses of the Old Testament in the New* (Chicago: Moody, 1985), 177–94.

But in the second century the tension between the OT and the church once again surfaced, this time under the leadership of the great heretic Marcion. Marcion was a wealthy shipowner from Sinope in Pontus (northeast Asia Minor) who was an active church member until he was excommunicated ca. A.D. 144. For him the OT was to be totally rejected and its God declared the *demiurge,* an inferior being who created and ruled over the world but who was not good in the same sense that the God and Father of the NT was.

While none of his writings have survived, we can construct large portions of his *Antitheses* from the extensive quotations found in Tertullian's work *Against Marcion.* Marcion vigorously sets forth the self-contradictory nature of OT revelation. The gospel was entirely new and had nothing that preceded it or with which to compare it. In fact, he began his *Antitheses* (based on Pauline phrases):

> O wealth of riches! Folly, power, and ecstacy!—Seeing there can be nothing to say about it, or to imagine about it, or to compare it to!

Marcion strongly (and in our judgment, rightfully) attacked the use of allegorization. But his purpose was to avoid difficult passages in the OT; and for him, each new difficulty was another reason why the church should pay no attention either to the OT or to the God of the OT. And while many of the difficulties he discussed were real, he was not beneath stooping to introduce trivial and contrived difficulties as well—e.g. when he argued that the God of Adam was ignorant and had to ask in the Garden of Eden, "Where art thou?" (Gen 3:9 KJV).

He did, however, retain the OT narratives, but this was merely to point up the *Antitheses* between law and grace. Robert M. Grant[11] observed in this connection that Marcion's reevaluation of history is the same as that of the Cainites, an obscure sect described by the church father Irenaeus. For the Cainites, the real heroes of the OT were Cain, Esau, Korah, and the people of Sodom. They in turn were hated by the evil creator-god because he could not harm them, for Judas had revealed this mystery in his act of betraying Jesus. The God of the OT seemed both powerless to move against his enemies and distorted in his values when his

---

[11]Robert M. Grant, "The Place of the Old Testament in Early Christianity," *Interpretation* 5 (1951): 195–96.

favorites exhibited a lower standard of morality than did his foes. This convoluted history of the Cainites went this way:

> Cain and those who are like him and the Sodomites and the Egyptians and those who are like them, and absolutely all the nations which walked in every combination of wickedness, were saved by the Lord when he descended to Hades, and they hastened to him and he took them up into his kingdom. But Abel and Enoch and Noah and the rest of the righteous and the patriarchs about Abraham, with all the prophets and those who pleased God, did not share in Salvation. . . . For they knew that their God was always tempting them, and suspecting that he was tempting them at that time they did not hasten to Jesus nor did they believe his proclamation; and therefore their souls remained in Hades.[12]

Toward the middle and second half of that same second Christian century, a similar attack on the OT was launched by some Ebionites. Our chief informant on this aberration is Epiphanius.[13]

The Ebionites rejected David and all the prophets but held to the one true prophet, who, changing form and name, continued appearing down through the ages, now as Adam, now as Moses, now as Christ, but always restoring truth where it had been lost or corrupted by others. This one true prophet was sinless, omniscient, immortal, and able to foreknow all things.

Over against this one true, male prophet, claimed the Ebionites, stood Eve, the introducer of sin, error, death, and *female* (or false) prophecy. To her is attributed all lust, war, greed, unchastity, idolatry, sacrifice, etc. In fact, everything in the OT that is unworthy of God or gives a distorted representation of him—including the sins of the patriarchs, the approval of sacrifice, the practice of polygamy, the murders, and all similar acts—are all part of the errors introduced by her!

In some ways, what is proposed here is not very different from some modern minimalistic attitudes: it is " . . . to test the parts of the Old Testament which show marks of imperfection, error, or defective morality, by reference to the underlying unity of revelation, which is assumed to be true, pure, and consentaneous throughout, and the ultimate touchstone of which is the perfect

---

[12] Irenaeus, *Against Heresies,* ed. W. W. Harvey, 2 vols. (Cantabrigiae: typis academicis, 1857), 1.27.2 (the best complete edition to date).
[13] James Orr, "The Old Testament Question in the Early Church," *The Expositor,* 5th ser., 1 (1895): 347–53.

teaching of Jesus Christ."[14] The problem with all such solutions is twofold: (1) it presumes its criticism of what constitutes imperfection, error, and defective morality is itself infallible, and (2) it presumes that what has been isolated as the whole, even though it is intermingled in the "erroneous" parts, is perfectly isolated and is in and of itself automatically useable by all readers of the text as an absolute divining rod to separate the good from the bad. But this presumes an inspiration or revelation for each reader in each generation that is at least as noble as that which these objectors have denied to the autograph!

Ebionism was not the most difficult challenge the church faced, however. The single most precarious crisis precipitated in the second century, or in any age, was that of Gnosticism. In the balance hung the question of whether Christianity would be derived from a body of revealed doctrines or whether it could be the result of countless emanations and a chaos of speculations.[15] Orr recounts:

> In the bewildering variety of Gnostic systems, no feature is more constant than the distinction perpetually made between the Demiurge [postulated in the OT] ... and the Supreme God revealed in the fulness of time by Christ. So essential does this feature appear to Neander, that he uses it (Baur also to some extent) as the principle of his classification of the Gnostic systems, dividing them according to the attitude they severally take up [sic] to the Old Testament, viz., whether their attitude is one of pure negation, or whether they recognize a certain subordinate worth in the Old Testament revelation.[16]

Regardless of the class of Gnosticism, however, it was alleged that the two Testaments came from two different gods, the OT being decidedly inferior, limited, and morally deficient.

Many of the movements of the modern era return to the heretical Gnostics for their roots, for the Gnostics were the first to impugn the integrity and genuineness of the Pentateuch, the normativity of the moral instructions of the law, and more. In Gnosticism's more speculative aspects, Basilides might be called its Hegel, and Valentinus (the poet and mythologist) might be labelled

---

[14]Orr, "The Old Testament Question," 352.
[15]See Hatch's *History of the Church*, 2:39, as cited by Orr, ibid., 353–54.
[16]Orr, ibid., 354.

its Schelling;[17] but in its destructive higher critical results, it was the forerunner of Julius Wellhausen.

So significant had the question of the place of the OT in Christianity become that most of Irenaeus' fourth book *(Against Heresies)* was devoted to this question. Thus, the Gnostics, Marcionites, Cainites, and Ebionites labored to demonstrate the self-contradictory character of the OT, while Irenaeus, Tertullian, Hippolytus, and Clement of Alexandria strove to resist these charges against the OT and Christianity.

Not until the nineteenth and twentieth centuries have we seen as serious an attack made on the OT as was mounted in the second century. We will have an opportunity to investigate the nature of this challenge in more detail in chapter 3 of this present work, but for the present it should be noted that critical research with its heavy emphasis on historical-critical methodologies forced the OT far into the past and out of reach for Christians.

Thus, while the message and events of the OT were being properly placed in the cultural and historical milieu in which they were first delivered, the church was left with no answer to the question of the text's present relevance or application—if there were any answers beside a straightforward "No."

It would appear that the church has made very little progress in describing just how the OT relates to the Christian. In the more lucid periods of church history, she has spent the majority of her time and efforts working on the formal question: is the OT an authority for the Christian? During the second and 'sixteenth centuries, she made great progress on this problem, but she did little with the material question: what are the procedures by which the OT can authoritatively be brought over for appropriation in the current issues, needs, and questions of the twentieth-century church?

THE QUESTIONS THAT THE OLD TESTAMENT POSES AS *THE* CHRISTIAN PROBLEM

Can the OT be a proper source for anything affirmed in the life of the church? If so, how? and by what legitimate means, since the text was not addressed to us? This overall question can be reduced to a few more exacting questions that should help steer us in these seldom navigated waters.

---

[17]James Orr's suggestions, ibid., 355.

The first question is obviously this: is the God of the OT the same as the God of the NT? Even though we have put most of the second-century talk about a "demiurge" behind us, the feeling still seems to persist that the deities of both Testaments cannot be made to square with each other.

But the early church specifically taught that the unity of the OT and NT was to be found in the same God: "God, having spoken in the past at many times and in numerous ways to the fathers through the prophets, has spoken to us in these last days by the Son" (Heb 1:1–2a, my translation). Believers during both the OT and NT eras shared the one and only most high God. Even in the form of revelation, Hebrews 1:1 uses the identical verb to refer to each ("spoke"), so that there was historical continuity and a revelation that was substantially one and the same. Thus, Calvin in his commentary on this passage concurred: " . . . he [the writer] sets before us one God . . . because God, who is always like himself, and whose word is unchanging, and whose truth is unshakeable, spoke in both together."[18]

But there is more to this argument than merely linking the revelations of both Testaments to the same God. Indeed, the central message of the NT leads us back to the God of the OT. As Walther Eichrodt concluded,

> . . . in the encounter with the Christ of the Gospels, there is the assertion of a mighty living reality as inseparably bound up with the OT past as pointing into the future. *That which binds together indivisibly the two realms of the Old and New Testaments—different in externals though they be—is the irruption of the kingship of God into this world and its establishment here.* This is the unitive fact because it rests on the action of one and the same God in each case; that God who in promise and performance, in Gospel and in Law, pursues one and the selfsame great purpose, the building of his Kingdom.[19]

Still some will say that the Yahweh of the OT is not identical with our understanding of the God revealed in Jesus Christ.[20] Yahweh still is viewed as a national God whose activity centers on

---

[18] Jean Calvin, *Commentaries on the Epistle of Paul the Apostle to the Hebrews,* trans. John Owen (Grand Rapids: Eerdmans, 1948), *in loco.*

[19] Walther Eichrodt, *Theology of the Old Testament,* trans. John Baker (London: SCM, 1961), 1:26.

[20] John Goldingay, *Approaches to Old Testament Interpretation* (Downers Grove: InterVarsity, 1981), 29.

his people Israel and who is this-worldly in his concerns. Like the Manichaeans of the fourth century A.D., many find Yahweh to be an alien deity because he is jealous (Exod 20:5), he commands the extermination of all Canaanites and Amalekites (Deut 7:1–5), and he orders and directs evil (Isa 45:7; Amos 3:6).[21]

But the objections are too narrowly conceived. Yahweh chose Israel to be a special people so that Israel, in turn, would be a blessing to all the families of the earth (Gen 12:3)—"the Gentiles" (Isa 42:6), "all the ends of the earth" (Ps 67:7). Even her external blessing was to be only an indicator of the internal work of grace.

All attempts to force a wedge between Yahweh and the God and Father of our Lord Jesus Christ must disregard the evidence. Indeed, John declares that the Yahweh that Isaiah saw "high and exalted" in the heavenly vision of the temple (Isa 6:1) was no other than Jesus and his own glory (John 12:41). Thus there are a number of reasons that give us confidence in making this connection.

A second question arises out of the first. Must we, on account of the continuity observed in the same God of revelation and promised kingdom plan, accept the OT in its whole as well as its parts? Or, is there for the Christian a canon within the OT canon? Must the unity and usefulness of the whole OT be maintained at the price of surrendering a literal interpretation and accepting an allegorical and symbolical method of understanding the OT (as was assumed by the early church)?

The tug of war between the temporal character of the OT and its abiding nature has continued almost without remission. But once we have admitted that there is an organic spiritual unity to the OT and the NT, must we conclude that all that is not part of this line must therefore "lead to Judaism" and must "draw the reader away from Christ?"[22]

It must be honestly conceded that the OT contains parts that were indeed temporary and, therefore, time-bound by their very nature (e.g., the ceremonial and ritualistic laws and the once-for-all aspects of its historic episodes). But our contention is that there was also a built-in warning with each of these temporary parts that alerted us to the fact that they would become obsolete. Accordingly,

---

[21]For detailed rejoinders to these and other charges against the character and acts of God in the OT, see Walter C. Kaiser, Jr., *Toward Old Testament Ethics* (Grand Rapids: Zondervan, 1983), 247–69.

[22]Th. C. Vriezen, *An Outline of Old Testament Theology*, 2d. rev. ed. (Newton, Mass.: Charles T. Branford, 1970), 100.

all the tabernacle instructions were given as a model, or "pattern" (Exod 25:9, 40; Heb 8:5), of the real, which remained separate from the ceremonial institutions themselves. Nevertheless, behind the temporal and historical lay a principle—a truth meant to outlive its temporal or historical illustration. Too frequently the church has incorrectly assumed that when it had seen the collapse of the temporal institution, it had also thereby witnessed the end of all truth or obligation to any undergirding principles that the institution or historical event illustrated for a former age. But surely this is either a positivistic reading of history or a superficial handling of the data that assumes that the surface reading is all that is necessary for the interpreter and that there are no universals or abiding truths taught in the antecedent Scriptures that easily inform that institution or historical event and that obligate both the ancient and modern reader. Our position would be to avoid the positivism and superficial reading and to search for underlying universals, abiding truths, found in the texts prior in time to the recording of the text under investigation.

In no sense, then, can Christians pick and choose what belongs to the whole and what should be consigned to one of the obsolescent parts. The text must give its own clear literary signals even in this work of distinguishing what is temporal, cultural, and historically conditioned. Yet, in these places our involvement as Christians is not finished when these texts are so identified, for even there we must still ask what in the character and nature of God, what of the preceding theology in its doctrinal or moral truth, underlies and informs these texts? Only then have we grasped the extent of the OT claim has on the Christian.

A third disturbing question will follow once the previous two have been answered. How can the expectation of the promise-plan, or kingdom of God (which dominated both Testaments), be the same, since Christianity was viewed as a new beginning with a "New Covenant?" How can we have it both ways—continuity and a radically new beginning?

Yet once again the contrasts are overdrawn and the distinctions are not true to their biblical depictions. Both OT and NT communities were, like the Qumran community and John the Baptist's preaching, dominated by an expectation that the Messiah would return and would effect a renewal of the world. On this point there were large areas of agreement and overlap. But Jeremiah's promise of a "New Covenant" (Jer 31:31–34) appears to many to mean that the program announced to Abraham and David has been superceded, or at least attenuated. However, this confusion results from attaching a modern meaning to the word "new." In Jeremiah's usage it meant only to "renew," as can be seen from the use of the same Hebrew word for the "new moon." This is also true of most of the contents of the previous promises made to Abraham, Isaac, Jacob, and David.[23]

Once more the question is put to the OT in an attempt to discover some place from which the widely felt, but as yet undocumented, rupture between the Testaments might emanate. The fourth and final question put to the OT as a Christian problem is this: are not the objects of faith, the method of salvation, the theology of repentance and sin, and the life of faith so different in the two Testaments as to belong to two separate systems?

If this is so, the NT surely missed that contrast and instead argued the reverse—at least in two famous Pauline chapters (Rom 4 and Gal 3). In fact, Paul uses Abraham and David as his models for Christian justification by faith alone (Rom 4:1–17). And in Galatians 3:8 the essence and substance of the "good news," or "gospel," that Paul preached is equated with the promise made to Abraham in Genesis 12:3: " . . . in your seed shall all the nations of the earth be blessed" (my translation).

No less impressive are the theologies of sin, repentance, atonement, and salvation that are exhibited in the Hebrew word "to atone" or in the events of Passover (Exod 12) or Yom Kippur (Lev 16). There is no doubt, of course, that in the NT these matters are heard more clearly, frankly, and usually more explicitly; nevertheless, a fair, straightforward reading of the OT text with its own informing antecedent theology will often lay the groundwork for a concrete, if not at times also an abstract, display of the same truth in its rudimentary and seminal forms.

THE NT TEACHING PASSAGE ON THE RELEVANCE OF THE OT FOR THE CHRISTIAN

The most definitive statement from the NT on how the OT is to be used and what roles it must play in the life of believers is to be found in 2 Timothy 3:16–17, Paul's admonition to Timothy (my translation):

---

[23]Walter C. Kaiser, Jr., "The Old Promise and the New Covenant: Jeremiah 31:31–34," in *The Bible and Its Literary Milieu: Contemporary Essays*, ed. Vincent L. Tollers and John R. Maier (Grand Rapids: Eerdmans, 1979), 106–20.

> All Scripture is God-breathed (*pasa graphē theopneustos*) and
> is profitable for
> > teaching,
> > reproof,
> > correction, and
> > training in righteousness,
> that the man of God may be complete,
> > equipped for every good work.

Before we take up the four uses that Paul assigned to the OT, four other items in these verses merit a brief comment, and all center around the first three words of this text: *pasa graphē theopneustos*.[24]

The subject of this text is "Scripture," *graphē*. But it may be understood in several ways: (1) an individual passage of Scripture, (2) the Scripture (OT) as a whole, or (3) in the plural, all parts of Scripture. Since Paul had just finished referring to the "sacred writings" (*hiera grammata*, v. 15), it is clear that he has the OT writings in mind. Here, however, he changed from the plural noun *grammata* to the singular noun *graphē*. Thus, his meaning is either that "all Scripture [OT] as a whole is God-breathed" or alternatively, "each and every passage [which comprises the whole of the OT] is God-breathed." On either reading, the claim is that the OT in its totality, or in each and every one of its parts, is the product of the divine breathing-out.

This high claim is strengthened by the first word, *pasa. Pas* can be understood in a collective sense, "whole, all, entire" or partitively meaning "each, every." Normally the anarthrous noun with *pas* would indicate the partitive "every" is the proper translation (e.g., Matt 7:17 *pan dendron agathon*, "every good tree"), but the collective "all" does occur in anarthrous situations (e.g., "all [*pas*] the whole of Israel," Acts 2:36). Since *pas* has the emphatic position in the sentence, perhaps it is best to translate it here as "all" Scripture is inspired. Nevertheless, if some still object, it may be translated "every," if the verb is correctly placed in the sentence.

The third item is the placement of the verb in this sentence. Since there is no verb in the Greek sentence, the question then

---

[24]I am indebted for the general outline of this discussion (even though we differ on minor points) to Terence P. McGonigal, "Every Scripture is Inspired: An Exegesis of II Timothy 3:16–17," *Studia Biblica et Theologia* 3 (1978): 53–64; also see Walter C. Kaiser, Jr., "A Neglected Text in Bibliology Discussions: I Corinthians 2:6–16," *Westminster Theological Journal* 38 (1981): 307–10.

revolves around this problem: is the verbal adjective *theopneustos* ("God-breathed") to be placed in the attributive position ("every *God-breathed* Scripture is . . . ") or in the predicate position ("all Scripture is God-breathed"). While good arguments can be raised for both positions, J. N. D. Kelly[25] presents four arguments why it must be taken as a predicate: (1) both *theopneustos* and *ōphelimos* ("profitable") must be taken together in a predicate sense, since they are linked by *kai* ("and"), otherwise the sentence would have no real predicate; (2) if *theopneustos* is an attributive adjective, then *kai* is pointless in the sentence, even if one tries to read "every inspired Scripture is *also* profitable," since the "also" would not be linked to anything else and the statement would be somewhat tautological; (3) the attributive construction would imply that some of the *graphē* was not inspired, but Paul's reference to the "holy writings" (v. 15) would rule that out; and (4) there is a similar construction in 1 Timothy 4:4, where two adjectives are connected by *kai*, and all scholars understand them to be predicative.

Prior to Kelly's work, E. K. Simpson[26] had also given his four arguments for preferring a predicate translation: (1) it is a curious specimen of anticlimax with a tautological effect to say "every God-breathed Scripture is useful;" (2) if *theopneustos* had been intended as an attributive adjective, it should more properly have been placed before *graphē* rather than after it; (3) Paul has the habit of dropping the copula, especially in his opening sentence, and the closest parallel is in 1 Timothy 4:4, which no one translates "every good creature of God is also not one of them to be rejected"; and (4) as early as Chrysostom, *theopneustos* was taken to be in the predicate position and *pasa graphē* was seen as referring to the *hiera grammata* of the preceding verse.

The fourth, and last, item is the meaning of *theopneustos*. Is it active (Scripture breathes God's Spirit) or passive (Scripture is the product of God's breath)? Or, to put it differently, is Scripture "inspired" in its *effect* or in its *origin*?

A. T. Robertson,[27] on the one hand, showed that a great number of Greek words ending in *-tos* had a passive meaning in function (e.g., *theodidaktos*, "taught by God," 1 Thess 4:9). On the

[25] J. N. D. Kelly, *The Pastoral Epistles* (London: A. & C. Black, 1963); 203, as noted by McGonigal, "Every Scripture," 63n.29. Also note the agreement of E. K. Simpson, *The Pastoral Epistles* (Grand Rapids: Eerdmans, 1954), 150.

[26] Simpson, *The Pastoral Epistles*, 150.

[27] A. T. Robertson, *A Greek Grammar of the New Testament in the Light of Historical Research* (Nashville: Broadman, 1934), 1095.

other hand, B. B. Warfield surveyed eighty-six words beginning with the element *theo-* and concluded that seventy-five of the eighty-six had "the sense of a result produced by God."[28] Thus, rather than claiming that God infused or breathed into the Scriptures or even into the writers an *effect*, the claim is that the Scriptures of the OT had their *origin* in God and came as a result of God's "breathing-out."

But how "useful" (*ōphelimos*, "profitable")[29] is the OT? Paul answers this inquiry with four *pros* clauses wherein he sets forth two positive and two negative functions of the OT.

The first useful function Paul finds in the OT is "teaching" (*didaskalia*). The Pastorals use this word no less than fifteen times, while in the Gospels and the other Pauline letters it occurs only six times. In five of these Pastoral occurrences it is qualified as "*sound* doctrine." Thus, it is clear that Paul urges the church to go to the OT to get her "doctrine" and her "teaching" material.

This in itself is revolutionary enough! Who would ever think that the NT believer, apart from the NT Scriptures, could go to the OT for any didactic purposes? But the claim is clear; the OT is most useful and profitable for "teaching." In fact, some literary and theological heights reached in the OT remain unrivaled by the NT, for all its own grandeur. For example, there is no more definitive statement on the nature of the atonement than Isaiah 53, nor is there any more detailed or majestic statement of the incomparability of God than Isaiah 40:12–31. Some doctrines are stated in their "chair passages" in the OT, never again to be reexplained except for allusions to them. Instances of this include the teaching on creation (Gen 1–2), the image of God in man (Gen 1), the fall of man (Gen 3), culture (Ecclesiastes), and romantic and marital love (Song of Solomon).

But the point is that the church spurns three-fourths of God's inscripturated revelation—a massive amount of biblical teaching—if she persists in constructing all of her theology from the NT, while shamefully neglecting the OT. It is this practice that will leave lacunae and imbalances in her teaching ministry. She must return to the profitable, didactic usage of the OT.

Paul notes that a second use to which the OT can be put is

---

[28]B. B. Warfield, *The Inspiration and Revelation of Scripture* (Philadelphia: Presbyterian and Reformed, 1978), 247, a reference I had forgotten until McGonigal, "Every Scripture," 63, reminded me of it.

[29]Only here and 1 Timothy 4:8 and Titus 3:8.

"rebuke" (*elegmos*). The evil in our lives needs to be reproved, and Scripture's work on the heart is a major step toward restoration.

The matter of Scripture's work on the human race may best be summarized by W. A. Bartlett:

> Reproof, then, must be understood as *much more than a mere rebuke,* a chiding for sin, as a *quid pro quo.* It is an appeal from a Holy God to sinful man, . . . the special object of which is to awaken in him a sense of his sin, a hatred of it, and a departure from it. It is an act of mercy far more than of punishment . . . The object of reproof is to show man his failure, to point out his mistake, to lead him once more towards the real aim of his existence.[30]

A better picture of how this OT reproof operates may be gained from observing wisdom and instruction at work in Proverbs. It is an admonition that both corrects and convinces, often in discipline of sorrow (Prov 3:11), in the correction of children (Prov 13:24; 22:15), or in general (Prov 1:23; 15:31–32).

The third use to which the OT can be put is "correction" (*epanorthōsin,* literally, "restoration to an upright position or to a right state" or "setting straight that which had become bent or twisted"). While we must guard against espousing the view that every punishment or form of suffering in the life of the believer is a "correction" from God, we must, nevertheless, recognize that "correction" is one of God's remedies for the removal of sin and for restoring people back to their temporarily forfeited position.

This concept of correction was one of the leading ideas in the whole of the wilderness experience.

> Remember how Yahweh your God led you all the way in the wilderness these forty years, to humble you and to test you in order to know what was in your heart, whether you would keep his commandments. He humbled you . . . to teach you that one does not live by bread alone, but by every word that comes from the mouth of Yahweh. . . . Know then in your heart that as a man disciplines [or corrects] his son, so Yahweh your God disciplines you . . . to humble and to test you, so that in the end it might go well with you (Deut 8:2–3, 5, 16—my translation).

------

[30]W. A. Bartlett, *The Profitableness of the Old Testament Scriptures* (London: Rivingtons, 1844), 170–71. In his note L, Bartlett quotes from Archdeacon Hare's sermons on John 16:7–11 ("The Mission of the Comforter"), commenting that Hare has "well-nigh exhausted the subject [of *elegchos*]."

Repeatedly the prophets return to the threats of punishment predicted in Leviticus 26 and Deuteronomy 28 as the fountainhead of their reasons why their audiences ought to repent immediately. If these warnings produced repentance and a reversal in direction, then the individual or the nation was spared the infliction of a more severe judgment from God for each fresh neglect of his call to turn back to him.

Those calls are still of "profit" to the contemporary church. All of us—our children, our nation, and our churches—stand in dire need of heeding the corrections mentioned in the OT, if we are going to live—and live abundantly.

The fourth profitable use to which the OT can be put is that of "instruction in righteousness." *Paidea* ("training" or "instruction") comes from *pais* ("child"). It originally applied to the rearing of a child. It implies the submission of the disciple to the rules of instruction given by the teacher—rules by which one can be built up or instructed into a completed human edifice.[31] It is a growth from childhood to adulthood, from weakness to strength, from immaturity to full development.

But the sphere of the growth promised from the OT Scriptures is "training in righteousness." *Dikaiosunē* (here translated as "righteousness") is the state of being *dikaios* ("just, righteous, upright") and conveys the idea that "all is as it should be." It must be a patient work, for it is a gradual training, often accompanied by pain as well as joy. The work is not an instantaneous one in which one can sit back and say, "I'm glad that part of my growth is over." Development in righteousness is a lifelong task, and one of the key sources for cultivating this is the OT Scriptures.

Unfortunately, many are of the opinion that all that is needed for Christian life and growth can be found in the NT. Paul unmasks that position as a lie and insists that there is much profit and utility to be found in the OT if one wishes to be trained in righteousness!

Paul concludes with a result clause: "so that the man of God may be complete, equipped for every good work." This *hina* clause cannot be a purpose clause, since the four uses of *pros* with an accusative have already indicated purpose, thereby making another purpose clause unnecessary. Furthermore, if the *hina* clause were a purpose clause, it would seem to say that this was the sole purpose of Scripture—"to equip God's minister for good work"; but verse 15 has already given a salvific purpose.

---

[31]Bartlett, *The Profitableness*, 245.

No, it is better to regard this *hina* clause as stating the results that Scripture will bring about when the four purposes found in the *pros* clauses are observed in the OT.

Scriptural, intellectual, emotional and volitional maturity will ensue from such a holistic reading and heeding of the OT. What is more, we shall be prepared to carry out every good work. This is a high claim indeed. Is it any wonder, then, that the Christian church limps along so anemically when it chooses, out of fear for the unknown or out of deliberate neglect, to avoid the OT? But the bold Pauline assertion is that the OT is most profitable indeed. Even on the matter of making one "wise for salvation through faith in Christ Jesus" (2 Tim 3:15), the OT can serve admirably well!

We must rediscover the OT once more as a most significant, profitable, and useful instrument in our personal and corporate growth in righteousness, in faith in Christ, and in preparation for every good work.

PART I

THE OLD TESTAMENT
AND SCHOLARSHIP

Chapter 2

The Old Testament as Part of the Canon

The designation "Old Testament" is in itself anachronistic, for nowhere in the first thirty-nine books of the Bible does this term occur. Actually, it was the Alexandrian church father Origen (c. 185–c. 254) who gave us this nomenclature, based in part on God's promise in Jeremiah 31:31 of a "new covenant"—hence his "New Testament." But both the label and the translation are misleading; it is only ecclesiastical convention that dictates our continued use of this term for that group of biblical books that the Jews referred to as "the writings," "the Scriptures," and "the Law and the Prophets."

But aside from what we call this collection, there are more pressing questions, such as: Which specific books shall we consider as part of this sacred collection? Who decided what books would be authoritative and which would not be so regarded? What were the criteria for normativeness and authority? What role did these specific books play in the nation of Israel in setting the standards for faith and practice in the life of the religious community? These are the questions that call for comment if the believing community is going to be able to point to this body of literature and use it in any normative way.

WHAT MAKES THE THIRTY-NINE BOOKS OF THE OT AUTHORITATIVE FOR THE CHURCH?

The Jewish historian Flavius Josephus (c. A.D. 37–c. A.D. 100) appears to be the earliest extant extra-biblical witness on the contents and limits of the OT canon. In his response to the anti-semite Apion, he wrote:

> We do not possess myriads of inconsistent books, conflicting with each other. Our books, those which are justly accredited, are but two and twenty, and contain the record of all time.
>
> Of these, five are the books of Moses, comprising the laws and the traditional history from the birth of man down to the death of the lawgiver. This period falls only a little short of three thousand years. From the death of Moses until Artaxerxes, who succeeded Xerxes as King of Persia, the prophets subsequent to Moses wrote the history of the events of their own times in thirteen books. The remaining four books contain hymns to God and precepts for the conduct of human life.
>
> From Artaxerxes to our own time the complete history has been written, but has not been deemed worthy of equal credit with the earlier prophets, because of the failure of the exact succession of the prophets.[1]

From later Christian testimony, which consistently referred to the same twenty-two book-count, it is possible to reconstruct a list of those twenty-two books and to show that that list includes the same books as our thirty-nine book list (as displayed on the next page).

Such discussions about which books are divinely inspired (and therefore authoritative, normative, sacred, and binding) led to the question of canonicity. Actually the word *"canon"* (from the Greek word *kanōn*, which in turn was borrowed from the Hebrew word *qāneh*, "a reed," or "a measuring rod," hence a "norm" or a "ruler") was first used in this technical sense by the church fathers in the fourth century (e.g., in the 59th canon of the Council of Laodicea, A.D. 363; in the Festal Epistle of Athanasius, A.D. 365; and by Amphilochius, archbishop of Iconium, A.D. 395).[2]

---

[1] Josephus, *Against Apion* 1.8.38–41 (Loeb 1:178–80).

[2] As supplied by George L. Robinson, "Canon of the Old Testament," *International Standard Bible Encyclopedia*, ed. James Orr (Grand Rapids: Eerdmans, 1939), 1:554. For full documentation, see Hermann Wolfgang Beyer, *"κανών,"* *Theological Dictionary of the New Testament*, ed. Gerhard Kittel and Gerhard

Five Books of Moses	Thirteen Books of the Prophets	Four Hymns and Precepts
1. Genesis	1. Joshua	1. Psalms
2. Exodus	2. Judges-Ruth	2. Proverbs
3. Leviticus	3. (1 & 2) Samuel	3. Song of Solomon
4. Numbers	4. (1 & 2) Kings	4. Ecclesiastes
5. Deuteronomy	5. Isaiah	
	6. Jeremiah-Lamentations	
	7. Ezekiel	
	8. The Twelve (the Minor Prophets)	
	9. Daniel	
	10. Job	
	11. (1 & 2) Chronicles	
	12. Ezra-Nehemiah	
	13. Esther	

Long before the expressions "canon" and "canonical" were invented, the NT was using the word "Scriptures" to denote those books that were sacred (Matt 21:42; John 5:39; Acts 18:24). Beginning in that same first Christian century, according to the Talmud, the phrase "defile the hands" was used by the Jewish community in connection with those writings that were deemed sacred, and hence they demanded that anyone who handled the writings had to wash his hands afterwards (before engaging in any other activity)—just as the High Priest had to wash his hands, not only prior to his putting on but also after he took off the holy garments of his office on the Day of Atonement (Lev 16:24). Thus both Jewish and Christian groups had a definite concept of canonicity, even if they used different terms to denote such.

There was more, according to the famous Jewish tractate on the Day of Atonement, *Yoma* 12b. Not only were the clothes worn by the High Priest supposed to be left in the Holy of Holies (Lev 16:23); they must also be hidden. Since they were no longer cultically serviceable and of course were never to be used for secular purposes, they must be abandoned to natural corruption. Similarly, Scripture manuscripts that became worn or had a prob-

Friedrich, trans. Geoffrey W. Bromiley, 10 vols. (Grand Rapids: Eerdmans, 1965), 3:601.

lem due to an error in their copying had to be hidden in a "treasure room" (*genîzāh*, from the root *gānaz*, "to gather, keep, treasure, conceal") in the sanctuary.[3] It was in one such genizah at Cairo that certain much discussed biblical manuscripts and a manual of discipline similar to the one discovered at Qumran were found.

The concepts "writings," "defile the hands," and "canon" certainly set the standard for an authorized group of books, but who had the right to declare a writing canonical? The most prevalent answer in some circles was that of a sixteenth-century Jewish teacher named Elias Levita (d. A.D. 1549): Ezra and his associates, the men of the Great Synagogue,[4] established both the correct text, the correct number, and the arrangement of the books of the Bible. But neither Scripture itself nor history gives us any warrant for linking Ezra or a "Great Synagogue" (a conclave that undertook an alleged canonical agenda, which agenda is unsupported by Nehemiah 8) to a closing of the canon. Neither is the tradition drawn from 4 Esdras 14—which supposes that all the sacred books were burned with the temple in 586 B.C., thereby necessitating that Ezra and his five companions rewrite them in forty days and forty nights—of much help either, for this too is completely unsubstantiated by any external historical data.

In our view, there never did exist a body of men such as the Great Synagogue with appropriate authority to fix the number or order of the books that would be the standard for faith and practice in the believing community. Even the frequently alleged work of the Council of Jamnia (or Jabne, a town not far south of Joppa, close to the Mediterranean coast) in its two meetings in A.D. 90 and 118 cannot be credited with declaring what is canonical and what is not. It is amazing how often scholars have cited each other with assurance that this Council in A.D. 90 settled the extent of the OT canon. This Jamnia hypothesis, concluded Jack P. Lewis, "appears to be one of those things that has come to be true due to frequent repetition of the assertion rather than to its being actually supported by the evidence."[5] Even the *Encyclopaedia Britannica's* adoption of this hypothesis sounded certain:

---

[3] See Albrecht Oepke, "κρθπτώ," *Theological Dictionary of the New Testament*, ed. Kittel and Friedrich, 3:981–84.

[4] Excursus A. in Herbert E. Ryle, *The Canon of the Old Testament*, 2d ed. (London: Macmillan, 1885), 250–83. Also, Hugo Mandel, "The Nature of the Great Synagogue," *Harvard Theological Review* 60 (1967): 69–91. Consult *The Massorah ha-Massoreth*, ed. and trans. C. D. Ginsburg (London, 1867), 119–20.

[5] Jack P. Lewis, "What Do We Mean by Jabneh?" *Journal of Bible and Religion* 32 (1964): 132.

After the destruction of Jerusalem by the Romans (A.D. 70) Jamnia became the home of the Great Sanhedrin. A meeting of Rabbis held there c. A.D. 100 discussed and settled the final canon of the Old Testament.[6]

Jamnia, however, gives no evidence of settling or even discussing the question of the canon. What was discussed, as Sid Z. Leiman has shown, was the interpretation of Song of Solomon and Ecclesiastes. But even these discussions were not binding, for they returned to the same questions a century later.[7] Moreover, the discussions arose because the canonical status of these two books was already assumed.

There is a better way to account for a set of authoritative books in the OT. The internal witness of the OT books themselves appears to favor a "progressive formation and canonization"[8] of the OT.

Within the corpus of the writings themselves there is both the assertion of the writers that their writings have been received from and guided by the revelatory and inspiring work of the Holy Spirit and the assertion that what has been written was to be collected with the other books that had made a similar claim and were likewise treated as authoritative.

The first such claim appears in Exodus 17:14, where, on the occasion of Joshua's victory over Amalek, Moses is instructed by Yahweh to "write this for a memorial in a book and rehearse it in the ears of Joshua." The authority for this act, so the text claims, was located in Yahweh himself, not Moses, the people of his day, or a later council. Clearly the writing was intended to be preserved "for a memorial."

It appears also that it was to be attached to a body of sacred literature already in Israel's possession, for Moses was told to write in "in *the* book," or *scroll* (*bassēper*). Moreover, provision was made for calling its contents to public attention in years to come, perhaps when Joshua would assume leadership of the troops once again during the conquest years.

---

[6] Edward Robertson, "Jamnia," *Encyclopaedia Britannica* (1970), 12:87, as cited by Robert C. Newman, "The Council of Jamnia and the Old Testament Canon," *Westminster Theological Journal* 38 (1975–76): 323.

[7] Sid Z. Leiman, *The Canonization of the Hebrew Scriptures: The Talmudic and Midrashic Evidence* (Hamden, Conn.: Archon, 1976), 121–24. See also Newman, "The Council of Jamnia," 338–44.

[8] I am indebted to my teacher Robert Duncan Culver for the general line of argumentation used here.

Provision is likewise made for the custody of each portion of the canon as it is written and for acquainting the people with its contents. The sacredness of this text was emphasized by placing the first completed portion of the OT alongside the ark in the Holy of Holies (Deut 31:24–26). Another copy was given to the king (Deut 17:18–19). Meanwhile, Joshua was urged "not [to] let this Book of the Law depart from [his] mouth; [he was to] meditate on it day and night so that [he would] be careful to do everything written in it" (Josh. 1:8, my translation).

On another occasion we read of an addition to "the Book of the Law of God" in Joshua's day, perhaps the best explanation for the eight or ten so-called "post-Mosaic" additions to the Pentateuch (Josh 24:26). Thus, a tradition of a growing canon was envisaged almost from the beginning of the composition of Scripture.

After Samuel wrote down his words on a scroll, he too "deposited [them] before the Lord" (1 Sam 10:25). We would therefore suggest that each fresh addition to the canon was immediately deposited in the sanctuary and thereby given its sacred and canonical status. Apparently, the king was to have his own private copy—either one that he himself copied (Deut 17:18) or at least one that was produced for him and then presented to him (2 Kings 11:12).

Later writers occasionally referred to each other's writings as being sacred and hence canonical. For example, with reference to Jeremiah 25:11, Daniel (Dan 9:2) denotes the prophetic writing of his predecessor Jeremiah as "the Scriptures, . . . the word of the LORD." Both Isaiah 8:16 and Jeremiah 36:1ff show an awareness of a written form of their prophecies almost from the beginning of their ministries. Later, Zechariah, in 520 B.C., refers easily to all the "former prophets" (1:4 KJV) whose writings have a definite form and an authoritative status in his view.

The statements of the OT, to the degree that they provide for laying up each new addition before the Lord and to the degree that they recognize the work of their colleagues and predecessors as "Scripture" or "the Word of the Lord," provide for their own process of "progressive canonization" apart from any external individual authentication or any adjudication from a particular group or body of people. The tests for canonicity were, in many ways, similar to the tests for revelation and inspiration. If the texts carried the requisite signs of authority and authentication of their writers, they were immediately placed before the Lord and thereby canonized.

WHAT ARE THE EVIDENCES AND LIMITS FOR GROWTH AND DEVELOPMENT IN THE OT?

Beyond the internal evidence of the OT, we are concerned with the witness of the church through the centuries, for our study of the OT as a Christian problem would be incomplete without seriously considering the testimony of the church.

How many books do our oldest lists enumerate for the OT, and in what order are they arranged in these lists? We are given at least two different enumerations. A twenty-two book count, as we have already seen in Josephus, was argued by Melito, Origen, Eusebius, Cyril of Jerusalem, Epiphanius, Jerome, and Augustine. No doubt they depended on the Jewish lists that connected this figure with the fact that there also were twenty-two letters in the Hebrew alphabet.

The idea of a a twenty-four book canon can be found in 4 Esdras 14:44–45, the Talmud's *Baba Bathra* 14[b], and the *Midrash Rabbah* on Numbers 14:4, 15, 22. The last named source associated this count with the fact that there were twenty-four priestly divisions. Nevertheless, the results would seem to be the same, as Aage Bentzen concluded:

> The difference is accounted for by assuming that Josephus combines Ruth with Judges, Lamentations with Jeremiah, and takes Ezra and Nehemiah as one book, while 4 Esdras probably regards Ruth and Lamentations as separate books.[9]

An eleventh-century Greek manuscript[10] containing the Didache and 2 Clement gives the number as twenty-seven, as does Epiphanius.[11] Audet places the sources for this list in the first half of the second century and possibly in the last half of the first Christian century. If this proves to be correct, then this list would be as old as the lists of Josephus and 4 Esdras. This list divides and counts the books of Samuel, Kings, and Chronicles twice; Ruth is separated from Judges, and Ezra from Nehemiah, while The Twelve remains as one book. Lamentations is either assumed to be part of Jeremiah or is missing. What is peculiar about this list is the order of the

---

[9] Aage Bentzen, *Introduction to the Old Testament*, 2d ed., 2 vols. (Copenhagen: G. E. C. Gad, 1952), 1:26, as cited by Newman, "Council of Jamnia," 345.

[10] Jean-Paul Audet, "A Hebrew-Aramaic List of Books of the Old Testament in the Greek Transcription," *Journal of Theological Studies* series 1 (1950): 135–54.

[11] Epiphanius, *Weights and Measures*, 23.

books: (1) Joshua is included in the Pentateuchal list of books, and
(2) Ruth, Job, Judges, and Psalms precede the historical books of
1 Samuel through 2 Chronicles, which are followed by Proverbs,
Ecclesiastes, Song of Songs, Jeremiah, The Twelve, Isaiah, Daniel,
1 Ezra, 2 Ezra (=Nehemiah?), and Esther.

Even though there was no consensus on how the books were
ordered or even counted, there appears to be a great degree of
agreement on the actual books that were regarded as authoritative
and sacred. How, then, did the present order of books come into
existence, and what part did the three-fold division of the Hebrew
canon play in this process?

Little, if any, debate ever centered around the acceptance
of the five books of the law (=Torah). The first division of the
"Scriptures" appeared to be formally recognized as a literary unit as
far back as our records go. The second division bears the name
Prophets (i.e. *Nebî'îm*). The most ancient list known to us is
contained in tract *Baba Bathra* of the Talmud, folio 14[b]. The
Baraitha (with the views of the Tanaim—as distinguished from the
Gemara with the views of the Amoraim, who were the expounders
of the former group's notes) arranged the prophets this way:

> The rabbins have taught that the order of the prophets is
> Joshua and Judges, Samuel and Kings, Jeremiah and Eze-
> kiel, Isaiah and The Twelve.[12]

Notice that Daniel was not included in this list as one of the
prophets, but this does not imply that this list was fixed before
Daniel gained canonical recognition. Medieval Jews explained
Daniel's absence from this list by implying that there were degrees
of inspiration; the prophets sharing a fuller degree of inspiration
("the spirit of prophecy") than those writers who contributed to the
third section, the Writings (=*Kethûbîm*). This distinction is contrived and has no basis in fact or in the OT itself. Likewise the
modern Protestant distinction that Daniel had the *gift* of prophecy
but not the *office* of prophecy appears to fail, since some who were
not at first in the office of prophet were later called to exercise the
gift of prophecy, such as Amos (7:14). But what is most persuasive is
the fact that Jesus and his Jewish contemporaries referred with
comparative ease to "Daniel the prophet" (Matt 24:15 KJV).[13]

---

[12] *Baba Bathra,* 14[b].

[13] For a fuller discussion of this problem, see Robert Dick Wilson, "The Book of
Daniel and the Canon," *Princeton Theological Review* 13 (1915): 352–408,

That same tractate of *Baba Bathra* also listed an order for the books in the third division, known as the Writings (*Kethûbîm*):

> The order of the writings is Ruth and the Book of Psalms and Job, and Proverbs, Ecclesiastes, Song of Songs and Lamentations, Daniel and the roll of Esther, Ezra and Chronicles.

This order, which became the traditional order, appears to give some precedent for the threefold division of the canon, *viz.*, the Law, the Prophets, and the Writings. But this tripartite division of the OT Scripture reflects a later development that cannot be placed any earlier than the first Christian century.

Some have suggested that Luke 24:44 (with its Law, Prophets, and Psalms) would favor this threefold division, but the more general and fluid classification that is found more frequently is "the Law and the Prophets" (e.g., Matt 5:17; 7:12; 22:40; Acts 13:15) or "Moses and all the Prophets" (Luke 24:27).

It is true that the prologue to the Greek translation of *Ben Sirach*, written about 132 B.C., refers three times to a threefold division of the OT: (1) "The Law and the Prophets, and the other books which follow after them," (2) "The Law and the Prophets and the other ancestral books," and (3) "The Law itself and the Prophecies and the rest of the books." However, the grandson of Jesus ben Sirach, who translated Ecclesiasticus into Greek and added his own prologue, did not give a distinct name to this third section or give a full list of the books it contained.

Philo, who died about A.D. 40, says that the sect of the Therapeutae received "the Law, and the other Oracles uttered by the Prophets, and the hymns and the other [writings] by which knowledge and piety are augmented and perfected."[14]

Accordingly, even though there is a general feeling that roughly approximates a threefold division of the canon, there is no clear evidence that calls for it. Because of the limitations of the scrolls, skins, and traditional materials suitable for writing in the pre-Christian and early Christian centuries, no single scroll (or whatever) could have contained even a significant portion of the OT, much less the whole of it. Thus, the books could be arranged in any order that suited the pleasure of their owner. In fact, so diverse

---

reprinted in *Studies in the Book of Daniel*, 2 vols. (London: 1917; reprint, Grand Rapids: Baker, 1972), 2:9–64.

[14]Philo, *De Vita contemplativa*, 2:475.

is the actual situation that Robert Dick Wilson concluded, after giving pages of various canonical lists:

> ... there is no evidence to show that any Hebrew manuscript ever contained the books of the Old Testament canon as they are arranged in our Hebrew Bibles as now printed. Nor did either of the great schools of Hebrew manuscripts, the Spanish, or the German-French, have the books arranged as they are now printed; nor are they printed in the order given in the Talmud. Nor do they follow the order of the earliest printed Hebrew Bibles, such as the Editio Princeps of Bomberg, which put the five Megilloth immediately after the Pentateuch. Our Bibles agree with the Spanish and Massoretic manuscripts in the order of the Prophets, but with the German and French in the Hagiographa. The order in the Talmud differs from that of the editions in use at present. It differs, also, in the order of the books in the Prophets and the Hagiographa from the Massoretic, Spanish and German-French manuscripts. [Likewise] the Peshito Syriac version differs in the order.... Moreover, no one of the great Greek uncials, Vaticanus, Sinaiticus, Alexandrinus, and Basiliano-Venetus, agrees in order with any other one of them, or with any one of the Hebrew or Syriac sources.... In short, of more than sixty lists [surveyed], no two present exactly the same order for the books comprising the Old Testament canon; so that it can be affirmed positively that the order of those books [and their position in a certain division] was never fixed by any accepted authority of either the Jewish or Christian Church.[15]

It also follows, with Laird Harris's conclusion, that " ... such a view [of the fluid classification of the Law and the Prophets for the whole canon] effectively dispels the idea that the Old Testament canon grew in three stages."[16]

The most helpful text on the extent, order, and authority of the OT canon is Matthew 23:34–35. In the midst of his denunciation of the scribes, Jesus declared:

> Therefore I am sending you prophets and wise men and teachers. Some of them you will kill and crucify; others you will flog in your synagogues and pursue from town to town.

---

[15]Wilson, *Studies in the Book of Daniel*, 2:37–38.
[16]R. Laird Harris, *Inspiration and Canonicity of the Bible* (Grand Rapids: Zondervan, 1969), 147; see also *idem*, "Was the Law and the Prophets Two-Thirds of the Old Testament Canon?" *Bulletin of the Evangelical Theological Society*, 9:4 (1966): 163–72.

> And so upon you will come all the righteous blood that has been shed on earth, from the blood of righteous Abel to the blood of Zechariah son of Berekiah, whom you murdered between the temple and the altar (cf. Luke 11:49–51).

If the murder of Abel appears in the first book of the Old Testament (Genesis), and if the other murder referred to in Matthew 23:34–36 was recorded in the last book in the Jewish order of the books in the time of Jesus (2 Chronicles), "the natural inference is that the intervening books were also settled, in accordance with the traditional order, and that consequently the canon was closed" [already in Jesus' day].[17]

However, before such an assertion can be made, the identity of the Zechariah connected with the second murder must be established. Most commentators assume that Jesus is referring to that Zechariah whose prophecy and murder are related in 2 Chronicles 24:19–22.[18] What really locks in this identification is the fact that Zechariah was slain between the sanctuary and the altar. Whenever "the altar" is without any further specification, it invariably means the brazen altar, or altar of burnt offerings in the temple court, the place in the court where it was proper only for the priests to be, which indeed Zechariah was.

But if the Zechariah that Jesus is referring to is the one murdered in 2 Chronicles and not (1) the canonical prophet by the same name (Zech 1:1, 7), (2) the Zechariah mentioned in Isaiah 8:2 (Zechariah, son of Jeberechiah [a longer form of Berekiah]), or (3) the Zechariah killed by the zealots "in the middle of the Temple" just before the Roman destruction of Jerusalem in A.D. 70, what is the explanation of the patronym "son of Berekiah," while the writer of 2 Chronicles 24:20 called him "Zechariah son of Jehoiada"? Since Jehoiada was 130 years old when he died (2 Chron 24:15), it could well be that he was Zechariah's grandfather and Berekiah was his actual father. "Son of Jehoiada" would, therefore, be translated—as the expression "son of" often is elsewhere—"descendant of Jehoiada."[19]

---

[17] Roger Beckwith, *The Old Testament Canon of the New Testament Church and Its Background in Early Judaism* (Grand Rapids: Eerdmans, 1985), 222.

[18] Ibid., 230n.81, notes that this identification can be traced back to the second century in the Gospel of the Nazaraeans.

[19] Beckwith, ibid., 217–20, strongly favors a solution suggested by the rabbinical haggadah that links two different characters who have a similar name, and thus he believes that the Zechariah who was slain between the altar and the temple has a

Thus, the point remains: Jesus, with all his divine authority, placed his stamp of approval on the exact number of books as are now in our thirty-nine book canon. Indeed, from one end of Scripture to the other there was a trail of martyred prophets that included *all* the martyred prophets! For Jesus, therefore, the canon began with Genesis and ended with 2 Chronicles, just as it does in the traditional Hebrew order of the OT, and so the dynamic equivalent of Jesus' expression, considering our present English order of the OT books, would be: "all the righteous blood . . . from Genesis to Malachi."

MUST THE CHRISTIAN INCLUDE ISRAEL AND HER LAND IN A CONTEMPORARY THEOLOGY?

Another aspect of the question about the canon of the OT is the interrelationship of the law (*Torah*) to the prophets. But the extent to which the preaching of the prophets was dependent on the teaching of the law is only part of an even larger question.

According to the apostle Peter, "All the prophets who have spoken, from Samuel and those who came afterwards, also proclaimed these days" (Acts 3:24, my translation). Yet it is precisely this claim—that the prophets proclaimed a unified message and that it focused on the era of salvation that was to come—that modern literary-critical scholarship has found so difficult to accept in its own study of the prophetic texts. The general consensus of literary-critical scholarship has been that the pre-exilic prophets were prophets of doom and destruction—*Unheilspropheten*[20] —though this conclusion is far from the attitude reported to us from the apostles and Jesus.

Nevertheless, the uniform message of the pre-exilic prophets as preserved in our present Masoretic text linked the prophets' message of destruction with a message of restoration of Israel. Usually the messages of doom and destruction were concluded with a rosy-tinted message of the deliverance that God would effect in the final day of the Lord. Ben Sira's reading of the prophets from his second century B.C. vantage point reflected this positive note of

double identity with the minor prophet Zechariah, the son of Berekiah, the son of Iddo (Zech 1:1, 7).

[20]This point is made by Ronald E. Clements, "Patterns in the Prophetic Canon," in *Canon and Authority: Essays in Old Testament Religion and Theology*, ed. George W. Coats and Burke O. Long (Philadelphia: Fortress, 1977), 42–43.

future deliverance: "May the bones of the twelve prophets revive from where they lie, for they comforted the people of Jacob, and delivered them with confident hope" (Sir 49:10).

This opinion was not reserved exclusively for the twelve minor prophets, for, as Ronald Clements points out, Ben Sira understood all the OT prophets in the same way (Sir 48:17–25). Clements also noted that this reading can be traced back even further, for already in 2 Kings 17:13 one can see a certain connection between each of the prophets (prior to the fall of Samaria in 722 B.C.) and the Mosaic Law: "The LORD warned Israel and Judah through all his prophets and seers: 'Turn from your evil ways. Observe my commands and decrees, in accordance with the entire Law that I commanded your fathers to obey and that I delivered to you through my servants the prophets.' "[21]

The preferred explanation among many OT scholars is to attribute this development of eschatological hope in the prophets to post-exilic themes that have been read back into the pre-exilic prophets. But there is no end to this hypothesis, for one must presuppose that the same restoration-of-Israel theme must also be a retrojection in the law, too (e.g., in Lev 26:40–45). Yet these earlier prophets were just as much heralds of hope as were those who came after 586 B.C.

Once again Clements cuts through this problem. Even though he saw a process of "telescoping" and a "reinterpretation of prophecies to meet the exigencies of later situations," he nevertheless allowed that the prophets "spoke with one voice of the salvation that was to come."

> Already this is evident in the case of Amos, for . . . the hope of the restoration of Israel under a Davidic kingship expressed in Amos 9:11–12 is best understood as originally applicable to a situation in the eighth century. It is not necessarily therefore to be regarded as a post-exilic addition, but may be understood as a part of the hope that Israel would once again become a single united nation under a Davidic ruler, a hope which is entirely credible and appropriate in this [eighth] century. Particularly is this hope understandable after the fall of Samaria in 722 B.C.[22]

Accordingly, whether in the pre- or post-exilic prophets, a pattern of joining words of hope to threats of destruction eventually

---

[21] Ibid., 44.
[22] Ibid., 49.

became a chorus of voices that blended into one hope for the future. One of the most prominent themes for the future was that Israel would be restored to her land. The latter prophecies tended to cast their message of hope in terms of the same aspirations found in the previous prophets and the law itself. Thus, by means of an informing theology, or the analogy of antecedent Scripture, the latter prophets added greater specificity to some of the very same concepts, terms, and promises that had appeared in seminal form in earlier prophetic announcements cast against entirely different emergencies in the life of the nation. This unifying framework of terms, citations, and concepts reinforced the canonical status of what had already been revealed, and it provided an expectation that what followed in the more recent writings of the prophets was also part of that same authoritative corpus of materials.

We conclude, then, that judgment and promise, threat and hope are not such antithetical opposites that they could not coexist in the same pre-exilic prophecies. And dominating their most joyous expectation was the realization of restoration to the land of Israel, even as the patriarchs had been led to believe and the Deuteronomic legislation had promised.

But what of the land and state of Israel beyond the time of all the OT prophets? Is that promise of restoration to the land still effective in the twentieth century?

Undoubtedly, Israel's rejection of Jesus Christ as her Messiah is one of the great abnormalities of history. But does this rejection, along with her repeated failures to obey the laws or statutes of God in the OT, mean that the oft-repeated promise of restoration to the land (which had been given as an *everlasting* possession) has thereby been nullified as well?

Few issues draw more heated affirmations and denials than this one. To affirm that Scripture does expect Israel to be restored to her land creates such misgivings that some immediately charge that this is nothing less than a contemporary form of an antiquated Pietism, the *Schwärmer* of the Reformation revisited;[23] it is at best a bad judgment call, reversing a proper theological exegesis that should begin with the NT in order to explain such OT themes.

If we are to proceed "according to the Scriptures," our appeal must be to the entire canon—both OT and NT. Thus, in our attempt

---

[23] See John R. Wilch, "The Land and State of Israel in Prophecy and Fulfillment," *Concordia Journal* 8 (1982): 173.

to unravel this knotty issue, we will follow the same course that revelation took.

The Everlasting Promise of the Land

Most acknowledge that the promise of the land was one of the most basic elements of the Abrahamic Covenant. However, it was not until Genesis 17:7, 13, 19 that we are given a triple affirmation that this covenant was to be "an everlasting covenant" (*berît 'ôlām*), a promise first stated in Genesis 13:15 and continued in Genesis 48:4.

In Genesis 17:8 this everlasting quality of the covenant was again related directly to the promise of the land: "The whole land of Canaan, where you are now an alien, I will give as an everlasting possession to you and your descendants after you. . . . "

This raises the problem as to what is meant by the Hebrew word *'ôlām* ("forever, everlasting"). Except for some twenty uses where it clearly refers to the past, most of the over four hundred instances of *'ôlām* refer to endlessness or indefinite continuance into the distant future. "When applied to things physical [such as "the land"], it is used in accordance with the revealed truth that the heaven and earth shall pass away, and it is limited by this truth."[24] However, impressive as this divine promise is, all too many have objected to the word "forever" and qualified it in too many ways.

What makes more sense is the argument that views the covenant as a whole. It is impossible to maintain that the messianic (the heir; seed) and salvific ("all nations be blessed") parts of the covenant were most certainly "eternal" and "everlasting" without simultaneously treating the third part of the covenant (i.e., the land) in the same way. What rule of hermeneutics allows us to say two-thirds of the promise is "eternal," while one-third has already been fulfilled? Unless the text of Scripture itself signals such a division of its unified covenant, wherein all three parts are so intimately united, it is an act of treason against its lordship over us arbitrarily to assign varying values according to our best insights.

But did not Scripture do just that—indicate that the land promise had been fulfilled? Joshua 21:43–45, 23:14–15, and Nehemiah 9:8 emphatically state that the Lord had fulfilled (*bā'* in 21:45 and *bā'û* in 23:14) the promise given to Abraham (e.g., "So

---

[24]Robert B. Girdlestone, *Synonyms of the Old Testament*, 2d ed. (1897; reprint, Grand Rapids: Eerdmans, 1956), 317.

the Lord gave Israel all the land he had sworn to give their forefathers. . . . Not one of all the Lord's good promises to the house of Israel failed; every one was fulfilled" (Josh 21:43, 45).

Here we must distinguish, first of all, between what had been accomplished in *principle,* in that all the main objectives had been reached, and what had yet to be done by way of "mopping up." There are numerous indications from Joshua 13:1 to Judges 3:5–6 that much remained to be done; for Israel never completely removed the Canaanites, nor did her borders at any time, even under David and Solomon, reach the northernmost extremity[25] mentioned in the promise. Even though 1 Kings 8:65 would appear to include everything from north to south, ("from Lebo Hamath to the Wadi of Egypt"), yet other passages once again modify our understanding of what was involved, for we are specifically told that Philistia was not within Solomon's administrative districts (1 Kings 4:21; 2 Chron 9:26). Likewise, the coastal area of Phoenicia, especially that above Tyre, was under Sidonian, not Israelite, rule. Accordingly, we cannot agree with the conclusions of Philip E. Hughes:

> And so we see how the promises to Abraham of old were, in their externals at least, quite definitely fulfilled,— how his seed . . . inherited the promised land in accordance with the limits which God had foretold. Nor is this a mere personal conclusion, but one that is attested in the plainest possible terms both by the Scriptures of that time . . . and also by those of a later time."[26]

The Conditionality of the Covenant

Even though this issue must be faced in chapter 7 (pp. 151–55), it always lies just below the surface of much theological debate. Many protest: were there not certain conditions connected with the fulfillment of this promise of the land? And is it not a fact that Israel failed miserably to meet those conditions because of unbelief and injustice to others? Furthermore, did not Jeremiah

[25] See our discussion of this problem, Walter C. Kaiser, Jr., "The Promised Land: A Biblical-Historical View," *Bibliotheca Sacra* 138 (1981): 303–5. The north boundary is probably *Nahr el-Kabir,* "The Great River," which today forms the boundary between Lebanon and Syria on the north, just south of the modern coastal hamlet of Sumra.

[26] Philip E. Hughes, "The Olive Tree of Romans XI," *Evangelical Quarterly* 20 (1948): 26.

18:7–10 formally state that in fact all prophecies were conditional? What is repeated more frequently throughout the prophets than Leviticus 26 and Deuteronomy 28—the alternative prospects for Israel, depending on her obedience or lack of it?

We would agree with the conditional argument except in those covenants where God obligated himself and not the other party. These exceptions would be unilateral, not bilateral, covenants; therefore, unlike social contracts, which are null and void when one of the contracting parties fails to live up to the specified conditions, unilateral covenants where God is the sole party depend totally on his faithfulness.

The following covenants must be excluded from the conditional class: the Noahic Covenant, the Abrahamic Covenant, the Davidic Covenant, the New Covenant, and the Covenant of the New Heavens and the New Earth. There is no record in any of these five covenants that God had a contracting party that agreed to certain obligations when the covenant was made.

This is not to affirm that subsequent obedience is not required if some or all of these five covenantal benefits are to be enjoyed. On the contrary, obedience is demanded if one is to enjoy the benefits of the Abrahamic-Davidic-New Covenant; however, failure to *participate* in the benefits will not thereby frustrate the plan of God as announced in the covenant. Even if some people do not *participate* in these benefits, they must, by virtue of their being part of Israel or (even more critically) of the messianic line, *transmit* these benefits to their successors.

The Restoration to the Land

Did not Israel return from the Babylonian exile and thus fulfill the prophetic promise that she would be restored to her land? Had not Isaiah prophesied that God would "reach out his hand a second time to reclaim the remnant" (Isa 11:11)? And did he not promise to "assemble the scattered people of Judah from the four quarters of the earth" (Isa 11:12) in a context of the Messiah being revealed to the nations of the world—that "shoot from the stump of Jesse" (Isa 11:1)?

If the *first* return was the Exodus out of Egypt under Moses (and it was), could we not regard the return from Babylon after Cyrus' decree in 536 B.C. the fulfillment of the *second* return?

We think not, for in 518 B.C., some eighteen years after the decree and Zerubbabel's return, Zechariah is still promising the same reassembling of Israel from the nations of the earth.

> I will strengthen the house of Judah
> and save the house of Joseph.
> I will restore them. . . .
> Though I scatter them among the peoples,
> yet in distant lands they will remember me.
> They and their children will survive,
> and they will return.
> I will bring them back from Egypt
> and gather them from Assyria.
> I will bring them to Gilead and Lebanon,
> and there will not be room enough for them.
>
> Zech 10:6–10

Clearly, then, the plans for a restoration to their land had not been terminated or fulfilled in the return from the Babylonian exile. Moreover, that return from Babylon had not been from all over the world, from its four quarters; it had only been a return from Babylon. Thus, it could not have been the long-awaited second return.

Others will agree with these points but will attempt to solve the problem by placing Isaiah's predicted return of Israel a "second time" from the "four quarters [or "corners"] of the earth" (Isa 11:11–12 KJV) in a spiritual context. Since the new return is pointedly linked with Messiah's being revealed to the nations of the world, these objectors argue, can we not say that "this new gathering of Israel's remnant (Isa 11:16) has been occurring simultaneously with the evangelization of the Gentiles (see Rom 11:11, 14)? This remnant is then identical to those Jews who acclaim Jesus as their Messiah and Savior, that is, the true Israelites according to St. Paul (Rom 9:6–8)."27

However, this move will not solve the exegetical issues involved. The focus of the Isaiah passage, as in literally dozens of other prophetic texts, is that it is the Lord who is moving to restore and repatriate his people, not the people themselves. It is still a difficult question to answer: does the return follow the conversion of the Jews or does their conversion come after their return? At times one has the impression that it is the former order, as in Deuteronomy 30, and sometimes the latter, as perhaps in Isaiah 11. But certainly Ezekiel 36:1–37:14 is very plain: first Israel returns

---

27Wilch, "The Land," 174.

and the scattered bones are gathered together, "but there was no breath (i.e., "life") in them." Since this passage in Ezekiel 36–37 seems to be the *sedes doctrinae,* or the chair teaching passage, it is best that we answer that Israel will probably be returned to her land by her Lord and will only subsequently be revived by a great revival and outpouring of the Holy Spirit. Therefore, we cannot accept Wilch's spiritualized interpretation, even though he wishes to employ "the Christocentric principle of hermeneutics."[28] His corollary to this principle, which he regards as the theological *crucis,* "is that the New Testament must always be the guide for interpreting the Old Testament; Old Testament passages may not become the basis for giving the primary direction for the interpretation of New Testament passages."[29]

What a pity! What on earth did the original audiences of the OT do until the New came? If they were in such a primitive state, how could Jesus have rebuked the two disciples on the road to Emmaus (Luke 24:25–27) and Nicodemus (John 3) so strongly? How could they have known messianic teaching, the new birth, or Holy Spirit theology? Yet Jesus roundly rebuked them with the hard-hitting term "fools" (Luke 24:25) and expressed amazement that Nicodemus in this pre-cross, pre-NT era was "Israel's teacher" and yet he did "not understand these things" (John 3:10). Given the explanation of the Christological principle of exegesis (as stated above), could not we, or the disciples, have sprung to the defense of such poor hapless souls as the Emmaus-bound disciples or Nicodemus and object: "But Lord, wait until they have the NT, then you can scold them!"

The irony of this discussion is this: without the real, literal, physical restoration of Israel to her land as part of the single covenant of God, there is no Christological element; for all three items are inextricably tied together: the heir (Messiah = Christology), the heritage (the gospel; Gen 12:3, cf. Gal 3:8), and the inheritance of the land. Break one and the others fall, for each is just as permanent as the others.[30]

When this is put together with the repeated claim of the prophets that God will return his people to their land "in the latter days" (e.g., Hos 3:5), the case is irrefutable. Jeremiah and Ezekiel

---

[28] Ibid., 174.

[29] Ibid., 173.

[30] Wilch's charge ("The Land", 173)—that this introduces the people and the land as "a kind of co-redemptrix" with Christ—misses the point by miles.

alone include twenty-five explicit statements about a return to the land (e.g., Jer 3:11–20; 12:14–17; 16:10–18; 23:1–8; 24:1–10; 29:1–14; 30:1–3; 30:10–11; 31:2–14; 31:15–20; 32:1–44; 50:17–20; Ezek 11:14–21; 20:39–44; 34:1–16; 35:1–36:15; 36:16–36; 37:1–14; 37:15–28; 39:21–29.[31] The evidence gets to be overwhelming when the other twelve prophets are included in the list.

The Land in the New Testament

Usually the counter charge is this: Christ foretold the destruction of Jerusalem and the dispersion of Israel (Luke 21:6, 20–24), but what did he or his apostles prophesy about the promised land or a return? Nothing!

That too is inaccurate. Romans 9–11 is the great teaching passage in the NT on this question. In fact, so important is the discussion of the Jew that it is impossible to discuss the issue of our salvation without raising the question of the Jew. Thus, Romans 9–11 is not a "parenthesis" in Paul's argumentation, as I had been taught and as many others still repeat; rather, it is intrinsic to his argument: "I am not ashamed of the gospel, because it is the power of God for the salvation of everyone who believes: first for the Jew, then for the Gentile" (Rom 1:16). Thus, Paul's whole argument about soteriology *must include, throughout the whole book of Romans,* the place of the Jew; it has not been restricted to Romans 9–11.

Paul mounts two very important arguments in Romans 11:11–12:

1. Israel's disobedience and dispersion was not the end of her calling. In fact, "She is and remains the link between the Messiah and the nations. She could be this link through her obedience, but even now, in her disobedience, she still fulfills her functions as a link."[32] As Romans 11:11 says,

---

[31] For one of the first studies on land theology in the prophets, see Elmer Martens, "Motivations for the Promise of Israel's Restoration to the Land in Jeremiah and Ezekiel," (Ph.D. dissertation, Claremont Graduate School, 1972), 172–96. There are also indirect prophecies on this theme (Jer 30:18–22; 31:23–25; 33:1–18; Ezek 28:20–26; 34:17–31).

[32] Hendrikus Berkhof, *Christ, the Meaning of History,* trans. Lambertus Buurman (Richmond: Knox, 1966), 142.

"because of their transgression, salvation has come to the
Gentiles. . . . "

2. If all this good has come as a result of Israel's failure,
think of it: what will happen to the Gentiles (indeed, the
whole world) when their full inclusion comes? (Rom 11:12).

Several amazing facts are unveiled here. First of all, in the
context of speaking about God's election of Israel and the patriarchs, we are reminded once again that "God's gifts and his call are
irrevocable" (Rom 11:29). Did we not argue above that that
covenant was unconditional (on man's part) and unilaterally obligat-
ing only to God? "Oh, the depth of the riches of the wisdom and
knowledge of God" (Rom 11:33)!

In the second place, what is this "fullness" (RSV "full
inclusion," or "full number"—*plēroma,* Rom 11:12)? Verse 12 must
be studied in connection with verse 25, where the same word is
used for the "full number" of the Gentiles that must come to Christ
in faith during the time of Israel's "failure." After that "full
number" (*plēroma*) (v. 25) has been reached, then comes Israel's
opportunity for her "full number" (v. 12). When this total number
of Gentiles that God intends to be saved comes, it will be the end of
the age (i.e., eschatological times). The gathering of Gentiles goes
on throughout all of history, but when the "fullness," or "full
number," comes, we will have arrived at the time when Messiah
wraps up the historical process. Thus, Romans 11:25 is similar to
Luke 21:24—"Jerusalem will be trodden down by the Gentiles
until the times of the Gentiles are fulfilled" (RSV). Jesus has this
comment: "When you see these things happening, you know that
the kingdom of God is near" (Luke 21:31).

In spite of the fact that all interpreters agree that the term
"Israel" ten out of eleven times points unmistakably to the Jews in
distinction from the Gentiles, many balk on the eleventh usage in
Romans 11:26 ("and so all Israel will be saved"). Indeed, the more
common interpretation views this text in Paul as requiring a large
scale conversion of the nation of Israel just before or at the time of
Christ's second coming after the "full number" of the Gentiles has
been gathered in.

But Anthony A. Hoekema poses two objections to this
interpretation. First, Romans 11:26 does not say "And *then* (implying the Greek word *tote* or *epeita*) all Israel will be saved," but it
has *[kai] houtōs* ("thus, so, in this manner"), a word describing
manner, not temporal succession. "In other words, Paul is not

saying, 'Israel has experienced a hardening in part until the full number of the Gentiles has come in, and *then* (after this has happened) all Israel will be saved.' But he is saying, 'Israel has experienced a hardening in part until the full number of the Gentiles has come in, and *in this way* all Israel will be saved.'"[33]

Second, to limit the salvation of Israel to the end times does not do justice to the word "all" in "all Israel." This last generation is only the capstone and a fragment of all those Jews who have ever lived on earth and who have also believed.

These are two excellent challenges, but they had already been met by Hendrikus Berkhof[34] thirteen years prior to Hoekema's publication. To the first he replied:

> We do not read "then" or "after this" but there is no reason to exclude the possibility that this "and so" is a future event. Paul is dealing with the historical order of God's activities, and only just before used the conjunction "until" (25). Yet, "and so" implies more than "until." However, it is less clear what the antecedent of "and so" is.[35]

Berkhof goes on to suggest that one could connect "and so" with "until the full number of the Gentiles has come in" (i.e., "because the full number of the Gentiles has come in, all Israel will be saved"). Or one could read "and so all Israel will be saved" (i.e., the last will be first and the first temporarily the last). Alternatively, in the rest of the words of verse 26, the phrase could depict both the result and the manner in which Israel will be saved: "The Redeemer will come from Zion; he will turn godlessness away from Jacob."

The point that both Hoekema and Berkhof miss is that Romans 11:27 linked this "and so" with "this is my covenant with them when I take away their sins." This can be nothing other than a reference to what Jeremiah calls the "New Covenant" (Jer 31:31–34) but which is referred to in some sixteen other passages as "my Covenant," the "Eternal Covenant," "The New Heart and New Spirit," etc. The contents of this covenant are a renewal and an expansion of the promises made to Abraham and David. Thus, we are back to the land promises again! Even more noticeable is the expansion of this land promise in the same contexts that one finds

---

[33]Anthony A. Hoekema, *The Bible and the Future* (Grand Rapids: Eerdmans, 1979), 144–45.

[34]Berkhof, *Christ, the Meaning of History*, 145–56.

[35]Ibid., 145.

the "New Covenant" discussed (e.g., Jer 31:35–40). Only if the sun and moon cease to shine will this promise be nullified, but the last time I checked, both were still operating; it would appear the promise is still in place.

John Murray, the late venerable Reformed theologian, after noting that verses 26–27 were quotations from Isaiah 59:20–21 and Jeremiah 31:34, commented: "There should be no question but Paul regards these Old Testament passages as applicable to the restoration of Israel. We cannot dissociate this covenantal assurance from the proposition in support of which the text is adduced or from that which follows in verse 28 ["on account of the patriarchs"]. Thus the effect is that the future restoration of Israel is certified by nothing less than the certainty belonging to covenantal institution."[36]

Therefore, even though the "and so" may not be temporal in its reference, it is sequential in thought and consequential in that it ties in the promises of the patriarchal-Davidic-New Covenant with the coming in of the "full number," or "full inclusion," of Israel. Once this is admitted, the unity and connectedness of the three elements of the promise (Messiah, gospel, land) come back into play for a fully developed theology.

What about Hoekema's second complaint against limiting this "full inclusion" to the end times? Once again, his failure comes in his refusal to see the past and present remnant of Israel as the foundation and guarantee that God would complete his work in a grand eschatological and climactic act. The prophets had depicted the remnant returning to the land (Isa 10:20–23) and becoming prominent among the nations (Isa 2:2; Mic 4:1) in the end day.

Another indication that Israel's conversion will be the immediate presage that the kingdom of glory has arrived is Romans 11:15—"For if their rejection means the reconciliation of the world, what will their acceptance mean but life from the dead?" (RSV). This "life from the dead" could be taken spiritually, but Scripture docs not use it this way.[37] It seems more natural to say that by this phrase, Paul means the reestablishment of Israel as God's people in their land again. Was not this the figure of Ezekiel 37:12, 14? Ezekiel heard the Lord say, "O my people. I am going to open your graves and bring you up from them; I will bring you back to the land

---

[36] John Murray, *The Epistle to the Romans*, 2 vols. (Grand Rapids: Eerdmans, 1965), 2:99–100.

[37] Berkhof, *Christ, the Meaning of History*, 144–45.

of Israel. . . . I will put my Spirit in you and you will live, and I will settle you in your own land." Thus, in this case, the mention of the "Redeemer," or "Deliverer," who "will come from Zion" is a reference, not, as Hoekema had hoped, to our Lord's *first* advent, but instead to his *second* coming.

Only in a holistic, canonical approach to interpreting Scripture can we begin to derive the richness, the depth, the wisdom and splendor there is to be found in the plan of God. To delete restoration to the land from the promise-covenant of God and to superimpose the NT over the OT would be to form a canon within a canon. The church has already been tested under this Marcionite logic, and we must once again refuse to capitulate to it or even to dabble with a "sanctified" (?) form of eisegesis, which exegetes the OT with NT eyeglasses.

Failure to grapple with the physical side of the plan of God opens us to the accusation raised by the 1904 Stone Lectures at Princeton Seminary by Willis J. Beecher:

> . . . If the Christian interpreter persists in excluding the ethical Israel from his conception of the fulfillment, or in regarding Israel's part in the matter as merely preparatory and not eternal, then he comes into conflict with the plain witness of both testaments. . . . Rightly interpreted, the biblical statements include in their fulfilment both Israel the race, with whom the covenant is eternal, and also the personal Christ and his mission, with the whole spiritual Israel of the redeemed in all ages.[38]

---

[38]Willis J. Beecher, *The Prophets and the Promise* (Grand Rapids: Baker, 1970), 383.

Chapter 3

The Old Testament as an Object of Criticism

Few individuals have had a more dramatic influence on the way Scripture would be interpreted in this century than Johann Salomo Semler (1725–91), for he is usually designated as the father of the technique that specialized in treating Scripture as an object of criticism and historical scrutiny. For many modern exegetes the key issue necessitating the historical-critical method would be encapsulated in Semler's assertion that "the root of the evil [in theology] is the interchangeable use of the terms 'Scripture' and 'Word of God.'"[1]

It was this unexpected tension between the human and the divine, between fact and interpretation, between what a text meant in the past and what it now means in the present, that has forced a whole new agenda for all who would wish to interpret the Bible and still claim to be conversant with the achievements and discussions of the scholarly world in the last two hundred years.

What is not immediately clear to those who are new to these

---

[1]Johann S. Semler, "Abhandlung von freier Untersuchung des Kanon," *Texte zur Kirchen- und Theologiegeschichte,* 5 (Gutersloh, 1967), 43, 47, 55, 58, as cited by Gerhard Maier, *The End of the Historical-Critical Method,* trans. Edwin W. Leverenz and Rudolph F. Norden (St. Louis: Concordia, 1977), 15.

discussions is that the terms *historical* and *critical* have taken on specialized meanings and methodologies. For example, there are two basic definitions for the word *criticism* in the expression *biblical criticism.* According to the *Oxford English Dictionary,* the first is: "The action of criticizing, or passing judgement upon the qualities or merits of anything; *esp.* the passing of unfavourable judgement; fault-finding, censure." The second is: "The art of estimating the qualities and character of literary or artistic work; the function or work of a critic."

Unfortunately there is much in contemporary biblical criticism to justify the use of this first definition. However, the second definition is more appropriate of those who, like James Orr in his article entitled "Criticism of the Bible" in the well-known conservative *International Standard Bible Encyclopaedia,* use it to describe "higher criticism": the domain of biblical introduction that takes up questions of date, authorship, genuineness, sources, destination, and purpose.[2] Even though Orr warned that destructive use of criticism (the kind that is closer to the first definition) " . . . tends to widen out illimitably into regions where exact science cannot follow it, where, often, the critic's imagination is his only law,"[3] he affirmed that "it would be wrong, however, to deny the legitimate place of 'higher criticism,' or belittle the great services it is capable of rendering, because of the abuses to which it is frequently liable."[4]

However, to speak of *the* "historical critical" method is in itself a most dubious procedure. It "is not a uniform method but rather a set of assumptions thought to be operative in doing historical research. . . ."[5] Those assumptions appear to be best summarized by George A. Kelly as the three governing principles of the historical-critical method: "(1) *autonomy*—the research scholar [will] make up his own mind in light of the evidence; (2) *analogy*—the credibility of a past event [is] tested in the light of its similarity to the modern experience; [and] (3) *causality*—the conclusion or datum is part of a cause-effect series."[6] Each of these principles

[2]James Orr, "Criticism of the Bible," *The International Standard Bible Encyclopaedia,* ed. James Orr, 5 vols. (Grand Rapids: Eerdmans, 1952), 2:748–53.

[3]Ibid., 749.

[4]Ibid.

[5]Archie L. Nations, "Historical Criticism and the Current Methodological Crisis," *Scottish Journal of Theology* 36 (1983): 63.

[6]George A. Kelly, *The New Biblical Theorists: Raymond E. Brown and Beyond* (Ann Arbor, Mich.: Servant, 1983), 21.

deserves a fuller explanation, but even with these provisional definitions it is clear that Semler's sentence still touches the heart of the problem: can such critics be judges of Scripture and still have a remainder called the Word of God that will judge the critics and all its readers?

One of the most serious areas where this bifurcation erupted was in the tension that modern scholars felt between the picture drawn from a critically assured minimum found in the alleged brute facts of history and the kerygmatically necessary picture of OT persons and events demanded by a theology of belief. What was the connection between history and belief, and for how much of OT history could modern historiography vouch? This question must take the chief place in our investigation of the OT as the object of criticism.

IF JERICHO BE NOT RAZED, IS OUR FAITH IN VAIN?

The fundamental problem that underlies all the numerous issues in the study of OT history was best summarized by Walter Eichrodt: it is "the discrepancy between the picture of history constructed by critical study and the salvation-history portrayed in the utterances of OT faith. . . . "[7] The discrepancy, as viewed by many today, is a choice between "actual" history and believed history. In their view there were few, if any, *bruta facta* in the OT on which to ground one's confession or faith; instead, faith would need to go beyond any minimal assurances that historical criticism could yield.

In spite of what appears to be a scholarly consensus on this bifurcation of faith and history, another group of scholars have argued that belief was grounded in real history. Roland de Vaux, one representative of this group, wrote: "If the historical faith of Israel is not in a certain way founded in *history,* this faith is erroneous and cannot command my assent" (my emphasis).[8] The argument is similar to the apostle Paul's famous challenge: "If Christ be not raised, your faith is in vain; you are still in your sins" (1 Cor 15:17, my translation): or put it in George W. Ramsey's turn of phrase, "If Jericho be not razed, is our faith in vain?"[9]

---

[7]Walter Eichrodt, *Theology of the Old Testament* (London: SCM, 1960), 1:512.
[8]Roland de Vaux, "Method in the Study of Early Hebrew History," in *The Bible in Modern Scholarship,* ed. J. P. Hyatt, (Nashville: Abingdon: 1965), 16.
[9]George W. Ramsey, *The Quest of the Historical Israel* (Atlanta: Knox, 1981), 107–24.

It is necessary to gain some understanding of the key role that Ernst Troeltsch (1865–1923) played in systematizing the historical-critical method and especially the role that the principle of analogy played in this method. The dilemma posed in the tension between scientific historiography and OT theology is this: The historian employs the principle of analogy, and that precludes any and all unique events, since he must assume that the events of the past are analogous to those he experiences in the present. As Van A. Harvey observed, "Without the principle of analogy, it seems impossible to understand the past; if, however, one employs the principle of analogy, it seems impossible to do justice to the alleged uniqueness of [a crossing of the Reed or Red Sea, or the capture of Jericho or a Mount Carmel descent of fire]."[10]

According to Troeltsch, historical criticism operates on three inseparable principles: criticism, analogy and correlation.[11] (1) The *principle of criticism* is that we can classify our judgments about the past, not as true or false, but only as claiming greater or lesser probability. (2) The *principle of analogy* indicates that our present experience is analogous to that of those in the past, and it allows for no occurrences that are unique or outside of this framework of experience. (3) The *principle of universal correlation* holds that all historical data are so interrelated and dependent that no change can occur at one point in the historical nexus without a change in all that surrounds it. Historical explanation of an event, in Troeltsch's definition, must be made in terms of its antecedents and consequences within the causal nexus of our spatial and temporal categories.

The Achilles' heel of Troeltsch's view is his principle of analogy; " ... it requires unnecessary assent to an ontological world-view which precludes the existence of God or his activity in history from the outset."[12] To be more specific, Troeltsch's principle of analogy, which is so central to most historical-critical

[10]Van A. Harvey, *The Historian and the Believer: The Morality of Historical Knowledge and Christian Belief* (New York: Macmillan, 1966), 32, as cited by Ted Peters, "The Use of Analogy in the Historical Method," *Catholic Biblical Quarterly* 35 (1973): 475.
[11]In his essay "Über historische und dogmatische Methode in der Theologie," first appearing in 1898 in *Theologie als Wissenschaft*, ed. Gerhard Sauter, *Theologische Bücherei* 43 (1971): 105–27. Also in *Gesammelte Schriften* (Tübingen: J. C. B. Mohr, 1913), 2:729–53. Also see Ernst Troeltsch, "Historiography," in *Encyclopedia of Religion and Ethics*, ed. James Hastings, 12 vols. (Edinburgh: T. & T. Clark, 1913; reprint, New York: Scribner, 1951), 6:716–23.
[12]Peters, "The Use of Analogy," 477.

methodologies as practiced in OT studies today, demands that there be a "fundamental homogeneity (*Gleichartigkeit*) of all historical events."[13] For him, all history must accede to being limited to the current range of our experience and research.

Wolfhart Pannenberg[14] (Professor of Systematic Theology at the University of Munich), however, correctly detected Troeltsch's overconfidence when he reduced all reality to the current range of experience and turned a *method* of investigating history into a *theory of reality*. Every event, without exception, Troeltsch claimed, could be comprehended in a "core of homogeneity." The realm of the transcendent was strictly precluded, and human experience set the norm for what could or could not have happened in the past.

But must we not be prepared, even as historians, to encounter, as Pannenberg warned, some events that may burst our analogies and set limits to what analogy can offer?[15] Pannenberg's solution is to distinguish between the *positive* use of analogy (in which a particular event is judged to be *more likely* an historical event if there are similar events known from other sources) and a *negative* use of analogy (in which an event is doubtful, since it has no other events similar to it that conform to "our present critically informed beliefs about the world"). It is the latter usage that Pannenberg finds spurious, for it exceeds its function as a methodology of investigating history and turns it instead into a conclusion about all reality and a world view in which everything conforms to a "core-homogeneity."[16]

In spite of the large scholarly consensus on the principle of analogy, at least two versions of Israel's earlier history emerged from use of the historical-critical method. The Albrecht Alt/Martin Noth school,[17] following Hermann Gunkel's method of form-criticism, judged that much could be ascertained about the written texts from the oral tradition behind the Scripture, but little, if anything, in the pre-monarchical period could be classified as historical. Over

---

[13] Troeltsch, *Gesammelte Schriften*, 2:732; Peters, ibid.

[14] Wolfhart Pannenberg, *Basic Questions in Theology* (Philadelphia: Fortress, 1970–71), 1:39–53; Peters, ibid.

[15] Pannenberg, *Basic Questions*, 1:48–9; Peters, ibid., 479.

[16] So summarizes Peters, ibid., 481.

[17] See the discussion on this school by Roland de Vaux, "Method," 15–29, and the response by George E. Mendenhall, 30–36.

against this German school was the American Baltimore school of William Foxwell Albright/George Ernest Wright/John Bright.[18] This school focused on the close parallels between the external sources of the Ancient Near East and the OT. The hope was that the extensive studies in Ancient Near Eastern linguistics, texts, pottery, stratigraphy, and archaeological artifacts would supply the controls necessary to establish the general reliability of the biblical texts.

While Evangelicals found the Albright/Wright/Bright school more objective—in that it appealed to some external controls (even though it shared many of the critical assumptions and results with most of the critical methodologies)—this school also failed to transcend the minimally assured results of scientific historiography and thereby to meet the needs of the community of faith. Fact and interpretation, event and word still remained separated from each other, even in the American school.

Once again it was Pannenberg who forged a new position in the debate by arguing against distinguishing historical facts from their meanings. In his view, "every event has its original meaning within the context of occurrence and tradition in which it took place."[19] In order to escape the traditional charges that salvation history is too provincial for the scientific interests of the historian, he broadened salvation history to a universal history that embraced reality in its totality and that was grounded in the unity of God, who works in both salvation and universal history. Thus, in Pannenberg's openness to all of reality and to a universal history, his world included a realm of the transcendent. It also provided for uniting facts with their meanings. Herein lies the possibility for a new starting-point in historical research. The ancient dichotomy between positivistic history and the language of faith is, therefore, overcome in a concept of a total reality and an original unity of facts and their meanings.

Without adopting the major presuppositional and philosophical baggage that Pannenberg's method of a universal reality would demand, we can certainly respond enthusiastically to his proposal that the original unity of historical facts and their meaning is the best starting position to begin OT studies. The modern dichotomy

---

[18]John Bright, *Early Israel in Recent History Writing* (London: SCM, 1956), evaluates and critiques the Alt-Noth School while setting forth the distinctives of his own school.

[19]Wolfhart Pannenberg, "The Revelation of God in Jesus Christ," *Theology as History* (New York: Harper & Row, 1967), 127.

between fact and meaning is itself already an "interpreted history, namely, interpreted on the basis of historico-philosophical premises."[20]

Now the whole point of this discussion simply put is this: Is there a necessary correlation between the factualness, or even the degree of historical truth, in a biblical account and the theological value and usefulness that history has for the life of faith?

Ramsey adamantly disagrees with the conclusions of such writers as John Warwick Montgomery, Clark Pinnock, and Francis Schaeffer, whom he summarily labels "fundamentalist theologians."[21] In particular, Ramsey feels the sting of Schaeffer's critique about divorcing faith from reason and thereby disinfecting faith from its historical verifiability. But Ramsey is unimpressed by this need for objective verification to detect where one should place genuine faith as opposed to a blind leap in the dark of subjective credulity. His complaint no doubt embodies one of the chief suspicions about all Evangelicals who claim simultaneously to hold a high regard for the claims of the biblical text while also affirming the legitimacy of their employment of every critical method and tool that proves its mettle when judged by the standards of truthfulness and fairness. His complaint is this: Evangelicals (his Fundamentalists) demand that we must first of all establish as probable that the past events (e.g., miracles) *did take place* and *are not fictitious* in nature[22] In other words, the Evangelical plays favorites and frequently lets the biblical writers get off too easy without challenging their accounts as a disciplined, critical news reporter would. Thus, the answer to the question "What happened?" is all too often a foregone conclusion for Evangelicals, moans Ramsey: it is whatever the biblical writers said happened. But this is not the work of a historian or a true biblical critic; it is "simply [being] a purveyor of tradition."[23] Ramsey concludes that "the Fundamentalist principle of verification" may be stated thus:

> Confirmation (or verification) of God's existence and activity comes through the occurrence of unlawful happenings which cannot be accounted for by natural factors.[24]

---

[20]Gerhard F. Hasel, *Old Testament Theology: Basic Issues in the Current Debate*, rev. ed. (Grand Rapids: Eerdmans, 1984), 101.

[21]Ramsey, *The Quest*, 108, a label that suggests that he is somewhat of a novice when it comes to understanding the history of his conservative contemporaries.

[22]Ibid., 111.

[23]Ibid.

[24]Ibid., 113. He italicized this whole definition in his text.

Unfortunately for Ramsey, he never quotes any of those he disagrees with for any part of this definition. I would have been surprised had he been able to do so; for it is one thing to admit elements of mystery in God's universe, but it is another to know that such are "unlawful" and that they can *never* be "accounted for by natural factors." As Ramsey admits, such a claim would call for omniscience, and no one but God deserves that attribution.

What Ramsey cannot adopt is the Evangelicals' approach to the historical claims of the Bible. We Evangelicals judge the events and details of those happenings to be innocent until proven guilty— in much the same way as the American system of jurisprudence demands the person be held to be innocent until proven guilty. In a previous generation, this approach was a prerequisite for any study in the humanities, be it Herodotus, Xenophon, or a writer from the Ancient Near East. The alternative negative critical approach, however, prides itself on adopting just the opposite approach: the text is untrustworthy except in those isolated portions where scholarship has been able to extricate a rare strand of historical fact.

But can faith be founded on anything less than fact, truth, or event? Granted, faith must exceed this starting point and go beyond historical fact and the limits to which reason at that point is able to go. But can faith be properly *placed* between competing claims, or rightfully *grounded* if it has not touched us visibly, really, and truthfully in our space/time world? This is not to say that faith must have *comprehensive* truth and facts (i.e., know every fact and have omniscient control of all historical events) in order to judge where God acted to reveal himself and his salvation for us sinners. But it does demand that there be *adequate* evidence, evidences that are rational, historical, experiential and revelational.

Ramsey thinks differently. "What is lost," he queries, "if the Jacob story is discovered—to consider another possibility—to be an out-and-out fiction, derived from *no* actual person"?[25] Very little, he answers, for the theological value exceeds all the discussions of secondary developments in the growth of the Jacob cycle. It is not all that essential that theology be based on historically accurate events or on actual persons! But what, then, has "theology" become? Who now is the "purveyor of tradition"? The apostle Peter would have bitterly protested: "We did not follow cleverly invented stories" (2 Peter 1:16).

Not more than three decades ago, many outside the Evangeli-

---

[25]Ibid., 122.

cal stream of scholarship voiced similar conclusions. For example, George Ernest Wright wrote, "In Biblical faith everything depends upon whether the central events actually occurred."[26] Likewise, Alan Richardson agreed: "The Christian faith . . . is bound up with certain happenings in the past, and if these happenings could be shown never to have occurred, or to have been quite different from the biblical-Christian account of them, then the whole edifice of Christian faith, life and worship would be found to have been built on sand."[27] And, as we have already quoted above, Father Roland de Vaux affirmed, "If the historical faith of Israel is not in a certain way founded in history, this faith is erroneous and cannot command my assent."[28] But their voice is being lost in the fast pace of contemporary critical studies; apparently it is a sufficient answer to label and lump George Ernest Wright, Alan Richardson, and Father de Vaux together with Montgomery, Pinnock, and Schaeffer as "fundamentalist theologians."

What shall we conclude then? Is our faith in vain if Jericho be not razed? Can we have criticism exclusively in the first sense supplied by the *Oxford English Dictionary,* ending with "fault finding," "censure," and "unfavorable judgments"?

History itself has already supplied her judgment on this procedure, for it is all too common today to hear the scholarly lament about the minimalistic inheritance, indeed, the vacuum, that negative criticism has bequeathed to her adherents. There appears to be very little, if anything, left on which to build a theology or a message. Surely the current theological bankruptcy of much of negative criticism is the best answer to our question.

Without Jesus' real resurrection from the grave, there is not Christianity, as the Apostle Paul insisted. Without the Exodus, there is nothing to the claim repeated 125 times in the OT, "I am the Lord God who brought you up out of the land of bondage." In like manner, if the evidence proves that Jericho was not destroyed or that Jacob was not a real person, can the attached claims to these dubious narratives warrant benefit or require faith and duty from any of us? We think not!

---

[26] George Ernest Wright, *The God Who Acts* (Naperville, Ill.: Allenson, 1952), 126.

[27] Alan Richardson, *Christian Apologetics* (London: SCM, 1947), 91.

[28] de Vaux, "Method," 16.

IF THE CRITICAL METHOD IS FOUND DEFICIENT, IS THERE AN EVANGELICAL ALTERNATIVE?

Nevertheless, I fear that all that has been said will be reduced to an argument about selecting between competing presuppositions. What, precisely, is a better and more adequate critical method, if the current model is found wanting in some major areas?

What is strikingly lacking in the whole debate is an extended methodological discussion as to how the tools of secular critical history may be applied to the Christian revelation. It is not enough to epitomize the task in Benjamin Jowett's famous phrase that the Bible must be interpreted "like any other book,"[29] for all admit to some kind of qualification that still allows this book to be the revelation of God. But what are those qualifications?[30]

Nigel Cameron, using Stephen Toulmin's *Uses of Argument*,[31] attempts to give us the anatomy of the historical critical model and a possible way out of the impasse of the last century. Laying aside the conventional syllogistic method of argumentation, Toulmin constructs this model:

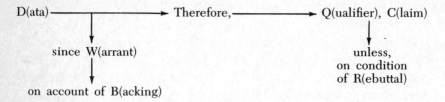

Thus, we move from D(data) to C(claim) justified by W(warrant) supported by B(backing), with Q(qualifier) representing the possibility of R(rebuttal).

Now the characteristic critical argument begins by assuming the methods of historical criticism, such as doubt, analogy, correlation, and autonomy. The D(data) represents the phenomena culled from the text of Scripture, such as historical improbabilities,

---

[29] Benjamin Jowett, "On the Interpretation of Scripture," in *The Interpretation of Scripture and Other Essays* (London: George Routledge and Sons, 1907); reprint from 1860 edition of *Essays and Review*.

[30] These questions were best raised by Nigel M. de S. Cameron, "Inspiration and Criticism: The Nineteenth-Century Crises," *Tyndale Bulletin* 35 (1984): 138.

[31] Stephen Toulmin, *The Uses of Argument* (Cambridge: Cambridge University Press, 1958). See also Harvey, *The Historian and the Believer*, 54; and Colin Brown, "History and the Believer," in *History, Criticism, and Faith*, ed. Colin Brown (Downers Grove: InterVarsity, 1977), 166.

insufficient evidence, modification of the material by an editor (or editors), discrepancies between and within accounts, comparisons with nonbiblical accounts, alleged supernatural occurrences, and literary genre.[32]

The resulting model, Cameron[33] suggests, is this:

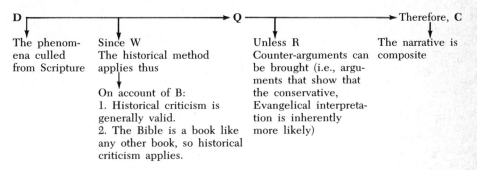

D ─────────────────────────────► Q ─────────────────────────────► Therefore, C

| The phenomena culled from Scripture | Since W The historical method applies thus | Unless R Counter-arguments can be brought (i.e., arguments that show that the conservative, Evangelical interpretation is inherently more likely) | The narrative is composite |

On account of B:
1. Historical criticism is generally valid.
2. The Bible is a book like any other book, so historical criticism applies.

The Evangelical position, Cameron contends, goes like this:

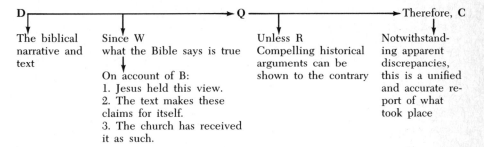

D ─────────────────────────────► Q ─────────────────────────────► Therefore, C

| The biblical narrative and text | Since W what the Bible says is true | Unless R Compelling historical arguments can be shown to the contrary | Notwithstanding apparent discrepancies, this is a unified and accurate report of what took place |

On account of B:
1. Jesus held this view.
2. The text makes these claims for itself.
3. The church has received it as such.

The point in debate, then, is not whether historical argument is applicable to the method; rather, it is *where* it should appear in the argument. Is it a *warrant* for reading the text or is it to be reserved as a *qualifier*, that is, a *condition* of rebuttal? Will our warrants justifying our moves from data to claim be *historical warrants* or *dogmatic warrants*?

Here is where the battle for or against the Bible is waged most fiercely. In common speech, the notion of criticism often

---

[32] This list reflects I. Howard Marshall's seven points of contact between historical criticism and the Bible, "Historical Criticism," *New Testament Interpretation: Essays on Principles and Methods,* ed. I. Howard Marshall (Grand Rapids: Eerdmans, 1977), 127–30.

[33] Cameron, "Inspiration and Criticism," 144–45.

carries the pejorative connotations we have previously noted: to criticize is to condemn, pass judgment, catalogue mistakes, and express a skeptical attitude. In etymology, the word "to criticize" signifies "to sift out, to divide from." But even more important is the epistemological stance that suggests that historical criticism is a way of knowing and a way of appropriating past traditions. This, in turn, raises the question of criteria.[34]

R. G. Collingwood cautioned that the critical historian, rather than

> relying on an authority other than himself, to whose statements his thought must conform . . . is his own authority and his thought [is] autonomous, self-authorizing, possessed of a criterion to which his so-called authorities must conform and by reference to which they are criticized.[35]

This autonomy of the critic is a warning that a new principle of authority has been introduced. Moreover, the critical historian

> *confers* authority upon a witness. He reserves the right to judge who or what will be called an authority, and he makes this judgment only after he has subjected the so-called witness to a vigorous cross-examination. . . . If the historian permits his authorities to stand uncriticized, he abdicates his role as critical historian. He is no longer a seeker of knowledge but a mediator of past belief; not a thinker, but a transmitter of tradition.[36]

These procedures and criteria turn out to be very expensive for the man or woman of faith. Again, Van Harvey explained:

> to enter the lists of the debate and to attempt to vindicate the truth of the sacred narrative, it was necessary to pay a costly price: it was necessary to accept the general canons and criteria of just those one desired to refute. One had, so to speak, to step onto the ground that the critics occupied. This was fatal to the traditionalist's cause, because he could no longer appeal to the eye of faith or to any special warrants. The arguments had to stand or fall on their own merits.[37]

---

[34] This point is made by Marlin E. Miller, "Criticism and Analogy in Historical-Critical Interpretation," in *Essays on Biblical Interpretation: Anabaptist-Mennonite Perspectives*, ed. Willard M. Swartley (Elkhart, Ind.: Institute of Mennonite Studies, 1984), 226.

[35] As quoted by Harvey, *The Historian and the Believer*, 40.

[36] Ibid., 42.

[37] Ibid., 105–6.

Cameron's solution is to appeal to the Bampton Lecturer for 1858, H. L. Mansel.[38] Proceeding from an argument that the infinitude of God means that there will be some matters pertaining to God that will not be fully understood by finite mortals like ourselves, Mansel applies the same principle to Scripture. Thus, rejecting one or more isolated portions of Scripture on the grounds that such element(s) is (are) repugnant to one's reason unleashes a principle that exalts man's reason over an infinite God. There is a proper use of reason in religious questions, he affirms, and that is not in deciding the *contents* of faith but the *evidences for* faith. Once these evidences have been accepted as sufficient and adequate for belief or trust, the entirety of revelation must be trusted. In his words:

> The objections urged against a religion are not like the weights of a scale, which retain their full value, even when outweighed by the other side:—on the contrary, they become absolutely worthless, as soon as we are convinced that there is superior evidence to prove that religion is true. . . . In a matter of which we are so ignorant and so liable to be deceived, the objection which fails to prove everything proves nothing: from him that hath not, is taken away even that which he seemeth to have. And on the other hand, an objection which really proves anything proves everything. If the teaching of Christ is in any one thing not the teaching of God, it is in all things the teaching of man: its doctrines are subject to all the imperfections inseparable from man's sinfulness and ignorance. . . . [39]

> Many who would shrink in horror from the idea of rejecting Christ altogether, will yet speak and act as if they were at liberty to set up for themselves an eclectic Christianity.[40]

Accordingly, once Christians are convinced of the truthfulness of the Christian religion, the believer is under obligation to accept it all. It is not only unreasonable but also irrational to substitute the authority of the believing subject in an eclectic *potpourri* of selected affirmations and Scripture texts over the infinite, speaking, God.

Cameron[41] analyzes the resulting model this way:

---

[38] H. L. Mansel, *The Limits of Religious Thought*, 5th ed. (London: John Murray, 1867), 4.

[39] Ibid., 161, as cited by Cameron, "Inspiration and Criticism," 154.

[40] Mansel, *The Limits*, 162, as cited by Cameron, ibid.

[41] Cameron, "Inspiration and Criticism," 155.

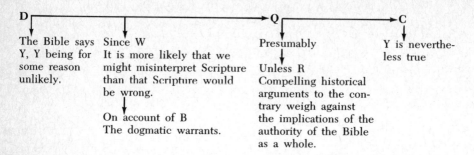

D

The Bible says Y, Y being for some reason unlikely.

Since W
It is more likely that we might misinterpret Scripture than that Scripture would be wrong.

On account of B
The dogmatic warrants.

Q

Presumably

Unless R
Compelling historical arguments to the contrary weigh against the implications of the authority of the Bible as a whole.

C

Y is nevertheless true

This, then, is the Evangelical alternative. The dogmatic warrant is substituted for the historical-critical warrant on the grounds that "every challenge to infallibility must carry sufficient weight to overthrow the whole principle of Biblical authority, or it must fall."[42] Nevertheless, the possibility of rebuttal still exists, and historical-critical arguments must be examined as one moves from data to claim at the level of qualifiers. In this sense, Evangelicals must remain open and proficient in all the critical methodologies, for these methodologies can be used as positive criticism—beside offering a negative check as possible qualifiers or giving potential rebuttals to the claims made by or on behalf of Scripture.

IF CRITICAL METHODS ARE TO BE USED, WHAT CONTRIBUTIONS MAY WE EXPECT FROM THEM?

John Barton, in a most candid exploration of such critical methodologies as structuralism, literary, form, redaction, and new criticism, concludes that they

> can take us some way towards a better understanding of what lies behind the biblical text, but they all seem to fail us if we look to them for help in reading the text as it actually meets us when we open a Bible. . . . The claim that any of these methods, or even all of them together, constitute the one "valid" way of handling the Old Testament seems to have an obvious flaw in it. The flaw is that there are questions we want to ask that none of these methods can answer for us. The methods we have got will simply not tell us what we want to know.[43]

---

[42] Ibid., 156.

[43] John Barton, *Reading the Old Testament: Method in Biblical Study* (Philadelphia: Westminster, 1984), 77–78.

But Barton's was not the first voice to be raised with this acknowledgment. In his 1980 presidential address to the centennial meeting of the Society of Biblical Literature, Bernhard W. Anderson summarized the situation in this manner:

> During the century of [SBL's] growth and service, much academic water has gone under the bridge and, as they say, many academic bridges have gone under the water. Perceptive members now say that the Society has reached a turning point, when "our fundamental methodologies for interpreting biblical texts" are in question and when even "the historical-critical method, in various forms the dominant *modus operandi* since the enlightenment, is under fire from many directions."[44]

Anderson's call was for a more serious regard for the final, or canonical, form of the text. In his view, scholars should move *through* criticism to "the second naivete," a post-critical posture that allows the text itself to speak directly to us.

Even more startling was the iconoclastic frankness of Walter Wink. Historical criticism, he alleged, was above everything else, an evangelistic tool to convert students from Fundamentalism to Liberalism.

> There can be little quarrel that the historical significance of the Graf-Wellhausen hypothesis (which no one today accepts as then formulated) was its usefulness as a method for destroying the conservative view of Biblical origins and inspiration, thereby destroying the entire ideology.[45]

> Far more fundamentally than revivalism, biblical criticism shook, shattered, and reconstituted generation after generation of students, and became their point of entree unto the "modern world."[46]

However, this drive for objectivity and scientific detachment in the form of biblical criticism, commented Wink, had "gone to seed" and was now "bankrupt" and a "dead letter":

> Simply but precisely put, the historical critical approach to biblical study had become bankrupt. Not dead: the critical tools have a potential usefulness, if they can only be brought

---

[44] Bernhard W. Anderson, "Tradition and Scripture in the Church," *Journal of Biblical Literature* 100 (1981): 5.

[45] Walter Wink, *The Bible in Human Transformation: Toward a New Paradigm for Biblical Study* (Philadelphia: Fortress, 1973), 12.

[46] Wink, *The Bible in Human Transformation*, 15.

under new management. But on the whole, the American scholarly scene is one of frenetic decadence. . . . Most scholars no longer address the lived experience of actual people in the churches or society.[47]

But there have been other voices as well. The conservative German Lutheran scholar, Gerhard Maier, issued his call for *The End of the Historical Critical Method*.[48] His objection was that the method created "a canon within a canon" by dividing the Scripture into divine and human components. Such a move removed the sovereign God, the authority of Scripture, and the church's spiritual functions from their legitimate roles and in their place installed critical evaluative judgments of those who as mortals also simultaneously claimed, as good churchpersons, to be under the authority of that Lord and the Word.

The irony of the situation was this: while dismissing objective controls in the area of an author's meaning, most contemporary theologians have gone to extreme lengths to avoid subjectivity in another area. Jay G. Williams offered this critique of this problem:

> In the [scholar's] attempt to avoid the apparently futile, sectarian quarrels of the past and to arrive at certainties, [they] have attempted to rid themselves of those subjective and communal biases which divided Christian scholars and to adopt a more scientific and detached attitude [of source and form criticism].[49]

But alas, bemoaned Williams, for "scarcely a word is said about the meaning of the text. It lies before the reader like an inert, dissected corpse."[50]

A similar cry came from O. C. Edwards, Jr.

> It has been assumed for many years in the theological seminaries of all the major denominations that responsible interpretation of the Bible is interpretation that uses the historical-critical method. Without wishing to deny that axiom completely, I do wish to propose that today the

[47]Walter Wink, "How I Have Been Snagged by the Seat of My Pants While Reading the Bible," *Christian Century* 24 (1975): 816.

[48]Gerhard Maier, *The End of the Historical-Critical Method,* trans. Edwin W. Leverenz and Rudolph F. Norden (St. Louis: Concordia, 1977).

[49]Jay G. Williams, "Exegesis-Eisegesis: Is There a Difference?" *Theology Today* 30 (1973–74): 226.

[50]Ibid., 224.

historical method is in trouble. The particular kind of trouble is . . . a failure of nerve.[51]

Even as long ago as 1941, J. N. Sanders had sounded forth the same warning.

> The application of the methods of historical criticism to the N.T. . . . is proving to be inadequate to achieve the aim which the N.T. scholar sets before himself—namely, that of understanding and expounding the N.T. This does not mean [he hastened to add] that historical criticism is without value. Its value is real, but it is only the preliminary [task] to the real exposition of Scripture, . . . which may be said to be achieved when one hears in the language of one's own time the message which one is convinced was meant by the author of one's text.[52]

With all of these calls for caution, many of my readers will expect that this Evangelical writer will summarily dismiss everything these methodologies have to offer and will not trouble himself to discern whether there are not some extremely helpful contributions here mixed in with some large doses of abuse. But this would be to misread my intentions and direction.

Naturally, Evangelicals will have no part of a methodology that demands prior allegiance to a philosophical grid or a *Vorverständnis* that imbibes in a flat-world spirit of modernity while simultaneously scaling down the textual claims of Scripture to sizes more to the liking of twentieth-century secular men and women. On the other hand, the careful and appropriately introduced employment of many of the tools of higher criticism cannot be an optional luxury—even for the Evangelical.

The Historical-Critical Method can be credited, at least partially, with a number of achievements. Along with Edgar Krentz,[53] we can include the following:

---

[51] O. C. Edwards, Jr., "Historical-Critical Method's Failure of Nerve and a Prescription for a Tonic: A Review of Some Recent Literature," *Anglican Theological Review* 59 (1977): 116.

[52] J. N. Sanders, "The Problem of Exegesis," *Theology* 43 (1941): 325. Note the last part of his quotation reflects the situation over forty-five years ago, before the autonomy of a text from the author's truth intentions become the current rage!

[53] Edgar Krentz, *The Historical-Critical Method* (Philadelphia: Fortress, 1975), 63–67, as cited by Willard M. Swartley "Beyond the Historical-Critical Method," in *Essays on Biblical Interpretation: Anabaptist-Mennonite Perspectives*, ed. Willard M. Swartley (Elkhart, Ind.: Institute of Mennonite Studies, 1984), 240–41.

1. A wealth of research tools such as grammars, lexica, concordances, original text editions, theological dictionaries, histories, and critical commentaries;

2. A "better grasp of the original grammatical and *historical sense* of the Bible;"

3. An appreciation for the ethos, language, geography, and history of the Ancient Near East and Graeco-Roman world as a backdrop against which to interpret the biblical text; and

4. A method for appreciating "the *time-conditioned, historical character* of the Bible."

There are additional positive features, but what "objections or modifications" did he offer?[54]

1. The historical-critical method is secular and is unable to handle the biblical claims of divine revelation or its unique events in history.

2. Because faith claims cannot be handled by the historical-critical method, use of the method by believing historians leads, Krentz believes, to intellectual dualism.

3. Biblical critics exhibit disagreement over the appropriateness or necessity of evaluating the content of a text for its veracity.

4. Historical criticism tends to champion itself as the only way to read the Bible.

5. Historical research objectifies the claims of the text, distancing the text from the reader, thus frustrating the effort to read the Bible as revelation to/for the church.

The most prized achievement of the historical critical movement, however, is its most dubious—in light of more recent studies, such as the one from Hans W. Frei, *The Eclipse of Biblical Narrative: A Study in Eighteenth and Nineteenth Century Hermeneutics*.[55] It was its claim that it was able to reconstruct the sources

---

[54]Krentz, *The Historical-Critical Method*, 67–72, as cited by Swartley, "Beyond the Historical-Critical Method," 241–42.

[55]Hans W. Frei, *The Eclipse of Biblical Narrative: A Study in Eighteenth and Nineteenth Century Hermeneutics* (New Haven: Yale, 1974). cf.. Eugene M. Klaaren, "A Critical Appreciation of Hans Frei's *Eclipse of Biblical Narrative*," *Union Seminary Quarterly Review* 37 (1983): 283–97; Cornel West, "On Frie's *Eclipse of Biblical Narrative*," *Union Seminary Quarterly Review* 37 (1983): 299–302.

that lay behind the texts now forming Scripture. But it is this point that has proven to be so sterile for the church and so lethal to the claims of Scripture.

In one of the great reversals of our time, the literal sense became separated from what the text means. In an attempt to reconstruct the historical events and the sources behind the Scriptural text, this reversal meant that the sense of what a text said became grounded in and oriented to a reference *behind* the text instead of allowing meaning to reside in the text itself. Thus, the subject matter, the setting, and the "pre-history" of the text became disassociated from the biblical narrative itself.

But to create a special sub-stratum underneath the text (whether it be hypothetical sources, overall subject matter, or the the historical ethos of the times when the text was written) or to develop a separate authorial intention (emotional, psychological, spiritual, or what have you—all except the author's own truth-intention) that could be considered apart from the text is tantamount to literary treason. The text and the text alone must first be listened to on its own terms. The meaning adheres in the text, not in the times, the audience, the subject matter, or the historical reconstructions of its history or the sources behind the text.

But concern for the text has gone too far if, with the New Criticism, it is asserted that a text has a life of its own apart from "what the author intended." The classic statement of this false dichotomy was announced by W. K. Wimsatt and M. C. Beardsley in 1946 in their essay, "The Intentional Fallacy." This essay contended that what the author intended was no part of a valid literary criticism. They affirmed that "the design or intention of the author is neither available nor desirable as a standard for judging the success of a work of art."[56] While they appeared to be talking about a standard for judging the "success" of a work, they in fact were concerned with "meaning" itself, not the degree of ability an author had in getting his ideas across. To divide a text from its author's truth-intention is like cutting out the heart of a person. The text means little or nothing if it has not come from someone who has gathered the word into a text form.

Consequently when Hans Frei makes the object of interpretation a nonreferential theory of biblical narratives and states that

---

[56]W. K. Wimsatt and M. C. Beardsley, "The Intentional Fallacy," *Sewanee Review* 54 (1946): 468–88; also in *On Literary Intention,* ed. D. Newton-de Molina (Edinburgh: Edinburgh University Press, 1976), 1–13.

their subject matter is to be found neither in their contents nor the author's intention but in their narrativity (i.e., the meaning of a narrative is in its narrative shape), he too has usurped the position that should be occupied solely by the author.

> New Critics, structuralists and proponents of "canon criticism" all agree that the essential flaw in asking about the intentions of an author, rather than about the inherent meaning of a text, is that to do so is to abandon literary criticism for psychology. A question about intention is a question about the state of someone's mind.[57]

But this is most certainly overdrawn. Surely we can distinguish between asking "what was the writer's emotional state?" or "what was going through the writer's mind at the time of writing?" and the question that we believe is germane here, "What did the writer mean by what was written?" Our generation desperately wants to be free of the author and any accompanying criteria for truth. Meaning cannot be determined by text, narrative, or canon *per se*; it must be attached to its author's truth-intention.

Thus, despite all their positive contributions in forcing us to focus on the text itself, it is also time that canon criticism, structuralism, and new criticism face some very shaky planks: (1) treating texts as if they were artifacts, (2) declaring the authorial intention irrelevant, and (3) saying that a work has meaning within itself or that it draws its meaning from its corpus or canon—just so long as we do not say that what it means is what its author meant![58]

In addition to taking the text itself, its structure, and its canonical location seriously, the contributions of form criticism (with its aid in identifying the proper genre) are likewise most helpful. But if form criticism must also involve the hypothetical assignment of certain elements or sayings in the text to particular settings that have conventional, rather than actual, locations in space and time, then we must once again demur. To look only for the sociological conditions under which certain sets of words may have originated and to which they may have belonged is again to search for that phantom text that lies *behind* the text; instead, until that text is shown to be guilty—using criteria that operate well when applied to numerous types of similar genera from outside the Bible and during the same general period and cultures—one should honor the text that stands in its wholeness before us.

---

[57] Barton, *Reading the Old Testament*, 168.
[58] Ibid., 171, 179.

Finally, redaction criticism focuses on the organizing purposes and ways in which sections of a particular book were arranged so as to reinforce the message already in the direct prose or in the indirect narrative. However, when the search focuses on the archivists or collectors to the disadvantage of the meaning of the author's text and when theories of what lies *behind* the text control the interpreting process, we have once again been diverted from our true mission.

As Barton warned, "The more impressive the critic makes the redactor's work appear . . . the more also he reduces the evidence on which the existence of those sources was established in the first place."[59] In fact, the text begins to appear to be so coherent, continued Barton, that no divisions of any sort are any longer warranted, and the sources and redactor vanish much as the rabbit does in the magician's hat. Thus, the hat that contained the redactor is lifted, and "not only is the redactor gone, but Moses himself has stepped into his shoes: a very frightening prospect indeed for a higher critic of [non-Evangelical outlook]."[60]

The only way forward—after having made some decision about the truthfulness of Christianity and the claims of Christ, the apostles, and prophets in Scripture—is to adopt the doctrinal warrants of Scripture and to apply all the methods of criticism, albeit in necessary modifications where their focus causes conflicting allegiances or fruitless searches for the text *behind* the text. But none of these methods must prevent us from asking the questions we need to ask of the text. The text can only mean now what it meant then, even though its significances and applications may have multiplied enormously.

Scripture was meant to be read and meant to be understood. Anything that aids this process must be welcomed, but when it rears a tyrannical head and wants to dominate and subject all other methods to its unique way of getting at a special feature in the text, its imperious demands must be seen for what they are and promptly put back in their proper place.

---

[59] Ibid., 57.
[60] Ibid.

PART II

THE OLD TESTAMENT AND THEOLOGY

Chapter 4

The Old Testament as
the Promise-Plan of God

One of the most vexing questions is the one that revolves around the quest for an organizing center and unifying theme for the OT. The discipline that normally has been charged with locating, describing, and arguing for this center has been OT Biblical Theology. However, that is the discipline that has come to the almost uniform decision that the OT has too much variety, diversity, and multiplicity of themes, events, and teachings to be brought into so confining a position. Can this conclusion be sustained?

THE SEARCH FOR A CENTER OF OT THEOLOGY: VALID OR USELESS?

OT Theology, as a discipline, has experienced a most unusual renaissance in the last decade, though some had predicted its early demise.[1] But in spite of all this recent activity in research and writing, Walter Brueggemann summarizes the prevailing mood

---

[1] For further discussion, see Walter C. Kaiser, Jr., "Old Testament Theology (history and content)," in *Dictionary of Christian Theology*, ed. Sinclair B. Ferguson and David F. Wright (Leicester: Inter-Varsity, forthcoming).

in OT scholarship by saying, "It is clear that the organization of an OT theology is now a quite open and unresolved question."[2]

In fact, so weary are some that there is a restless agitation to move beyond what is now popular to regard as the compulsion to search for a center, or *Mitte* point, in OT Theology.

But is this possible? No! Not as long as the discipline is named OT Theology—in the singular. It must systematize, and as it systematizes it calls for some type of organization. "Why"? asked Walter Harrelson.

> Because theology by definition has to do with the systematic ordering of thought; it involves comparison and contrast, the relating of this understanding or practice to that one, and the critical evaluation of life, thought, and ethos in light of the claims made within the tradition as to the truth and the fundamental meaning of it all. . . .
>
> The demand then for some qualitative and quantitative modalities of the relation of Yahweh to reality that will show themselves to be central, all-inclusive, and capable of being shown, by critical thought, to be central and all-inclusive *derives from this understanding of theology as a systematic endeavor.* . . . One must *systematize the variety* before one has done the theological task.[3]

We could not agree more heartily. As a contribution, then, to this search for an organizing paradigm, we would urge all future OT theologies to take a "diachronic" shape (i.e., to trace the revelation of God in its chronological and historical sequence) and to identify an inductively derived "focal point" that supplied the organizing center to which the successive writers in the OT contributed as this center emerged from its seminal form to a more fully developed concept.

In our judgment, the best contender for this textually derived "focal point" is what the NT calls the "promise" (*epangelia*) but which the OT knew under a constellation of words and a network of

---

[2]Walter Brueggemann, "A Shape for Old Testament Theology I: Structure Legitimation," *Catholic Biblical Quarterly* 47 (1985): 28. The same assessment had been given by E. Würthwein, "Zur Theologie des Alten Testaments," *Theologische Rundschau* 36 (1971): 185—"We are farther apart today on an agreement on content and method of OT Theology than we were fifty years ago." See also Gerhard Hasel, "A Decade of OT Theology: Retrospect and Prospect," *Zeitschrift für die alttestamentliche Wissenschaft* 93 (1981): 165–84.

[3]Walter Harrelson, "The Limited Task of Old Testament Theology," *Horizons in Biblical Theology* 6 (1984): 60–61 (his emphasis).

interlocking and developing features. The substance of this "promise" was most frequently, but not exclusively, embodied in the *content* of the various covenants. One must be careful not to fix one's attention on the external shapes of the covenants *per se,* for they are all too numerous and too varied (both in the individuals and in the groups addressed) and too distracting in that they tend to divert attention to the *form* and away from the more vital aspect: the *content* of the covenants.

But before we argue the case for recognizing "promise" as the center of OT theology, let us take up some of the current objections to this whole endeavor. For most, all such discussions about a center are much too static and restrictive: no one center can embrace the entire OT in all of its multiplicity of themes and writings.

However, what usually motivates this objection is not the demands of the text as such but the modern post-Enlightenment grids that are imposed over the text by various currents of modernity and certain forms of criticism. Since there are so many diverse sources from which the biblical text was originally welded, goes the contemporary argument, the chances of identifying a continuing stream of thought, much less a *Mitte* (a center, a fundamental idea, or a central concept), is negligible—and if it were to be found, it is more an accidental imposition than a deliberate choice of the biblical writers (and editors). However, we cannot agree with the majority of the conclusions championed by source, tradition, redaction, or form criticism. The working assumptions that undergirded these conclusions were first developed and employed in fields outside of biblical studies. In fact, before these methods were used in biblical studies, many had been used in the field of Western literature. But because of a "kind of circularity"[4] in their arguments, almost all scholars in the humanities have abandoned most, if not all, of these methods long ago, while those in the biblical field continued to hold fast to most aspects of these grids.

Furthermore, this argument for diversity implies heterogeneous sources—materials and trains of thought with no organizing mind behind it all. But what shall we say, then, about all the textual claims for the divine source that the text repeatedly stresses as the fountainhead of its disclosures? Must the price for our modernity be

---

[4] John Barton, *Reading the Old Testament: Method in Biblical Study* (Philadelphia: Westminster, 1984), 5. "I try to show how each method, however modestly it is applied, always brings in its wake some kind of circularity in argument."

the omission of this evidence, which could be the single most important reason for suspecting that perhaps there is a unifying factor in all the multiplicity of details, styles, and genres?

The major alternative to denying any type of center is the growing consensus[5] that God as Yahweh is the new *dynamic* unifying center in place of an organizing *principle* that systematizes the OT materials.

But surely this is hardly an adequate center. It only states the noun without giving us any predicate. Our question must then be this: Yahweh does/is *what*? Is it God's presence, his promise, his kingdom, his covenant, one of his attributes, or one of his saving acts that forms the center? Theology is the study of who God is and how he relates to his works and the peoples of the earth. But to isolate the unique name of God as Yahweh and to stop there is to tantalize the academy as they wait to hear the other shoe fall. Yahweh is and will do *what*?[6] As Gunneweg chided, "[The] subject [of theology] is not God himself, but men and their experiences of God, their attitude to existence in the face of the question about God, their understanding of themselves, the world and God as this is expressed in the texts of Scripture."[7]

Neither will it save the situation by declaring that this is a "dynamic unifying center" as opposed to the old search for "an organizing principle" that systematizes the whole of the OT. This merely assumes that the stating of issues in tension (dialectic or in an existential modality) will more adequately suit the situation than any approach that asks for a coherence or correspondence test for truth. This decision appears to favor the spirit of pluralism in modernity more than it represents the claims of the writers, and thus it must be judged to be anachronistic.

The debate between the so-called "static" view (which searches for a center to OT Theology) and the "dynamic" view (which recognizes a multiplicity of themes) is not an exegetical question. It is, instead, an epistemological question, and advocates

---

[5] Gerhard Hasel, "Major Recent Issues in Old Testament Theology: 1978–1983," *Journal for the Study of the Old Testament* 31 (1985): 51n.139. He lists a number of advocates of this dynamic center: C. R. North, G. E. Wright, P. R. Ackroyd, F. Baumgärtel, J. Lindblom, A. Heschel, K. H. Miskotte, E. Jacob, A. Deissler, H. J. Stoebe, H. J. Kraus, S. Wagner, J. Zengel, and himself.

[6] Ibid., 40, knows that some regard "God as the center" as an "empty formula" (*Leerformel*).

[7] A. H. J. Gunneweg, *Understanding the Old Testament* trans. John Bowden (Philadelphia: Westminster, 1978), 93.

of the "dynamic" view tend to espouse, whether deliberately or unintentionally, the theory of truth that denies that there can be Truth with a capital "T"—absolute and from God. Thus, the debate over the source, unity, and trustworthiness of revelation has shifted from an exegetical confrontation to the more removed issue as to how we can know truth on philosophical grounds. But, once the conclusions have been stated, the effects will still be very similar for this question of a theological center. If we only "know" things as they appear to us in an existential tension—or, as radical empirical philosophy would say, in dynamic categories of becoming—then the static categories of being that have shaped classical theology in the past have indeed been replaced.

This is not to claim that indeed all who espouse multiple themes and centers for OT theology have done so out of reaction to so-called "static" forms of theology. Some are frankly bewildered by the sheer plethora of detail in the OT and therefore join in the chorus of modern scholars without realizing that they have thereby also bought into another system, one which is antithetical to their own. It also is a signal that too little attention has been paid to the "informing theology"[8] that is found in the midst of all the detail. In fact, the case for diversity has already been subtly built into the agenda for many OT readers, since they have erroneously been taught to read the Bible backwards, i.e. to interpret it from the viewpoints and meanings found in the NT.

Of course, the Christian reader cannot pretend that the NT does not complete the OT. It does, indeed! But it is a methodological fault to expect the NT use of a word or phrase to unlock the depths of a similar word or phrase in the OT without letting the OT writer speak his own mind first. Such a leveling off of OT words and phrases with similar NT words and phrases would eventually product a flat Bible and some such hermeneutical dictum as: things similar to each other are ultimately and fully equal to each other, since the final or most recent statement of them is the most in-depth and developed meaning applicable for all in the series (i.e., from the OT through the NT). Surely all will denounce such a practice as

---

[8] See the discussion of this point in Walter C. Kaiser, Jr., *Toward an Exegetical Theology* (Grand Rapids: Baker, 1981), 134–40. Also idem, *Toward an Old Testament Theology* (Grand Rapids: Zondervan, 1978), 22–25, on the necessity of deriving both the structure and the content of an OT Theology on *inductive* and *exegetical* grounds instead of deductively imposing categories and grids over the text.

eisegesis (i.e., reading meaning into a text) rather than *exegesis* (i.e., reading meaning out of a text).

Without attempting to impute NT values to OT texts, there still remains the legitimate question for all Christian readers of the OT: what estimate did the early Christian church place on the OT? How did they view this issue of a center? Did the writers of the NT ever reflect on the question of a dominating concept or theme in the OT and the plan of God?

THE NT "PROMISE" AS THE CENTER
OF THE PLAN OF GOD

No one in modern times has stated the NT's espousal of the "promise" as the center of the plan of God in both Testaments better than Willis J. Beecher[9] in his Stone Lectures at Princeton Seminary in 1904. Beecher did not formally organize his promise-doctrine into a complete theology, but this has now been done in my programmatic study entitled *Toward an Old Testament Theology*.

Beecher defined the promise this way:

> God gave a promise to Abraham, and through him to mankind; a promise eternally fulfilled and fulfilling in the history of Israel; and chiefly fulfilled in Jesus Christ, he being that which is principal in the history of Israel.[10]

Should it be objected that it is the announcement of the kingdom and its anointed king the Messiah that is the most prominent feature in the NT, Beecher has a ready answer: "But it is on the basis of the divine promise that [the NT] preachers proclaim the kingdom, and when they appeal to the Old Testament in proof of Christian doctrine, they make the promise more prominent than the kingdom itself."[11]

The first fact to be observed is that there is only one single promise (*epangelia*) that, according to the NT writers, has been unfolding as the plan of God since it was first announced in the OT. Thus Paul, on trial for preaching that Jesus was the Messiah, concluded for King Agrippa:

[9]Willis Judson Beecher, *The Prophets and the Promise*, (New York: Thomas Crowell, 1905; reprint, Grand Rapids: Baker, 1963), 175–94.
[10]Ibid., 178.
[11]Ibid., 178–79.

> And now it is because of *the promise* God made to our
> fathers that I am on trial today. This is *the promise* our
> twelve-tribe nation is hoping to see fulfilled as they earnest-
> ly serve God day and night. It is about this hope, O King,
> that the Jews are accusing me (Acts 26:6–7, my translation
> and emphasis).

Paul's hope was located in the promise.

It is expected that someone who is on trial and whose life is
on the line would "formulate most carefully the central article of
[one's] creed."[12] The most surprising fact is that the apostle did not
base his appeal to Agrippa on a number of scattered predictions in
the OT (which would be accurate enough *in substance* but certainly
not scriptural *in form*).[13] Instead, Paul founded his case on a single,
definite, all-embracing promise. And the context clearly indicates
what promise Paul meant—the same one given to Eve, Shem,
Abraham, Isaac, Jacob, and David. Thus, the offense for which Paul
stood accused was the offense that that promise included the
Gentiles as well as the Jews!

In some forty passages spread through half the books of the
NT, the NT uses the word "promise" to summarize the heart of the
OT message. These forty passages leave no doubt that all the
revelation concerning the past, present, and coming kingdom of
God and its Messianic King Jesus form one continuously unfolding
doctrine encapsulated in the promise—the second important fact
about the promise doctrine. This promise sums up all its hopes in
Jesus as the Messiah and is unequivocally identified as the one
made to Abraham (Heb 6:13–15) and to which Isaac and Jacob were
"heirs [together] with him of the same promise" (Heb 11:9);
indeed, it is that same promise in which we Christians share as
"heirs together with Israel" (Eph 3:6).

No less an authority than Claus Westermann came to much
the same conclusion. For him, the history of the OT was not
adequately " . . . described by establishing the points along the
journey of the people at which some form of a promise was given
and then stretching a line from these points to the fulfillment of the
various promises."[14] Instead, he correctly perceived an "unbroken

---

[12] Ibid., 179.

[13] Ibid., 178, my emphasis.

[14] Claus Westermann, "The Way of the Promise through the Old Testament," in
The Old Testament and Christian Faith: A Theological Discussion, ed. Bernhard
W. Anderson (New York: Harper and Row, 1963), 214.

line of *transmission* of the promises,"[15] which he further explained in this manner:

> If, from the angle of the New Testament, one sees just individual points of the various promises made at some time or other only from the viewpoint of whether or not they are fulfilled in Christ, then he has not at all seen what is decisive about the life of these promises in the people of the Old Covenant: namely, how they gave constant support to the people of God step by step along their way and thus, being received and passed on from one generation to another, constituted a decisive element in the people's journey toward the hour of fulfillment.[16]

The promise of the Messiah, then, was not a set of scattered predictions sprinkled through the OT like so many spots where occasional diamonds might be garnered from the landscape; instead, the promise of the Messiah was like a continuous stream that was constantly giving refreshment and fulfillment to the people along the way throughout the whole OT.

Another qualification about the promise emerges: this one promise-plan, or promise-doctrine, contained so many specifications that it is also possible to speak of "promises" in the plural. However, even in this somewhat infrequent use of the plural form of the term, the definite article will frequently be employed to show that these were not just "promises" in general, or scattered predictions. On the contrary, they were recognized as constituent parts of a specific group of interlinked words of divine encouragement that left a distinctive trail of hope and warning throughout both Testaments: "The promise."

So broad was the audience addressed by this promise that in a most amazing declaration, Paul announced to the church at Rome that God had made Christ a servant of the Jews in order to "confirm *the promises* made to the patriarchs" (Rom 15:8–9, my emphasis) and also so that the Gentiles might come to praise God even as the OT had anticipated (Rom 15:9–12).[17] Just as Israel had inherited the covenants, the giving of the law, and the service, so they had also received, "the promises" (Rom 9:4). Instead of limiting this promise exclusively to a Jewish audience, believers are exhorted

---

[15] Ibid., his emphasis.
[16] Ibid., 214–15.
[17] Paul refers here to four OT texts (2 Sam 22:50 = Ps 18:49; Deut 32:43; Ps 117:1; Isa 11:10).

not to become lazy but to imitate those who by means of faith and patience "inherit the promises" (Heb 6:12 KJV). Thus, twentieth-century Gentiles who are now NT believers, who once were "excluded from citizenship in Israel and foreigners to the covenants of the promise" (Eph 2:12) have now in Christ been made "fellow citizens with God's people and members of God's household" (Eph 2:19).

The promise-plan of God is indeed multi-faceted and all-inclusive. Some of the major specifications in this single promise doctrine can be diagrammed as follows:

1. *The word of blessing that the gospel was also for Gentiles.*

Rom 1:2	"The gospel he promised beforehand through his prophets"
Gal 3:8	"God would justify the Gentiles . . . All nations will be blessed."
Gal 3:14	"The blessing given to Abraham might come to the Gentiles."
Gal 3:29	"If you belong to Christ, then you are . . . heirs according to the promise."
Eph 2:12	"[Once] foreigners to the covenants of the promise"
Eph 3:6	"Sharers together in the promise in Christ Jesus"

2. *The Promise of the gift of the Holy Spirit*

Luke 24:49	"I am going to send you what my Father has promised."
Acts 1:4	"The gift my Father promised"
Acts 2:33	"The promised Holy Spirit"
Acts 2:38	"The gift of the Holy Spirit"
Acts 2:39	"The promise is for you . . . and for [the Gentiles]"
Gal 3:14	"We [Jews and Gentiles] might receive the promise of the Spirit"
Eph 1:13	"You were marked in him with . . . the promised Holy Spirit."

3. *The Promise of resurrection from the dead.*

Acts 26:6–8	"God has promised our fathers that . . . God raises the dead."
2 Tim 1:1	"The promise of life that is in Christ Jesus."
Heb 9:15	"The promised eternal inheritance"
Heb 10:36	"You will receive what he has promised."
2 Peter 3:4	"Where is this 'coming' he promised?"
2 Peter 3:9	"The Lord is not slow in keeping his promise."
1 John 2:25	"This is what he promised us—even eternal life."

4. *The promise of redemption from sin*

Rom 4:6–8   " ... Blessed are they whose transgressions are forgiven ... "

James 2:21–23 " 'Abraham believed God, and it was credited to him as righteousness.' "

5. *The promise of Jesus the Messiah*

Luke 1:69–74   "He has raised up a horn of salvation for us ... (as he said ... long ago)."

Acts 13:23   "From this man's descendants God has brought ... Jesus, as he promised."

Acts 13:32–33 "[The] blessings promised to David"

Rom 4:13   "His offspring received the promise that he would be heir of the world."

Rom 9:9   "The promise was stated: ... 'Sarah will have a son.' "

Gal 3:16   "The promises were spoken to Abraham and ... 'to your seed,' meaning ... Christ."

Gal 4:23   "His son by the free woman was born as the result of a promise."

Heb 8:6   "He is mediator ... founded on better promises."

Heb 11:11   "He considered him faithful who had made the promise"

This is not to slight the other specifications in this single promise; they included the promise of the inheritance of the land (Acts 7:17), the promise of life (Eph 6:2; 1 Tim 4:8; cf. the connection between the OT wisdom theology and the promise), the promise of the New Heavens and the New Earth (2 Pet 3:13), the promise of the second coming of Christ (2 Pet 3:4, 9), and the promise that all who believe would be heirs together with the living God (Gal 3:29; 4:28; Eph 2:12–13).

In the fourth place, the NT writers did not restrict the operation of this promise to a limited period of time. On the contrary, they regarded this promise as eternally operative and irrevocable. It was the writer of Hebrews that connected the ancient promise given to Abraham with the "immutability" of God's eternal counsel. Moreover, he continued in Hebrews 6:13–18, God made sure there would be no mistaking his will and intentions when he confirmed the promise he had offered to the OT patriarchs, confirmed it by two unchangeable things in which it is impossible that God should lie and recant: his word (in Gen 12:2–3) and his oath (in Gen 22:16–18). Paul also affirmed the irrevocable character of this promise when he agreed that the Mosaic covenant could not, nor did it, disannul the promise made four hundred and thirty years earlier (Gal 3:15–18), for "God's gifts and his call are irrevocable" (Rom 11:29).

The final point we wish to make about the NT use of the promise doctrine as the apostles' way of summarizing the quintessence of the OT message is, as Beecher has already pointed out, that the NT writers associated the promise with many key OT phrases and special terms that had by NT times assumed distinctive theological meanings. Thus, the NT freely alludes to "the last days," "the day of the Lord," "my messenger," "the Messiah," "the Servant of the Lord," "the Son," "the kingdom," "my Chosen One," "the Holy One," and many others. It is clear that they view themselves as contributing to an ongoing stream of revelation. Theirs was not an innovative commencement of a radically new offering. They were part and parcel of what God had done in the past and was continuing to do in their day and in the future.

Do we not, therefore, have more than adequate basis for viewing "the promise" as the Bible's own center for the whole plan of God? It would appear that this is the only fair way to proceed.

THE OT "WORD" AS THE CENTER OF THE PLAN OF GOD

Since we have strenuously insisted that no center should be imposed as a grid over the OT, not even from the later NT revelation, what internal and inductive clues does the OT itself possess that would have led us to suggest already that the promise is that center? Since I have already argued this case in some detail in my *Toward an Old Testament Theology*,[18] it will probably be best if it is merely sketched out here for the sake of capturing the full argument.

The OT never formalizes the promise doctrine under one concept or title; instead, it uses a constellation of terms that exhibit its multi-faceted nature and comprehensive provisions. The first term to be used, in the order of the OT canon as we know it today, is "blessing" (or "to bless") in Genesis 1–11. Under this rubric, God pledged in this word to do something either for all creation (e.g., Gen 1:22) or more particularly for mankind (Gen 1:28).

Following the pre-patriarchal material of Genesis 1–11, the terms begin to multiply. But a careful study of the content and the

---

[18]Kaiser, *Old Testament Theology*, especially 32–35.

textual connections made between these terms shows that although they are variously labeled, they constitute a unified whole. Some of the words by which the OT promise is known are God's "oath," "rest," "blessing," and "word."[19] Even the verb *dibber*, usually translated "to speak," in over thirty OT instances should be translated "to promise," according to Foster R. McCurley, Jr.[20] The divinely promised items included: (1) the land (Exod 12:25; Deut 9:28; 12:20; 19:8; 27:3; Josh 23:5, 10), (2) blessing (Deut 1:11; 15:6), (3) multiplication of God's people Israel (Deut 6:3), (4) rest (Josh 22:4; 1 Kings 8:56), (5) a Davidic dynasty and throne (2 Sam 7:28; 1 Kings 2:24; 8:20, 24–25; 1 Chron 17:25–26; 2 Chron 6:15–16; Jer 33:14), and (6) all good things (Josh 23:15).

In addition to this constellation of terms and this burgeoning list of items that identified the substance of what was promised, several formulae assisted in epitomizing the central plan of God in the theology of the OT. Some of these formulae appeared in both OT and NT with such frequency that they became the hallmarks of that biblical theology.

The most prominent of these formulae was the tripartite formula, which announced: "I will be your God, you shall be my people and I will dwell in the midst of you." The first part of this formula was inaugurated in Genesis 17:7–8 and 28:21. The second part came on the eve of nationhood (Exod 6:7), the final portion coming as the tabernacle theology (Exod 29:45–46). Altogether, this tripartite formula appears in *both* Testaments some forty times.

Other formulae included: "I am Yahweh, who brought you up out of Ur of the Chaldeans," (e.g., Gen 15:7, my translation) or the formula found almost 125 times in the OT: "I am Yahweh your God, who brought you out of Egypt, out of the land of slavery" (e.g., Exod 20:2, my translation).

Add to this impressive litany of words and formulae the accumulation of OT metaphors—especially those that related to the messianic descendant from Abraham and David. This scion was to be the "Seed," "Branch," "Stone," "Root," "Lion," "Servant," and "Messenger of the Covenant."

Nevertheless, in spite of this impressive array of material, none of the aforementioned data would produce the case we have

---

[19] There are, for example, several references just to the content of the divine oath (Gen 26:3; Deut 8:7; 1 Chron 16:15–18; Ps 105:9; Jer 11:5).

[20] Foster R. McCurley, Jr., "The Christian and the Old Testament Promise," *Lutheran Quarterly*, 22 (1970): 401–10, especially 402n.2.

argued for had it not been for the fact that there is an interlocking network of allusions made by the succession of writers in the OT. If we were to take just the *content* and *recipients* of the various covenants, they alone would form a fixed, but continuing, core around which most OT theology could be gathered. It is from this fixed and growing core that meaning was found in the emerging revelation as the OT grew. Thus, the promise became God's stated declaration that he would freely do or be something for a distinctive line of men (beginning with Eve's son, Shem, and continuing through Abraham) with the result that through this line he could also be something for all men, nations, or nature itself. Whether that "something" he would do would be an act of salvation/blessing or an act of judgment would depend on what response men and women made to the Man, or Seed, of promise.

THE AMOUNT OF CONTINUITY AND DISCONTINUITY THE TESTAMENTS SHARE

Article 25 of the Belgic Confession gives us one of the few creedal guidelines the church has formulated as to how the OT is to be read and applied. It confesses:

> We believe that the ceremonies and figures of the law ceased at the coming of Christ, and that all the shadows are accomplished; so that the use of them must be abolished among Christians: *yet the truth and substance of them remain with us in Jesus Christ,* in whom they have their completion. In the meantime *we still use the testimonies taken out of the law and the prophets,* to confirm us in the doctrine of the gospel, and to regulate our life in all honesty to the glory of God, according to his will (my emphases).

Thus, even though we are urged to "use the testimonies taken out of the law and the prophets," we are not told how we may accomplish this.

Perhaps dealing first with several false positions might help us profit from the mistakes or myopic stances of previous answers to this problem.

The traditional answer in past centuries went like this: whatever the NT repeats from the OT, or alternatively, has not changed in basic principle, remains in force. While this appears at first to offer great promise as a guideline for defining what is discontinued and what has continued from the OT to the NT and the church, it evaporates under the strain of hard exegesis. As a matter of fact, Matthew 5:17–19 makes it clear that unless the heavens and the earth have disappeared, we should definitely count on all the minutia (in Jesus' hyperbole: "the jot and tittle") and all the commands remaining in force for all believers in all times until all have been accomplished! Our Lord does not give even the slightest degree of comfort to the position that the NT is the hermeneutical divide in determining for contemporary readers the proper quotient and its remainder from the OT revelation.

A second approach is at least as old as Gisbertus Voetius (1588–1676). Voetius had carried on a debate with another able Dutch Calvinist, Johannes Cocceius (1603–1669), who in turn represented a third approach on this question of continuity between the Testaments. In fact, so serious were their controversies that their polemics have left a cleavage in Calvinistic theology to this present day. Voetius argued that since God is eternal and his decrees are eternal, all differences between the Testaments could only be temporal and bearing on circumstances. God's decree of election was just as eternal as were his salvation and justification. Therefore, the OT text could be used just as well as the NT, for both would teach the same thing. This emphasis on God's person and action rested its case on using systematic theology as a hermeneutical grid over the OT to determine what is permanent, preachable, and personally applicable today. It tended to foster a "static" view of theology and the text.

Cocceius's objection was that theology must not override the historical differences of each of the epochs of revelation. Thus, for example, the question of the permanence of the Sabbath for those in the New Covenant emerged as one major difference between Cocceius and Voetius. Cocceius's view turns out to be "dynamic," with history and exegesis determining relevancy for the reader of the OT.

But we are ultimately disappointed, for now we are placed in the uncomfortable position of choosing between God and his works, between eternity and history, between the theological derivative of Scripture and the exegetical method by which we derive that theology, and between choosing to side either with the case for the unity or the case for the diversity of the Testaments.

Each of the preceding three positions exhibits major problems. Since the first position was so easily explained, the status of arbiter of all alleged disputes, conflicts, or tensions between the two Testaments was assigned to the NT. But with this new hierarchy of Testaments the old Augustinian hermeneutical advice that "The

Old is in the New revealed and the New is in the Old concealed"[21] had given way to what Willem A. Van Gemeren had humorously rechristened as "the Old is by the New restricted and the New is on the Old inflicted."[22] But the immediate danger of reading the NT into the OT is that the church will be stripped of those aspects of hope, promise, and judgment that are in the OT passages but not repeated in the NT.

A recent review article by a Dutch Calvinist expressed this concern of the tyranny of the NT.

> There is not just a movement from the New Testament to the Old Testament, in which the spiritual nature of the Old Testament promise is accentuated . . . but also there is a place for the opposite movement, in which we direct ourselves to the New Testament from the Old Testament, emphasizing the wholistic nature of the redemption, including the earthly and creatural, which in the whole of inscripturated revelation, both in the Old Testament and the New Testament, is proclaimed. This balance in understanding of the whole of Scripture, in which both the place of the Old Testament and New Testament are recognized, is in our conviction one of the most fundamental characteristics of a reformed hermeneutic of the Scriptures as revelation of God.[23]

We agree with this call for balance and for a forward reading of the OT into the NT text. To import "prior conclusions" from the NT into the OT is outright *eis*egesis and worthy only of our rejection, no matter how noble its goals are.

What, then, shall we conclude? To what extent does the NT correct, jettison, or modify the literal-natural interpretation of the OT law and prophets? The question of the law can be treated below in chapter seven, but at the heart of the use of the OT prophets lies the question of Israel. Can the Christian still expect (1) a restoration of the Jewish people to their native land, (2) a large conversion of

---

[21] His full statement was: *"multum et solide significatur, ad Vetus Testamentum timorem potius pertinere, sicut ad Novum dilectionem: quanquam et in Vetere Novum lateat, et in Novo Vetus pateat."* Augustine, *Quaestiones in Exodum*, 73.

[22] Willem A. Van Gemeren, "Israel as the Hermeneutical Crux in the Interpretation of Prophecy (II)," *Westminster Theological Journal* 46 (1984): 268.

[23] C. Graafland, *Het Vaste Verbond. Israel en het Oude Testament bij Calvijn en het Gereformeerd Protestantisme [=The Firm Covenant: Israel and the Old Testament in Calvin and Reformed Thought]* (Amsterdam: Uitgevery Ton Boland, 1978), 99, as translated by W. A. Van Gemeren, "Israel as the Hermeneutical Crux," 281.

Jews in the future, and (3) a future glorious kingdom composed of Jews and Gentiles? What is the present and future import of the OT prophecies regarding the Jewish people, their land, and their participation in the kingdom of God? Do all such prophecies bearing on these questions have any more than a typological significance?

The case for the unity of the total canon as set forth in the promise-plan of God exhibits some real advantages when facing these types of questions. The promise doctrine encompasses both the spiritual and the *material* aspects of revelation. Rather than sporting an unbiblical gnosis that rips the material universe and disconnects the material blessings of God from his spiritual gifts, it argues that in Christ all things cohere (Col 1:15–23) and that his plan embraces food, drink, paycheck, and national boundaries (cf. Eccl; Matt 6:33; Acts 17:26).

But even more importantly, it refuses to view fulfillment in the Bible as a static fact that is limited to one particular event. W. J. Beecher, the father of promise theology, held to a "cumulative fulfillment," that is, "a promise . . . may begin to be fulfilled at once [when the predictive word was first uttered] and may also continue being fulfilled through future period after period."[24]

But this is almost the same as the "gradual progression," or progressive realization, hermeneutic of John Calvin. For him, fulfillment was not a static state of perfection; it was a process that often took the reader through the OT, the NT, and the entire history of the church on into the future.[25] O. Palmer Robertson, even though he introduces typology as his principle of interpretation when the OT touches on the material aspects of Israel's promises, still agrees with this progressive hermeneutic: his term is "multi-staged fulfillment."[26]

The promise in Isaiah 52:11 that Israel would be restored from exile is not to be limited to either the NT or the OT; it includes the time "down to Christ's last coming, when all things shall be fully accomplished."[27] Said Calvin:

---

[24] Beecher, *The Prophets and the Promise*, 129.

[25] See the illuminating discussion by Van Gemeren, "Israel as the Hermeneutical Crux," 275–97.

[26] O. Palmer Robertson, *The Christ of the Covenants* (Grand Rapids: Baker, 1980), 298–300.

[27] John Calvin on Isaiah 54:2, as cited by Van Gemeren, "Israel as the Hermeneutical Crux," 277.

> This prophecy is maliciously restricted by the Jews to the deliverance from Babylon, and is improperly restricted by Christians to the spiritual redemption which we obtain through Christ; for we must begin with the deliverance which was wrought under Cyrus . . . and bring it down to our own time.[28]

Instead of viewing the NT as the sieve through which all the OT must be pushed or even as the final fulfillment of the OT, we must view the NT as the next installment in the ongoing revelation and plan of God. As such, the NT confirms the OT expectations by giving additional examples as to how the OT hope continues to be fulfilled. This gives the present-day church assurance that the OT promises will finally be consummated in that future day of the Lord just as the prophets had led Israel, and now the church, to believe. Therefore, it will be proper "to include a hope for Israel in every generation."[29] And if it be objected, as it surely will, that the NT says precious little about the restoration of the Jews to ancient Canaan, the two answers of Van Gemeren[30] will be used. First, even though Jerusalem was destroyed in A.D. 70, the Jews remained in significantly large numbers in Judah and Galilee. Thus, the topic of restoration to the land was hardly germaine. Secondly, the apostles' focus was on the conversion, not the restoration, of the Jewish people.

Therefore, neither Israel, nor her land, conversion, or participation in God's future kingdom and lordship should be the occasion for anyone's stumbling. Nor should the language of the prophets automatically be transcribed into typological equivalences because of some importation of some prior conclusions from the NT or systematic theology. The promise of God embraces the national, material, and spiritual aspects of both the Old and New Testament into one single all-inclusive plan of God.

The example of the land of Canaan as a permanent bequest of God cannot be a barrier, therefore, to solving the question about the amount of continuity or discontinuity in the Testaments. Nor can the issue of the law be made into a dividing wedge for those who seek to describe the precise amount of continuity and discontinuity that exists between or even within the Testaments.

---

[28] John Calvin on Isaiah 52:11, as cited by Van Gemeren, ibid.

[29] Ibid., 284–94. (It is regrettable, however, that Calvin, in his comments on Isaiah 52:11, attributed malice to the Jews but let Christians get off with a mere charge of impropriety.)

[30] Ibid., 293–94.

The solution to this problem can be stated as follows: only where the text itself (in either Testament) signals the reader that the author clearly intended the material to have a limited application or a built-in obsolescence can we dare to conclude that the material in that section is discontinuous and of no permanent or literal authority. This is not to say that that same material may not, however, have behind it an abiding principle that is clearly taught in the abiding and continuous revelation of God. The question of continuity and discontinuity cannot be solved by imposed philosophical or imposed theological categories over the text of Scripture; the text must remain sovereign! It will give its own signals in the very context in which the suspected discontinuous text appears. Thus, we would solve the problem of the number and location of these texts that are time-conditioned by appealing to an exegesis of the affected passages.

Chapter 5

The Old Testament as
a Messianic Primer

The doctrine of the Messiah in the OT is at the heart of the promise-plan of God. In fact, according to some 558 separate citations in rabbinical writings, there are 456 OT passages that refer directly to the Messiah or to messianic times.[1] It must be conceded that the Rabbis used highly stylized and subjective methods of exegeting a good number of these texts; nevertheless, even with what remains when this list is reduced, the statistics are still impressive and present an eloquent testimony both to the sheer number of texts that are available from the OT and to the strong Jewish expectation of a promised deliverer of the Jews in the OT.

DID THE OT WRITERS CONSCIOUSLY
ANTICIPATE THE MESSIAH?

In spite of these statistics from the Rabbis of the pre-Christian and early Christian centuries, all too frequently OT scholarship has remained extremely skeptical about a messianic consciousness among the OT writers. Typical of this judgment are

---

[1]Alfred Edersheim, *The Life and Times of Jesus The Messiah*, 2 vols. (Grand Rapids: Eerdmans, 1953), 2:710–41.

the conclusions of Joachim Becker: "There is no evidence for true messianism until the second century B.C.,"[2] and "It is on the threshold of the New Testament that we first encounter a real messianism."[3] However, Becker is simultaneously aware of the fact that "Such a conclusion would contradict one of the most central concerns of the New Testament which insists with unprecedented frequency, intensity, and unanimity that Christ was proclaimed in advance in the Old Testament. Historical-critical scholarship can never set aside this assertion of the New Testament."[4]

In order to do justice to both the alleged historical-critical evidence for "the messianological vacuum"[5] and the persistent witness of the NT, Becker appeals to the exegetical method observed among the Essenes at Qumran and among the Rabbis in the Targums and Midrashim—namely, the *pesher* exegesis of the OT. This method of interpreting a text has several features: (1) the words of the OT prophets, especially, are taken to be full of secrets; (2) these hidden meanings are taken to be allusions to events that were to take place at the end of time; and (3) since the time of the end is near, the "prophecies" are applied directly to the interpreter's (in this case the NT writer's) own generation. Thus, while "the conclusions of historical criticism are inescapable,"[6] Becker is still willing to find a messianic interpretation in the OT, even though he feels it poses an "embarrassment"[7] and is "arbitrary."[8] He concludes his study with this amazing statement:

> To find Christ at every stop on our way through the history of Israel and the Old Testament is not only no deception but also a duty imposed on us by the inspired testimony of the New Testament, the meaning of which we must strive to understand.[9]

Even though Becker assures us that it will not be a "schizophrenic act of intellectual violence"[10] to accept at one and the same time the contrary results of the light of faith and the demands of

---

[2]Joachim Becker, *Messianic Expectation in the Old Testament,* trans. David Green (Philadelphia: Fortress, 1980), 50; also see 93.
[3]Ibid., 87.
[4]Ibid., 93.
[5]The title of Becker's chapter 12, ibid., 79–82.
[6]Ibid., 95.
[7]Ibid., 94.
[8]Ibid., 95.
[9]Ibid., 96.
[10]Ibid., 93.

historical and exegetical analysis, we cannot see any other way to regard such a deep bifurcation of faith and evidence.

We cannot agree with an alleged *pesher* exegesis of the OT, much less ground the doctrine of Messiah in such "arbitrary" and "embarrassing" NT *retrojections* [!!] over the OT text.[11] Rather than adopting a "yes" *and* "no" synthetic solution to the question "Did the OT writers consciously anticipate the Messiah?" ("Yes" by faith; "No," by evidence), we would boldly answer "*Yes*, they did." For many the difficulty lies in the area of the results of historical-critical exegesis. Some OT critical scholars have been influenced too adversely by their minimalistic philosophical and theological presuppositions and by their overly confident faith in the correctness of their late-dating of some of the key OT texts.[12]

Charles A. Briggs in his magisterial work, *Messianic Prophecy*, offered the same complaint about his generation that we could make a century later about our own:

> There is no section of Biblical doctrine which has been so little understood and so much abused as Messianic prophecy. The Scholastics have interpreted the Messianic passages in accordance with the Christian doctrine of the person and work of Christ, ... and they have ignored the organic system of Messianic prophecy in the Bible itself. They have neglected its varied phrases. They have seen neither the unity nor the variety of the organism. ... On the other hand, Rationalists have ignored the ideal element, and, in limiting the Messianic prediction to the local, temporal and circumstantial elements, determine the substance of the prediction by its external form, seeking in every way to exclude references to the Messiah and the redemption brought to the world through Him.[13]

The way to remedy both of these opposing abuses, according to Briggs, is:

> (1) to study each prediction by itself with the most patient criticism and painstaking exegesis in all the details;
> (2) to study it in relation to other predictions in the series and note the organic connection; [and]

---

[11] See my vigorous protestation of the use of *pesher* exegesis for Christian apologetical use of OT texts to establish the Messianic doctrine in my book *The Uses of the Old Testament in the New* (Chicago: Moody, 1985), 17–57.

[12] For my detailed arguments, see chapter 3, "The Old Testament as an Object of Criticism."

[13] Charles A. Briggs, *Messianic Prophecy* (New York: Scribner, 1889), 63–64.

(3) to study it in relation to Christ and His redemption.[14]

Neither in our view, nor in Briggs' recommendations, would this mean that we should force NT meanings into OT passages. That would be a clear case of eisegesis. Nor does this method advocate the employment of a double-sense theory for Hebrew prediction; each prediction has one sense. Each new prophetic contribution to the subject of messianism appears to belong to an organism wherein the prophets consciously allude to or explicitly quote the antecedent contributions to this same doctrine so as to yield an ongoing series, a unity of subject-matter and a veritable informing theology of messianic thought. Thus, although each passage in the OT must be examined in its own context and on its own terms, special note must simultaneously be taken of its organic connections with the preceding revelation on the topic.

Instead of the NT transforming OT predictions of Messiah into histories or resorting to double or multiple meanings for these prophecies, we would urge that the *temporal prophetic* fulfillment be viewed as a whole. In Briggs' words,

> inasmuch as the prediction advances from the temporal redemption of its circumstances to the eternal redemption of Messiah, and it is part of a system of predictions in which the experience of redemption is advancing, it cannot be otherwise than that some of the elements of the predicted redemption should be realized in historical experience ere the essential element of the Messianic redemption is attained.[15]

Briggs does, however, disavow the term "successive fulfillment" to explain this legitimate phenomenon in messianic prophecy, since he felt this would work against the important fact that each prediction had but one sense. We believe it is possible, nevertheless, to argue for a single meaning for each passage while simultaneously arguing that that promise was being maintained by events, persons, and deeds in the temporal process. Thus, there was more than a *word* for the future; there often were *events* that served as earnests, place-holders, and elements of the predicted Messiah realized in the historical and temporal scene. They acted as encouragements for OT saints to believe that the total prediction would be realized in space and time in a climactic, total, and final

---

[14] Briggs, ibid., 65.
[15] Briggs, ibid.

way. Therefore, the "Messianic ideal should be realized in some of its phases ere the ideal itself is attained . . . "[16] concluded Briggs—and so do we.

One may ask, then, how much the OT writers were aware of this nexus of the temporal/historical realization of some elements and the ideal/climactic fulfillment in Messiah, his times, and his work. Or was their vision and understanding and the meaning of these passages strictly limited to their own times and without any intentional messianic references as far as they could tell?

The challenge raised in this question was clearly understood by David Berger and Michael Wyschogrod when they threw down the gauntlet in their book entitled *Jews and "Jewish Christianity"*:

> Christians can argue that the Hebrew Bible has hidden, profound meanings which are accessible once certain truths are already known from other sources. But let us be clear what this means. It means the verses we are talking about have a more obvious meaning which does not have anything to do with specifically Christian ideas. It means that they cannot be used to prove these ideas to someone who does not believe. . . . If God wanted to teach such ideas clearly in the Hebrew Bible, he could have made them as clear as they are in the Gospels. It seems to follow that God wanted people to be able to read the Bible without seeing these beliefs. In that case, quoting verses to prove these doctrines to non-Christians doesn't appear to make sense.[17]

As far as Berger and Wyschogrod are concerned, the temporal reference is all that the Hebrew author or that God meant to say. The Christian's belief that Jesus the Messiah was divine contradicts the repeated statements that the Messiah comes from David, not from God, argue these Jewish apologists. Berger and Wyschogrod, if pressed, think the best of all "Christian proof-texts"[18] is Isaiah 9:5[6], where the child Immanuel is called "mighty God" and "everlasting Father." But alas, they argue that three of the divine names are the subject of the sentence and the fourth name supplies the verb and object—i.e., "The mighty God, the eternal father, the prince of peace *is planning* a wonderful deed."

---

[16] Briggs, ibid. For more detail, see my discussion on "Double or Single Meaning?" in "Double or Generic Meaning?" in Kaiser, *Uses of the Old Testament,* 63–75.

[17] David Berger and Michael Wyschogrod, *Jews and "Jewish Christianity"* (New York: Ktav, 1978), 36.

[18] Ibid., 43.

But if the word "wonderful" (*pele'*) constitutes the object, and the remainder of the sentence supplies the subject of the participle "planning, counselling" (*yō'ēṣ*), we must (with Edward J. Young)[19] ask the following questions:

1. Why is this sentence given as the name of the child to be born, especially when *pele'* is used in the OT exclusively of what God, never of what man, has done? (The context is talking about a child's name.)

2. Why was a participle used instead of the more usual imperfect of some form of the verb "to be"?

3. Why is the Hebrew accent over *pele'* ("wonderful") a *telîšā*, one of the weakest of the disjunctive accents, and without the direct object sign, *'et* (as it appears in verse 10, for example)?

4. What is the purpose of heaping up epithets which do not contribute to the object, "a wonderful deed"? and

5. Is it not clear from the context that "Almighty God, Father of Eternity, and Prince of Peace" apply not to God, but to this child?

It would appear that this text is not only a so-called "Christian" proof text for the full deity of the Son to be born in David's house but also a "proof text" by which Isaiah was fully cognizant of Messiah's exalted nature. That "son" was no less than God, according to Isaiah.

Berger and Wyschogrod likewise hold that the translation "The Lord, our Righteousness" in Jeremiah 23:5–6 is a mistranslation, for it would make the coming king to be the Lord (one who is divine). In their view, it makes a statement not about the coming Messiah but about God himself: "The Lord *is* our righteousness."

But once again, several internal factors in the OT text lead us to reject the denial that the Messiah is divine. In fact, significant evidence exists for Messiah's deity and the author's awareness of this fact.

In the first place, the "righteous Branch" (*ṣemaḥ ṣaddiq*) promised by Jeremiah had already been promised by Isaiah 4:2 as the "Branch of the Lord" (*ṣemaḥ YHWH*), a genitive of source, or

---

[19] Edward J. Young, *The Book of Isaiah*, 3 vols. (Grand Rapids: Eerdmans, 1965), 1:332–33. Young, *in loco*, discussed how Samuel David Luzzatto tried to avoid the messianic implications of this name by translating it in his 1885 commentary as: "A wonderful thing is counselling he who is the mighty God, the everlasting Father, the Prince of Peace."

origin, since what lies behind the idea appears to be 2 Samuel 23:5 ("will not God *cause to sprout* [*yaṣmîaḥ*] all my salvation and all [my] desire?"—my translation) and Psalm 132:17 ("I will make a horn *sprout* [*'aṣmîaḥ*] for David; I will set up a lamp for my Messiah.").[20]

Secondly, the one who speaks in Jeremiah 23:6 is not a human being, as is true when symbolic names are given—such as "Yahweh-yireh" (given by Abraham in Gen 22:14), "El Elohe Israel" (given by Jacob in Gen 33:20), "El Bethel" (given by Jacob in Gen 35:7), "Yahweh, my banner" (given by Moses in Exod 17:15), or "Yahweh, Peace" (given by Gideon in Judg 6:24). Yahweh himself states that the name of the "branch" shall be "Righteous Branch" and that he shall be called by the name "The Lord our Righteousness."

Thirdly, the phraseology that introduces this name is most unique. "The Lord does not say: His name is or shall be (e.g., Gen 17:5b; Ezek 48:35), nor: Call Him (Gen 16:14; 33:20; 35:7; Judg 6:24), nor: Call His name (Gen 16:11, 13; 21:3; 22:14; Ex 17:15), nor: This shall He be called (Jer 33:16)."[21] Instead, *two* facts are stated here: "This [is] his name" (i.e., that which describes the very nature and essence of the "Branch"), and ["This is] what some shall call him" (i.e., the name that is given to him by the Lord God himself).

Lastly, the tradition of the Masoretic pointing indicates that the best translation is "The Lord our Righteousness." The conjunctive *mêreᵏā* under Yahweh clearly connects that word with Ṣidqēnû ("Our Righteousness"). Moreover, the dividing line, *pāsēq*, after Yahweh evidently indicated that *ṣidqēnû* was not regarded as the predicate of "Yahweh" (i.e., "Yahweh is our righteousness"); instead, "Our Righteousness" was a second name. "Yahweh," then, denoted his nature, and "Our Righteousness" signified his work.[22] This reading by the Jewish Masoretes is all the more remarkable

---

[20] A late Phoenician inscription (c. third century B.C.) from Farnaka, Cyprus, uses ṣemah ṣedeq ("the righteous sprout"), meaning an individual who was the legitimate heir to the throne. Likewise, a similar fifteenth century B.C. Ugaritic Kret epic calls Kret *špḥ ltpn* ("The shoot, or progeny, of *Ltpn*"). See Walter C. Kaiser, Jr., "Ṣemah," in *Theological Wordbook of the Old Testament*, ed. R. Laird Harris, Gleason L. Archer, Jr., and Bruce K. Waltke, 2 vols. (Chicago: Moody, 1980), 2:769–70.

[21] Theo. Laetsch, *Bible Commentary: Jeremiah* (St. Louis: Concordia, 1962), 195. Contrast the introductory formula in Jeremiah 33:15–16 and Laetsch's discussion of it on 269–70.

[22] This point is also made by Laetsch, ibid., 193.

when one remembers that the Christian church was appealing to this passage to demonstrate the deity of Jesus.

Our goal in citing Isaiah 9:6 and Jeremiah 23:5–6 is to indicate that the OT itself deliberately looked forward to the Messiah and openly, even if enigmatically, described him as fully divine.

Our interpretation is not a Christian eisegesis of these texts. In the tract *Baba Bathra* of the Jewish Talmud we read that Samuel B. Nahmeni said in the name of Rabbi Johanan (A.D. 200–279):

> The following three will be named with the name of the Holy One, blessed be He: The Upright, as said above [Isa 43:7]: "Everyone that is called by My name";—the Messiah, as it is written [Jer 23:6] "And this is His name whereby He shall be called: The Lord Our Righteousness";—and Jerusalem, as it is written [Ezk 48:35]; "And the name of that city shall be from that day: The Lord is there."[23]

To this affirmation could be added *The Midrash Tehillim* (A.D. 200–500) on Psalm 21:1:

> God calls King Messiah by His own name. But what is His name? Answer: Yahweh is a man of war [Exod 15:3]. And concerning Messiah we read: Yahweh Our Righteousness. And this is His name ... [Jer 23:6].

Midrash Mishle, a commentary on Proverbs (A.D. 200–500), has this to say:

> R. Hunna [c. 212–297] said: Eight names are given to the Messiah, which are: Yinnon [Ps 72:17, sprout], Shiloh, David, Menachem ["Comforter," as in Lam 1:16], Yahweh, Our Righteousness, Branch [ṣemaḥ], Elias.

And Rabbi Abba Ben Cahan (c. A.D. 200–300) answered the question "What is the name of Messiah?" by saying (in *Echa Rabbathi* on Lam 1:16): "Yahweh is His name, and this is proved by 'This is His name' [Jer 23:6]."[24]

Of course, not all Jewish interpreters would concede that Jeremiah meant King Messiah with a divine nature, but the fact that some did and the fact that the OT may legitimately be understood as

---

[23]This citation and the ones immediately following are cited by Laetsch, *ibid.*, from Rodkinson, *The Babylonian Talmud*, 13:212.

[24]Laetsch, ibid., as cited from Schoettgen, *Horae Hebraeicae*, 200; Calov, Ad Jer 23:6, 427A.

saying such without any NT or Christian overlay is most significant to the point we are attempting to establish: the OT writers did consciously and knowingly write and point to the Messiah as being a special son born in the line of David with the special divine nature that belonged to God alone!

IS JESUS CHRIST THAT ANTICIPATED MESSIAH?

It is one thing to argue that OT writers looked forward to a future Messiah; it is another thing to demonstrate that Jesus most adequately meets all the criteria laid out in the Hebrew Bible.

Now the best way to accomplish this task would be to adhere to the methodological strictures laid out in my previous chapter on the promise-plan: a diachronic but systematic ordering of the evidence. However, to do so in the short scope of a chapter would be foolish, since the only proper forum for such a thorough case would be an OT biblical theology text. This I have already offered in programmatic form in my *Toward an Old Testament Theology*.

In this chapter, therefore, it would seem best if the case could be boiled down to those especially difficult areas where the major objections are raised so frequently by Jewish as well as Gentile readers.

The most emotion-laden issue is this: How can Messiah be expected to appear on earth twice, while Jewish interpreters, if they look forward to the coming of Messiah at all, connect it solely with the coming era of tranquility, peace, and harmony on earth? If the Messiah can come only after a time of universal peace has been established, the Christian claim that there are two advents and that Jesus of Nazareth came as the Messiah about two thousand years ago are both open to easy refutation. Where in the Hebrew text of the *Tenak* can the two comings of Messiah be substantiated? This will be the heart of the identity question if Jesus' claims are to be validated.

Probably no text speaks more directly to this question of the two comings for the one Messiah than Zechariah 12:10—"They will look on me, the one they have pierced, and they will mourn for him as one mourns for an only child, and grieve bitterly for him as one grieves for a first born son." Typical of recent Jewish understanding of this verse is that of Gerald Sigal.[25] Sigal denies that one can

---

[25]Gerald Sigal, *The Jew and the Christian Missionary: A Jewish Response to Missionary Christianity* (New York: Ktav, 1981), 80–82.

equate "me" with "him" of verse 10 and refer both to Jesus. In his view, "The only admissible interpretation is . . . that the Gentile nations shall look to God, whom they have attacked by the persecution, death, and general suffering they inflicted on the nation Israel ('him'), whose dead will be mourned by the surviving Jewish people."[26]

Several problems appear in this interpretation. Implicit is the translation "because of him whom" (*'ēt 'ašer*) "they (i.e., the nations) have pierced."[27] However, the Hebrew expression simply means "whom" and no more. But even more important is the unnatural supposition that the subject of the first verb ("shall look")—i.e., Israel—is different from the subject of the second verb ("pierced")—i.e., the nations. Since the two occurrences of "they" are separated in the text solely by the prepositional phrase "on me" and the pronominal expression "whom," it would be more than somewhat cavalier to interpolate any additional words (e.g., "[whom the nations] were piercing")—an attempt to introduce a new subject without any grammatical or textual warrant! The fact must be faced by all interpreters: the same crowd that participated in the piercing of God are those who in "that [eschatological] day" will look intently on him and mourn as one mourns when he or she has lost an only son in death.

The textual and theological difficulties introduced by the expression "they shall look *on me*" (*'ēlay*; emphasis mine) are well known. It is true that fifty Hebrew manuscripts support (mainly as *Qere*, i.e., marginal readings) "on him" (*'ālâw*), as docs Lucian's Septuagint.[28] The fifth word beyond this one in verse 10 is "upon him" (*'ālâw*), but such switches from the first person to the third person are fairly common in Hebrew.[29] Moreover, John 19:37 and Revelation 1:7 read "upon him whom they pierced." Nonetheless, the MT reading of "on me" should be retained on the principle of *lectio difficilior* (= "more difficult reading"). Furthermore, Yahweh is the speaker, since he was the one who promised to pour out the

---

[26] Sigal, *The Jew and the Christian Missionary*, 82.

[27] This point and the ones that follow are suggested by David Baron, *The Visions and Prophecies of Zechariah: The Prophet of Hope and of Glory* 1918; reprint, (Fincastle, Va: Scripture Truth, 1962), 437–55.

[28] S. R. Driver, *The Minor Prophets* (Edinburgh: T. C. and E. J. Jack, 1906), 266. But Rahlf's edition of the LXX does not adopt Lucian's reading ("on him") but reads *pros me* ("on me").

[29] Gesenius, *Hebrew Grammar*, 1350, 144a, as cited by Merrill F. Unger, *Zechariah* (Grand Rapids: Zondervan, 1963), 217.

spirit of grace and supplication, and thus the naturalness of the first person ("on me").

Naturally, everyone immediately remarks that it is impossible to pierce God, since God is Spirit (Isa 31:3; John 4:24). Some go on to change the text in order to be rid of the difficulty. But the mystery in this text is that the one who was pierced—and mourned for, like one grieves over the loss of an only son—is at the same time one in essence and being with the God who speaks and who will pour out the spirit of grace and supplication in that future day when Israel shall suddenly recognize what had escaped her previously. The situation is exactly as Douglas Moo has described it:

> Piercing is often used as a figure of speech for death in the OT and the mourning following the piercing in this passage confirms the fact that a death is represented. The one pierced has been identified with an historical personage; an unknown martyr; God ("pierce" interpreted psychologically = mock); or the king (in humiliation rites). However, piercing is never used in the sense of mock in the OT and the other hypotheses fail to do complete justice to [*'elay*] "to me." The pierced one must be identified as a representative of God.[30]

Along with this analysis it should be observed that (1) "the first person occur[s] over and over again in this chapter (vv. 2, 3, 4, 6, 9, 10) and in every case refers *to the Messiah*"[31] and (2) Zechariah 11 had just referred to the rejection of Yahweh's representative (viz, the Good Shepherd, whose rejection would be followed by terrible punishment). One can only conclude that it is the Messiah who alone fits all the particulars mentioned here. It is the Messiah who is divine and who will be rejected and pierced only to be deeply mourned for and finally appreciated by all those who previously had rejected him, especially by Israel.

But if Zechariah 12:10 anticipates earth's finest hour—"that day," when Messiah comes to restore paradisiacal conditions—it must also recognize that he was the same Messiah who had been pierced sometime prior to that triumphal advent. Herein lies the strongest OT case for two comings of one and the same Messiah. Such a recognition will not be regarded by Jews as irreconcilable

---

[30]Douglas J. Moo, *The Old Testament in the Gospel Passion Narratives* (Sheffield, England: Almond, 1983), 212.
[31]Unger, *Zechariah*, 217.

with faith in God, nor will it be thought of as being in opposition to the great affirmation of the *Shema*, that the Lord our God is one; indeed, the two comings of Messiah will be altogether in harmony "in that day" with both of these legitimate concerns, for then "they shall look *on me*." Yahweh and his Servant are here identified as one and the same.

More timid exegetes need not be intimidated by the accusation that such exegetical results for Zechariah 12:10 are due to Christian presuppositions. In fact, some of the more ancient Jewish interpretations of this prophecy applied Zechariah 12:10 to Messiah ben Joseph. Aben Ezra (A.D. 1088–1176), understood this passage this way: "all the heathen shall look to me to see what I shall do to those who pierced Messiah, the son of Joseph."[32] Abarbanel (Rabbi Dan Isaac ben Jehudah, A.D. 1437–1500), with an eye to Rashi and Kimchi, opined, "It is more correct to interpret the passage of Messiah, the son of Joseph, as our Rabbis of blessed memory have interpreted it in the treatise Sukkah, [*Babylonian Talmud, Sukkah,* 52a] for he shall be a mighty man of valor of the tribes of Joseph, and shall at first be captain of the Lord's host in that war [against Gog and Magog], but in that war shall die."[33]

Of course, the Bible knows nothing about a Messiah ben Joseph. David Baron believes that this two-Messiah theory—Messiah son of David and Messiah son of Joseph—can be traced back to the third or fourth century A.D. Its invention may well have come as the Talmudists' attempt to grapple with the irreconcilable pictures of suffering and glory that are found in depictions of the Messiah. But instead of referring to two different persons, we would commend the solution that there are two separate advents of the one Messiah.[34]

Even more amazingly, the same individuals who despised and rejected this Servant (Isa 53:3), the one whom they, along with Gentile unbelievers, pierced, will one day look attentively, hopefully, and trustingly on that same one. Then the enormity of such a treacherous act will come home with such a full impact that a bitter

---

[32] As cited by Baron, *Visions and Prophecies of Zechariah,* 440–41.

[33] Ibid.

[34] It may well be that the Rabbis intended none other than Jesus by the epithet Messiah ben Joseph (Baron, ibid., 441n.2)! Note that after the blowing of the ram's horn at the Feast of Trumpets, God's mercy is sought in Judaism today through "Jesus, The Prince of the presence of God, the metatron," i.e., the One who shares the throne of God.

lamentation will ascend from family after family and individual after individual (Zech 12:10–14).

WHAT ARE THE KEY MESSIANIC TERMS AND PASSAGES IN THE OT?

Surprisingly enough, the term "Messiah" appears only some thirty-nine times in the OT, only nine of these references referring exclusively to that coming person we are focusing on in this chapter. But if one were to ask the OT prophets what their choice of terms for this designated person would be, no doubt they would have said "servant of the Lord." This term appears thirty-one times in Isaiah 40–66, with twenty of the references—all in the singular—appearing in the section that climaxes in that most significant chapter—Isaiah 53. The eleven references to "servant" in the plural ("servants of the Lord") all appear after Isaiah 53.[35]

It is exceedingly important, however, regardless of what word or series of terms are chosen to refer to this personage, to treat the OT passages as a series of promises and not simply as predictions or independent prognostications of some eschatological event. To treat these OT references as promises means that we will need to take more into consideration than just the mere predictive word and its final or ideal realization. We have already argued in our chapter on the promise-plan of God that three things are simultaneously in mind here: (1) the divine word of revelation, (2) the historical means by which parts of that predictive word were progressively experienced in a series of results by which the eventual realization was turned into a historical reality in the lives, offices, events, and situations of those who were in the line of custodians of that promise, and (3) the climactic and final fulfillment of that word in the eschatological era.

We may organize the terms and the passages that are involved in the messianic promise under five historical rubrics: (1) the roots of the messianic promise in the pre-patriarchal times, (2) the heart of the messianic promise in patriarchal times, (3) the enlargement of the messianic promise in the Mosaic and monarchial times, (4) the exposition of the messianic promise in the times of the pre-exilic prophets, and (5) the maturation of the Messianic

---

[35] Willis J. Beecher, *The Prophets and The Promise* (1905; reprint, Grand Rapids: Baker, 1963), 270–88. See also Walter C. Kaiser, Jr., *Toward an Old Testament Theology* (Grand Rapids: Zondervan, 1978), 215–17.

promise in exilic and post-exilic times. Each is worthy of a brief discussion.

The Roots of the Messianic Promise

Three promises are given as God's gracious gift following the three human debacles in Genesis 1–11. These three tragedies were the Fall, the Flood, and the folly of the tower of Babel.

In response to the first debacle, God promised to send a "seed" through Eve, which "seed" would deliver a lethal blow to the head of "the serpent" (Gen 3:15). It is true that many have balked at a high Christological understanding of Genesis 3:15, implying that neither Eve nor the writer of Genesis could have had even a smidgen of such an advanced idea. But, is it not also true that the startling fact announced in this text is not that the woman, or the man, or the serpent will be avenged in this contest? It is that an unnamed male descendant will deliver the knockout blow, even though his own heel will be bruised somehow in the fray.[36]

The second gracious word comes from Genesis 9:27. Whoever this promised male deliverer is, he will be a Semite, for "[God!] will dwell (*šākan*) in the tents of Shem." Most interpreters prefer to have Japheth dwell in Shem's tents (whatever that means), but we presume, in keeping with the ordinary rules of Hebrew grammar, that a clause that has an unexpressed subject has the same subject as the preceding clause where the subject is expressed. Moreover, to use the direct object of the preceding clause as the subject of the next would be highly unusual, unless some textual or contextual signal indicated its legitimacy. Thus, we have connected the "blessing" of God with his indwelling among the Semitic people as the divine relief for man's second debacle.[37]

The payoff promise, which came as God's response to the earth's third crisis in this period, is found in Genesis 12:1–3. Five times some form of the word "to bless," or "blessing"—a key term, one that summarizes the theology of Genesis 1–11—appears in these three verses. But the most important declaration from God was that one Semite, named Abraham, had been chosen by God in order that (note the *waw* of purpose or result) he might be a blessing; indeed, a blessing to all the families of the earth (which

---

[36] Kaiser, *Old Testament Theology*, 77–79.
[37] Ibid.

incidentally had just been named in Genesis 10).[38] God's means of doing this was to be through the perpetuation of that "seed" promised to Eve and now continued in Abraham's descendants.

The Heart of the Messianic Promise

In the emerging Promise-Plan of God, the central figure of hope he offered (Gen 12–50) to the three fathers of the nation Israel (Abraham, Isaac, and Jacob) was an heir who would perpetuate the promised line and complete the hope offered to Eve about the final victory of her "seed" over "the Serpent". The references to this heir are numerous in the patriarchal narratives (Gen 12:3, 7; 13:14–16; 15:4–5, 13, 18; 16:10; 17:2, 7, 9, 19; 21:12; 22:17; 26:24; 27:28–29; 28:14, etc.). It became clear that not only was this seed a gift of God, but only God could maintain and preserve the life and mission of this heir, whether the threat was the issue of sacrificing the life of that son (Gen 22) or the jealous rivalries of brothers and parents who attempted to push their own plans in aiding or frustrating the divine plan (e.g., Isaac and Rebekah in the matter of the assignment of the will to Jacob and Esau; Gen 27–28). God alone could maintain his own promise, which he did by offering his word, not only repeatedly, but even with an oath (Gen 22:16; Heb 6:13–18).

Meanwhile, a series of fresh births of sons (e.g., Isaac and Jacob) continued the reality of the promise while testifying to the fact that they themselves were part of what was to be accomplished in their own historical times: a partial realization and fulfillment of the complete fulfillment that was to come in Messiah himself—and the end of this line of descendants.

Two other provisions were included along with the appearance of the seed: the *inheritance* of the land of Canaan as a gift to the patriarchs and their descendants as a perpetual component of that large Promise-Plan (Gen 12:1, 7; 13:15, 17; 15:7, 18; 17:8; 24:7; 26:2–3; 28:13); and the *heritage* of the good news that through Abraham's seed all the nations of the earth would be blessed (Gen 12:3; 18:18; 22:18; 26:4; 28:14). So excellent was this universal offer of the effects of the Seed's appearance and work that the apostle Paul labeled it the "gospel" (Gal 3:8).

The messianic line constantly narrowed from a male descendant promised to Eve, a Semite promised to Shem, a particular segment of the semitic peoples (later called Hebrews), to Abraham,

---

[38] Ibid., 82–83.

and finally to land in a particular tribe of the Hebrews—those descended from Judah, the fourth son of Jacob (Gen 49:8–10).[39] In fact, royal associations are already being made with this seed in that passage as well as in Balaam's prediction (Num 24:17). The scepter, symbol of royalty, would not depart from Judah "until he comes to whom it belongs" (cf. "Shiloh," Gen 49:10; Ezek 21:27).

The Enlargement of the Messianic Promise

During the Mosaic and monarchial eras of Israel's history, the three offices of Messiah are announced: prophet, priest, and king. Once again the OT oscillation between the one and the many, between all the people and the representative person of the Messiah who was to come, must be taken into account.

The whole nation is declared to be "my son," "my firstborn" (Exod 4:22–23; Deut 14:1; cf. Matt 2:15). They are also characterized as a "kingdom of priests" before the Lord (Exod 19:5–6). Even though an "everlasting priesthood" had been offered to Phinehas (Num 25:12–13), yet on the eve of the demise of Eli's house God promised that he would raise up a "faithful priest" and "build him a permanent house and he would walk before his anointed [Messiah] forever" (1 Sam 2:35, my translation). Later in the monarchy, David contemplated in Psalm 110:4, 6 this union of a "priest . . . after the order of Melchizedek" with a victorious "Lord" who would judge the nations. No doubt David was mediating on the unusual victory God had given to the man of promise, Abraham (Gen 14), over four foreign kings. This only stirred his mind to reflect on the greater future victory of one who was a priest-king after an order whose priesthood's ancestral roots were unknown; the success of this person (David's "Lord") was so certain that the God of the universe would say to him, "Sit at my right hand." For God to say to David something about a sovereign over David who was not the same as the speaking God, but who was nonetheless accorded royal dignity and divine equality, must have been mind-boggling indeed!

This man of promise was also to be a prophet like unto Moses (Deut 18:15–18). While this promise technically is not a collective singular noun nor a generic prophecy in the usual sense of the other messianic terms, all the same the word is used here also in a distributive sense. The context is dealing with classes of offices:

---

[39] For my discussion of Shiloh, see Kaiser, *Old Testament Theology*, pp. 95–97; especially n.17.

judge, king, priest, and prophet. Thus, while focusing on one prophet, Moses, we are led to expect from the context a succession of prophets, ending in "that prophet" often mentioned in the NT.

An expectation that the Messiah should be a prophet was common even before the days of Jesus and his ministry. The Samaritan woman concluded that Jesus was that "prophet" (John 4:19, 29). Similarly, the multitude by the Sea of Galilee, "This truly is the prophet that should come into the world" (John 6:14, my translation). Peter likewise quoted Deuteronomy 18:15 and applied it to Jesus (Acts 3:22–26), as did Stephen (Acts 7:37).

Few passages have extolled Messiah's potential kingship as clearly as the word given by Nathan the prophet in 2 Samuel 7. David's "seed" was to be adopted by God as "my son," God himself declaring he would be "his father" (7:14). But even more staggering was the overwhelming word in verse 16 that David's dynasty and kingdom would never end and that the authority of his throne would be established forever. When David heard this word, he whimpered, "Who am I, O Lord Yahweh, and what is my family that you have brought me to this place in life? And as if this were not enough in your sight, O Lord Yahweh, you have spoken about the dynasty of your servant for a great while to come. And then that this should be the charter for all humanity, O Lord Yahweh!!" (2 Sam 7:18–19, my translation).[40]

So a seed, a dwelling in the tents of Shem, and a blessing to Abraham were promised in the pre-patriarchal era. Then the patriarchal era added an heir, an inheritance, and a heritage of the gospel. Finally, during the Mosaic and monarchical epochs of Israel's history, God predicted the coming of a special prophet, priest, and king.

The Exposition of the Messianic Promise

With the establishment of David's dynasty and Solomon's temple, the messianic plan of God had reached a provisional plateau in its development. It is now possible to focus more on the world-wide implications of God's plan to send a "seed."

---

[40] For a defense of "charter" and the unusual terms in this text, see Walter C. Kaiser, Jr., "The Blessing of David: A Charter for Humanity," in *The Law and the Prophets*, ed. John Skilton (Philadelphia: Presbyterian and Reformed, 1974): 298–318, also Kaiser, *Old Testament Theology*, 149–64. Note also Psalm 89, a commentary on 2 Sam 7.

Almost immediately (if Joel and Obadiah may tentatively be placed at the head of the pre-exilic prophets and be located in the ninth century) the attention shifted to "the Day of the Lord." This "day" was to be a coming period of time when God would deal with Israel and all the nations on the face of the earth either in unusual outpouring of blessing or in unprecedented judgment—depending on how they had responded to his Messiah.

Samples of God's blessing in response to individual and national repentance ("turning" back to God) could be seen both in the *immediate* relief from the locust plague with the land's productivity restored once again (Joel 2:19–27) and in a *future* downpour of the Holy Spirit on "all flesh" without respect to sex, age, or race.[41]

The writers of Psalms and the pre-exilic prophets used a number of terms to refer to the Messiah. He was God's "Holy One" (*ḥᵃsîd*: Ps 16:10; Hos 11:9, 12), Yahweh's "Son" or "Firstborn" (Ps 89:26–27; Hos 11:1), his "Branch" (*ṣemaḥ*: Isa 4:2–6; Jer 23:5–8: cf. Post-exilic Zech 3:8; 6:9–15), his "servant" (Isa 42:1–4; 49:1–7; 52:13–53:12), a "Flower" or "Shoot" (Isa 11:1; 60:21), and a "Prince" or "captain" (*nāgîd*: Isa 55:4; cf. the exilic Dan 9:25; 11:22).[42] As Beecher concludes,

> Each [term] . . . is so universal that it might be applied to any person or personified aggregate, thought of as representing Yahaweh's [*sic*] redemptive purposes for mankind. Each one was primarily understood to denote either Israel or the contemporary representative of the line of David, or both, thought of as standing for Yahaweh's [*sic*] promised blessing to mankind. But in each case this contemporary person or personified person is a link in an endless chain . . . [which] looked forward to the future manifestation of the [Messiah] . . . in such glory as should eclipse all earlier manifestations.[43]

Indeed, Messiah would be born in Bethlehem of Judah (Mic 5:2) to the house and line of David (Isa 7:13–14) with authority and dominion equal with and as unending as that of God (Isa 9:6–7). And even though the Davidic house (dynasty) might appear to be tottering and in a total state of collapse, God himself would raise it

---

[41] See Walter C. Kaiser, Jr., "Participating In and Expecting the Day of the Lord. Joel 2:28–32," in *Uses of the Old Testament*, 89–110.

[42] See further on "Prince," Beecher, *The Prophets and Promise*, 340–42, especially n.1.

[43] Ibid., 342–43.

up, repair the "breaks" between the northern and southern kingdom so as to weld them into one nation once again, and restore Messiah's ruins from ashes in order that Israel might take possession (cf. Num 24:17–18) of Edom and all nations who have God's name called over them (Amos 9:11–12).[44]

The Maturation of the Messianic Promise

Just when it appeared that the fortunes of the Davidic kingdom were ended in the fiery holocaust of 586 B.C., Ezekiel and Daniel emerged with the most spectacular announcements of the reappearance of Messiah's kingdom.

From the valley of dry bones, God would resurrect the whole nation of Israel (Ezek 37:1–14), and the separated northern kingdom would be reunited with its southern counterpart so that they would be "one nation" under "one God" with "one king" over them, the "one shepherd, my servant David" (Ezek 37:15–28). All this would take place in keeping with God's "everlasting covenant."

No less dramatic is Daniel in his promise about the coming "Stone" that would crush all of the preceding and successive kingdoms of men in such a way that the kingdom of this stone would spread until it covered the whole earth (Dan 2). In fact, the "Ancient of Days" would grant to "the Son of Man," who would come from the clouds of heaven, all authority, glory, and kingship so that all peoples, nations, and tongues would serve his everlasting dominion, which would never pass away (Dan 7:13–14).

Messiah is described by Haggai in the post-exilic period as a "signet-king" in the person of the Davidic governor Zerubbabel (Hag 2:23). But Haggai's contemporary Zechariah saw him as God's conquering hero, who, even though he was smitten and sold for thirty pieces of silver (Zech 11:7–14), causing the people who had pierced him to mourn for him as one grieves over the death of an only son (Zech 12:10–13:1), still he would emerge on that final day of battle as most victorious (Zech 14). As Ezekiel had seen the "glory of the Lord" leave the temple and ascend from the Mount of Olives, so Zechariah predicts Messiah shall return (cf. Dan 7:13) and plant his feet on the Mount of Olives (Zech 14:4–5), thereby causing such seismic convulsions that the Mount of Olives would split, leaving a

---

[44] For more details, see Walter C. Kaiser, Jr., "Including the Gentiles in the Plan of God: Amos 9:9–15," in *Uses of the Old Testament*, 177–94.

new valley running through it from east to west. The battle that would ensue would be dreadful but final. This indeed would finally be the war to end all wars. Then God would be Lord, and Messiah's kingdom would be universal and without end.

But before Messiah would appear, Malachi warned us that a messenger would announce his coming, and the very owner of the temple would come to refine and purify all unrighteousness, which could not stand in his presence (Mal 3:1–3). Note once again that God who sends the preparing messenger is separate from "The Lord," the "angel of the covenant" who shall come and yet who is nonetheless the very "God of justice" (Mal 2:17) whom the people allegedly were deeply longing to see.

This by no means exhausts the doctrine or the veritable storehouse of texts and terms that deal with the OT's understanding and anticipation of the Messiah, yet it will be more than enough to substantiate why it was that Jesus of Nazareth was so exasperated with the dullness of his contemporaries (and with our generation on the same count and more) to grasp all that Moses, the prophets, and the Psalms had said about him and his coming (Luke 24:25–27, 44–47).

Chapter 6

The Old Testament as the Plan of Salvation

Too many contemporary readers come to the unfortunate conclusion that the salvation offered in the OT is on a do-it-yourself basis and therefore totally out of harmony with the offer graciously extended in the NT. And since there is a relative scarcity of words for faith or believing in the OT, many wrongly infer that both the concept and the practice were unimportant. But such a conclusion can be exposed as being extremely superficial, if not also just plain erroneous.

WAS THE OBJECT AND METHOD OF PERSONAL SALVATION THE SAME IN THE OT AND NT?

Fortunately, almost all who work on the OT doctrine of salvation will agree that "grace" is involved to some extent, but therein ends the agreement. The much quoted note in the *The Scofield Reference Bible* declared, "The point of testing is no longer legal obedience as the condition of salvation, but acceptance or rejection of Christ."[1] Meanwhile, covenant theology affirmed, "The

---

[1] *The Scofield Reference Bible* (New York: Oxford University Press, 1909), 1115n.2.

plan of salvation has always been one and the same; having the same promise, the same Saviour, the same condition, and the same salvation."[2]

But these two quotations could easily mislead many into thinking that the former position always held to at least two ways of salvation and the latter group never faltered in its view on the unity of the plan of salvation for both Testaments.

The real difficulty for both these groups is apparent when each is pressed to declare what was the object of the OT believer's faith. All too frequently the reply will be that the object of faith was "God." While it surely is claiming too much to say that the OT saints were fully conscious that the object of their faith was the incarnate, crucified Son of God—the Lamb of God, with all that that implies—it is likewise certainly claiming too little to say that OT believers were mere theists!

Accordingly, modern Evangelicals fall over each other making the point that "salvation has always been by grace through faith—plus nothing." But the qualifications that are immediately raised are disturbing. The key question continues to be: who or what was the object of the OT individual's faith? If God were the sole object in the OT and Christ is the sole object of faith from NT times to the present, then do we have a major disagreement and a strong contrast in the method of personal salvation for the two Testaments?

The best way to approach this problem is first to analyze the Hebrew word *he'emin* with its prefixial use of the letters *lamedh* ("he believed [that]") and *beth* ("he believed in").[3] This discussion in turn can be applied to Genesis 15:6, "Abraham believed in the Lord, and he counted it to him for righteousness" (my translation).

The basic word underlying the Hebrew word *he'emin* is *'āman*, meaning "it is firm" or "it is sure." But this belief can be divided into two types, depending on which prefix (*lamedh* or *beth*) is used. The first involves believing what a person says and accepting those statements as true and trustworthy. Thus, Joseph's brothers had a difficult time getting their father Jacob to believe *that* Joseph was still alive and in Egypt (Gen 45:26). Likewise

---

[2]Charles Hodge, *Systematic Theology*, 3 vols. (London: Thomas Nelson and Sons, 1872), 2:368.

[3]I am indebted to Gordon Wenham for this discussion in his 1975–76 annual conference lecture to the Theological Students' Fellowship at Queen's University, Belfast, Ireland, *Faith in the Old Testament* (Leicester, England: Theological Students' Fellowship, n.d.), 1–24.

Moses feared that the Israelites would not trust anything *that* he said (Exod 4:1).

However, belief *in* someone (*he'emin be*) is more of an endorsement of another person's character, not just relying on that person's statements. The OT does occasionally give us examples of faith in another human being; Israel is twice said to believe *in* Moses (Exod 14:31; 19:9), and Achish, King of Gath, is said to have believed in (i.e., trusted) David's character (1 Sam 27:12). However, this use of believe *in* with the preposition *beth*[4] is more frequently used of faith in God. This type of believing involves much more than accepting the statements made by or about someone; " . . . believing in asserts the total dependability of a person."[5] But upon *what* or *whom* is that dependence put?

According to the OT, faith in God involved believing what God has promised or commanded and believing in him and his person and character. Faith was evidenced when a person "believed *in* [God's] commands" (Ps 119:66, my translation) or when "the people feared the Lord and believed in the Lord" (Exod 14:31, my translation). In fact, the OT often coupled fearing God with believing in him. Israel was to "fear not [the Egyptians]" but to "stand firm and see the salvation of God" (Exod 14:13, my translation). But when Israel failed to fear God (as recorded, e.g., in Deut 1:29, 32), it was because she "did not trust in the LORD" (v. 32; cf. Num 14:9). Likewise, faith is linked with obedience, for unbelief is matched with rebellion against the commandment of the Lord (Deut 9:23). Unbelief and disobedience, then, are twins.[6]

The most important passage in the patriarchal narrative, however, is Genesis 15:6: "Abram believed *in* the Lord, and he credited it to him as righteousness" (my translation). The *hiphil* form of the verb "to believe" (*'āman*) is unusual in form, since it is in the perfect tense with *waw* and not, as one would expect, in the

---

[4]Franz Delitzsch. *A New Commentary on Genesis*, trans. Sophia Taylor (Edinburgh: T. & T. Clark, 1888; reprint, Minneapolis: Klock and Klock, 1978) argues for that usage (Exod 4:31; 14:31; 19:9; Num 14:11; 20:12; and Deut 1:32). See also J. Alfaro, "Fides in terminologia biblica," *Gregorianum* 42 (1961): 462–505. Alfaro's conclusion on 504 is "the notion of faith is basically identical in the Old and New Testaments: 'to believe' entails man's complete commitment to God who reveals and saves." See also Franco Festorazzi, " 'We are Safe' (Jer 7, 10): The Faith of Both Testaments as Salvific Experience," in *How Does the Christian Confront the OT?* ed. Pierre Benoit, Roland E. Murphy, Bastiaan Van Ierse, (New York: Paulist, 1967), 45–59.

[5]Wenham, ibid., 4.

[6]These connections were also made by Wenham, ibid., 5.

imperfect with a *waw conversive*. The unusual verb form, however, probably means that Abraham's faith had a permanence of attitude. He remained constant in his faith; he did not just believe this one time.[7]

The faith spoken of in Genesis 15:6 was a particular, and not a general, act of believing. While Hebrews 11:8–9 clearly says that it was *by faith* that he obeyed when he was called at least ten to fifteen years earlier to leave his city, Ur of the Chaldees (Gen 12:1), Genesis 15:6 is the first time that Holy Scripture expressly speaks of his faith.[8]

But if Abraham had already been justified as he left Ur of the Chaldees, why was his faith belatedly on this occasion credited to him as righteousness? Only the context and the narrative of Genesis 12–14 can help us answer this question.

It is the land promise that occupies our attention in Genesis 12, for the Lord, after reappearing to Abram (who had just reached Shechem), enlarged on the promise he had delivered to Abram back in Ur: "To your offspring I will give this land" (Gen 12:7). Unfortunately, due to fear of famine, Abram subsequently left that very land of promise. But if famines are under the control of God, what was its purpose here? And why should Abraham fear for his life if he believed in God and in his promises? Nevertheless, God's promise remained despite Abram's poor showing: indeed, it remained in spite of his half-truth lie to Pharaoh that Sarah was his sister.

The divine promise is put to the test once again (Gen 13). This time Abram resists the temptation to help make the promise come true and instead offers Lot and his herdsmen first choice of the same land promised exclusively to himself. That God approved of this act of faith and generosity is confirmed by Genesis 13:14; for here, once again, God repeats his promise about the land, adding a word about an incalculable number of offspring. Only after that did Lot expose himself to being taken captive, a snare from which he had to be rescued and which act once again proved that it was God who was blessing Abram and delivering him from his enemies (Gen 14:19).

[7]A Grammatical point made by H. C. Leupold, *Exposition of Genesis* (Grand Rapids: Baker, 1953), 1:477. Leupold refers to Eduard Koenig's *Lehrgebäude der Hebräischen Sprache: Part II Syntax* (Leipzig: Hinrichs, 1897), 367.i.

[8]Martin Luther, *Luther's Commentary on Genesis*, trans. J. Theodore Mueller, 2 vols. (Grand Rapids: Zondervan, 1958), 1:264.

Genesis 15 shifts, however, from the promise of the land to the concern about that promised male descendant. The call for Abram to believe appears already to be signaled in the opening words of the divine vision: "Fear not" (Gen 15:1; recall the linking of believing in and fearing God). Once again Abram's attempt, by his own works, to bring about God's promise had to be rebuked: his adoption of Eliezer of Damascus as his legal son was not according to God's promises—"This man will not be your heir" (Gen 15:4). This was good enough for Abram: "He believed in the Lord, and he credited it to him as righteousness" (v. 5, my translation).

What, then, was the object of Abram's faith? Franz Delitzsch answered: "The promise . . . has truly Christ for its object; . . . the faith in which he receives it, is faith in the promised seed."[9] Likewise, Leupold is just as adamant on the point, if not even more so than Delitzsch: "Now the question arises, 'Is Abram's faith different from the justifying faith of the New Testament believer?' We answer unhesitatingly and emphatically, No. The very issue in this chapter has been Abram's seed."[10]

Leupold does go on to qualify his answer somewhat as we all must, by saying that while Abram and the NT believer share Christ as one and the same object of saving faith, this is not to say that Abram possessed a full understanding of the Savior's future name, his future atoning work, or even the details of the freely offered and accomplished redemption. Yet in essence both the OT and NT believer had to put their trust in the Seed whom the Father had promised: that is where the similarity lies.

Traditional Evangelical theology can not let the issue rest with this exegesis; in fact, Evangelicals have done very little contextual exegesis on the Genesis 15:6 statement. Most tend to lean more heavily on the line of argumentation that Charles Ryrie restated so clearly:

> Did the Old Testament revelation include Christ as the conscious object of faith? From the inductive study already made [allegedly showing that God was the *sole* object of faith, but which affirmation is modified by saying that "this God was a Saviour"] it would seem that it did not. Furthermore, the two summary statements in the New Testament which deal with forgiveness in Old Testament times indicate the same. Both Acts 17:30 and Romans 3:25

[9] Delitzsch, *Genesis*, 2:7.
[10] Leupold, *Exposition of Genesis*, 1:478.

teach that Christ's relationship to forgiveness was unknown
in the Old Testament. In addition, there are several specific
statements which show the ignorance of Old Testament
saints regarding salvation through Christ—John 1:21; 7:40;
1 Peter 1:11.[11]

Likewise, Lewis Sperry Chafer,[12] after quoting Matthew
19:17, agreed:

> True to the Jewish dispensation, He said with reference to
> the law of Moses: "This do and thou shalt live"; but when
> contemplating the cross and Himself as the bread come
> down from heaven to give His life for the world, He said:
> "This is the work of God, that ye believe on him whom he
> [God] hath sent" (John 6:29). These opposing principles are
> not to be reconciled. They indicate that fundamental distinc-
> tion which must exist between those principles that obtain
> in an age of law, on the one hand, and an age of grace, on the
> other hand.

But these texts will not bear the weight they are being asked
to carry. The "times of ignorance" (Acts 17:30) referred to the
Athenian Gentiles, not Israel. Appropriate for Israel was the rebuke
that the two disciples received on the road to Emmaus, "Oh fools
and slow of heart to believe all that the prophets have spoken"
(Luke 24:25 KJV). The tolerance shown by the "forbearance" of God
for the sins committed "beforehand" (Rom 3:25) was only with
regard to the final work of satisfaction of the justice of God in the
death of Christ and not with regard to a special deal on sinning
without any culpability or record of the sins during the OT days
since they were done in ignorance! That some, in Israel, were just
as ignorant of the Messiah and his work (John 1:21; 7:40) as were
the two disciples on the road to Emmaus (Luke 24:25) does not
detract one iota from what they could and ought to have known. In
fact, 1 Peter 1:10–12 specifically affirms that the only item on
which those who had the Scriptures could plead ignorance was the
matter of "time" (i.e., *when* the Messiah would come). But that
there was a Messiah, that he would suffer, that he would be
glorified as King over all, that the royal glory came after suffering,
and that the prophets delivered their messages not only for Israel
but also for the church is flatly declared.[13]

---

[11]Charles Ryrie, *The Grace of God* (Chicago: Moody, 1970), 49.
[12]Lewis Sperry Chafer, *Grace* (Findlay, Ohio: Dunham, 1922), 92.
[13]See my detailed linguistic argument in Walter C. Kaiser, Jr., *The Uses of the Old Testament in the New* (Chicago: Moody, 1985), 18–23, 209.

Some will still persist in asking: "Was this the time that Abraham was saved and justified?" We will answer that it was not the first time he believed, but it is the first time that the Scriptures expressly mention his faith. It is appropriate to bring out his faith at this point because of the prominence that the text has now given to what has been there all along (since the ancient promise made to Eve)—the promise of the "seed"—but is only made explicit by the newly raised problem of the lack of an heir to be the Seed that was promised.

Thus, the passage connects the Seed (whom we can identify with Christ) as the object of Abraham's belief. As Martin Luther taught on this passage:

> ... here the Holy Spirit states emphatically [that he believed in God who promised] so that we should learn from this passage that all who (*after Abraham's example*) believe in Christ are justified. . . . Our righteousness before God is simply this that we trust in the divine promises (*of Christ*).[14]

Therefore, as Harold G. Stigers decided, it is not necessary to deny that personal salvation is being addressed here:

> Paul speaks of Abram's belief, not as an example of saving faith, but as the vehicle through which the grace of God is bestowed, and so he makes the point that God's promises and favors are not *earned* but come *through* faith (Rom 4). This is the meaning of Genesis 15:6: God would give Abram a son because he trusted God to do it. He therefore was of *right character*, righteous in the eyes of God.[15]

Likewise, George Bush sees Abram's act as a special deed on a single occasion that was made a matter of public and lasting record (i.e., remembered to his credit), and in that sense alone was he justified.[16]

Will this interpretation of Bush and Stigers hold up under the accounting figure ("credited it to him for righteousness") as well as the Pauline use made of it in Romans 4? Bush believes it will, for he

---

[14] Luther, *Luther's Commentary on Genesis*, 1:265 (translator's emphasis). See also Seth Erlandsson, "Faith in the Old and New Testaments: Harmony or Disagreement?" *Concordia Theological Quarterly* 47 (1983): 1–14.

[15] Harold G. Stigers, *A Commentary on Genesis* (Grand Rapids: Zondervan, 1976), 154 (his emphasis).

[16] George Bush, *Notes, Critical and Practical, on the Book of Genesis*, 2 vols. (New York: E. French, 1838–39), 1:244.

views Paul as appealing to Genesis 15:6 merely as an illustration. The fact that this was not the first time that Abram believed and the fact that Abram's faith did not (in Bush's view) have Christ as its grand object are the reasons why Bush is driven to say that this is a faith focusing only on one particular promise—an innumerable seed. But we have already shown that Scripture probably deliberately delayed its discussion of Abram's belief and justification so that it might make the strongest connection between the Savior (i.e., the One Seed) and Abram's justification in order that no one might dissociate justification from the Seed that was to come.

Was Abram's faith a work by which he merited righteousness or achieved some honorable mention? The subject of the accounting, reckoning, or crediting term is clearly and solely God. And even though this is the first time in Scripture that faith and justification are bound together, the intimate connection of this root ts-d-q[17] ("to justify") with salvation in subsequent texts leads us to conclude that Paul was on good exegetical and antecedent theology grounds when he argued in Romans 4:1–16 that Abram's salvation from sin was not "by works" but "by grace." Furthermore, in the context of Genesis 12–22, it is clear that every time Abram decided to extricate himself by his own works, he only dug himself in deeper. Only God's gracious gifts were effective in granting the blessings God had promised; therefore, only God's gracious act of crediting Abram with righteousness would likewise be effective. In fact, Abram was not in any position to do anything to save himself: his sin was all too evident both in his lying to Pharaoh about Sarah and in his adoption of Eliezer as his heir in spite of the promise of God. This, then, raises the problem of the OT saint's conception of sin.

WAS SIN IN THE OT MORE OF AN EXTERNAL OR AN INTERNAL PROBLEM?

There is hardly a page in either Testament that does not have at least one reference to the topic of sin. Traditionally the Hebrew vocabulary for sin has been divided into three major categories: (1) *deviation from* or *falling short of* the law or will of God (*ḥaṭṭā't* or *ḥāṭā'*),[18] (2) *rebellion against* or *transgression of* that law

---

[17]See Horace D. Hummel, "Justification in the Old Testament," *Concordia Journal* 9 (1983): 9–17.

[18]The Hebrew root involved (occurring some 580 times) is the most frequent OT root for sin.

(*peša'*),[19] and (3) *guilt* (*'āšām*) or *wickedness* (*rāšā'*) before God. Simon J. DeVries, however, divides OT sin vocabulary into six categories: (1) formal words (like *'ābar*, "to transgress"), (2) relational words (like *mā'an*, "to disobey"), (3) psychological words (like *'āwāh*, "to be twisted"), (4) qualitative words (like *rā'āh*, "to be bad, evil"), (5) words referring to consequences (like *'āmal*, "to do mischief"), and (6) words for the responsibility for sin (like *'āšam*, "to be guilty").[20]

Regardless of which system of categorizing we use, sin cannot be classified as bad luck or misfortune; rather, it is a personal and deliberate deviation or defection from the person, character, or word of God, the result being a state of feeling real cessation of fellowship with God. Sin is a calculated *act*; but sin is also a *state* of real guilt before God and exposure to his punishment for that guilt. This state of guilt not only follows individual acts of sin but actually precedes sin and gives rise to acts of deviation and defection from that will or law of God. Thus, David confessed that he had been born in iniquity and conceived in sin (Ps 51:5).

Unlike the mythologies of the Ancient Near East, which tended to associate sin with human creatureliness or with sexual generation, the Hebrew writers attributed the source of humanity's sin to the corrupted heart of individuals:

"Every inclination of the thoughts of [the human] heart was only evil all the time" (Gen 6:5).

"These people come near to me with their mouth and honor me with their lips, but their hearts are far from me" (Isa 29:13).

"The heart is deceitful above all things and beyond cure. Who can understand it?" (Jer 17:9).

The fact that God regarded the person and the person's inner attitude prior to and almost as the grounds for judging the person's deeds is best illustrated in the Cain and Abel narrative (Gen 4:1–15). The syntax of verses 3–5 easily supports this notion of assigning priority to the person and the person's heart attitude. Rather than placing the verb first, as is normal in Hebrew, the

---

[19] Some synonyms for *pš'* are the Hebrew roots: *mrd*, to rebel, revolt; *mrh* to be disobedient towards; *srr*, to be stubborn, obstinate; *m' l*, to act faithlessly or unfaithfully [e.g., in a breach of the covenant] and *sûg* to turn back [from God].
[20] Simon J. DeVries, *The Achievement of Biblical Religion: A Prolegomena to Old Testament Theology* (New York: University of America Press, 1983), 164.

subject "Abel" is placed first in verse 4. The emphasis on the individual is reinforced by linking the independent pronoun with the emphasizing particle *gam* and repeating the pronominal suffix on the verbal form in fourth position. A literal translation would be: "And Abel, even he, he brought."

This emphasis is now matched by the choice of his worship, for Abel gave of the first-born of his flock and from the fat pieces. This is to say that because he was, first, authentic in his attitude, he could then truly be generous and wholehearted in his act of worship; therefore he gave the choice portions to God.

Cain, on the other hand, gave more out of custom, formalistic worship and with little or no heart. It was not that he brought agricultural gifts in place of an animal or blood sacrifice. The word for sacrifice used here in connection with both men is *minḥâh*, meaning a "gift" or "tribute." It is the same word used of the grain offering in Leviticus 2.

God, however, discerned the difference, for he "had respect (= *šā'âh 'el*; note the priority placed on the person) for Abel, and [then] for his offering. But unto Cain and [then] to his offering he did not have respect" (vv. 4–5, my translation). Therefore, we affirm that the divine gaze is directed to the person first and only then to the person's worship or work. Only if the heart is found right can the individual's worship, service, or gifts be acceptable.

Too frequently people look "at the outward appearance," whereas "the Lord looks at the heart"(1 Sam 16:7). In his contrition over the Bathsheba incident, David had to learn this same truth the hard way. It was "a broken spirit; a broken and contrite heart" (Ps 51:17) that God was seeking. And this was the same battle that the prophets waged with those who attempted to substitute outward acts of piety for the necessary inward prerequisites for offering all sacrifices or gifts to God (Isa 1:11–18; Jer 7:21–23; Hos 6:6; Mic 6:6–8).

B. D. Eerdmans' attempt to argue in 1903 that "Old Testament ethics do not meddle with the inner thoughts of men"[21] failed because he did not notice:

---

[21]B. D. Eerdmans, "Oorsprong en betekenis van de 'Tien Woorden'" *Theologisch Tijdschritt* 37 (1903): 19–35, as reported also in B. Gemser, "The Object of Moral Judgments in the Old Testament," in *Adhuc Loquitur: Collected Essays by Dr. B. Gemser*, ed. A. vanSelms and A. S. van der Woude (Leiden: Brill, 1968), 78–95. Unfortunately, many have continued to agree with Eerdmans' thesis. For example, Th. C. Vriezen, *An Outline of Old Testament Theology*, 2d ed. (Newton, Mass: Branford, 1970), 393, concluded, "We must therefore agree with Eerdmans

(1) the place and significance that the OT gives to the heart,

(2) the emphasis the OT places on the thoughts, intentions, and deliberations of the wicked, and

(3) the capstone to the Ten Commandments did focus, contrary to Eerdmans' exegesis, on "desire," which pointed to the inner motives as being a proper realm for evaluating all acts.

Thus, we cannot agree with those who attempt to describe sin in OT times as being a matter more of the external act apart from any inner motive or heart attitude. This distinction is not only artificial but also entirely wrongheaded, and it cannot be sustained by the data of the OT text. The inner spiritual state of each person was indeed a matter of primary concern.

Some, however, objecting to such a personal and internal view of sin in the OT, will persist in pointing to the category of "sins in ignorance" (Lev 4:2, 13, 22, 27). Does not this category, argue our objectors, imply that most of the sin or guilt sacrifices (Lev 4:2, 22, 27; 5:17–19) were for sins that the Israelites had no idea were wrong or evil? And if that were so, how could the state of their heart attitude be a matter of concern or even enter into our description of the forgiveness process in the OT?

An alarmingly large number of students of the OT divide all sins into the two major headings of accidental and deliberate.[22] The Psalmist enumerated three major headings in Psalm 19:12–13: "Who can discern his *errors [š^egî'ôt]*? Cleanse me from my *hidden faults [nistārôt]*. Restrain your servant from willful sins *[zēdîm]*" (my translation). But if the first two categories of the Psalmist ("errors" and "hidden faults") are merely two subcategories of the "accidental" heading, as Jacob Milgrom[23] concluded, then it is clear that so-called "sins in ignorance" are actually "sins of inadvertence." Thus, the designation "unwitting" (KJV, NJV, RSV "ignorance")—i.e., "without wit," "without consciousness"—is impossible. The sins of *shegagah* are acts of negligence; the offender knows the law but violates it accidentally and without malice aforethought (e.g., in the case of accidental homicide—Num

---

when he says that the Israelite *did not know of sins in thought. . .* " (his emphasis). See my full discussion on this point in Walter C. Kaiser, Jr., *Toward Old Testament Ethics* (Grand Rapids: Zondervan, 1983), 7–10.

[22]See Exod 21:12–14, Num 15:27–31, 35:15–25, and Deut 19:4–13.

[23]Jacob Milgrom, "The Cultic ŠGGH and Its Influence in Psalms and Job," *The Jewish Quarterly Review* 58 (1967–68): 115–25; also chapter 11 in idem, *Studies in Cultic Theology and Terminology* (Leiden: Brill, 1983), 122–32.

35:22ff; Deut 19:4–10; Josh 20:2–6, 9). There is also the sin of inadvertence, where the person acts without fully knowing all the facts—the ignorance was not about the law but about the circumstances—such as in the case of Abimelech's taking Sarah, whom he thought was Abraham's sister (Gen 20:9), or when Balaam was unaware that an angel was in the donkey's path (Num 22:34: "I have sinned. I did not realize you were standing in the road"). Thus, the sinner who commits a sin of inadvertence is conscious of the act, even if he or she is not always aware of its consequences.

Milgrom makes the same point about two famous texts: Job 6:24 ("Teach me and I will be silent, and make me understand my inadvertence")[24] and Job 19:4 ("If indeed I erred inadvertently, it is I [emphatic position of 'with me' justifies 'it is I'] who should be conscious of my inadvertence").[25] Job's claim is that "he should be conscious of his sins—but he is not!"[26] Milgrom explains further:

> Thus, from the friends' viewpoint, God punishes *NSTROT* [= "hidden faults"] and the sinner's consciousness of his act is not essential for God to punish him. Job, on the other hand, will not admit to the justice of God punishing any other wrong but inadvertent wrong, the *ŠGI'OT* [= "sins of inadvertence"], acts of which Job at least was conscious when he did them though he may not have known they were sinful until later. He demands a bill of particulars. . . . [27]

In fairness to Milgrom, however, it must be pointed out that he feels that Job's friends were championing the traditional view found in Leviticus 4, while Job becomes the first to proclaim that God holds individuals accountable for only conscious sins. We cannot agree with this stratification of the biblical evidence, for it exceeds the categories of the text itself.

The sin of a "high hand" (*beyād rāmâh*, Num 15:17–36) is, in our view, something altogether different from the previous categories. It involved blasphemy against the Lord and contempt for the Word of God (Num 15:30–31). This is similar to what is called the blasphemy of the Holy Spirit in the NT (cf. Heb 10:26–39). As such it becomes an unpardonable sin, since it represents high treason and revolt against God. Its symbol is the clenched fist upraised in a

---

[24] Milgrom, "The Cultic ŠGGH," 121, his translation.
[25] Ibid., 122, his translation.
[26] Ibid., 122.
[27] Ibid., 123.

menacing position against God in heaven. Such sustained treason or blatant blasphemy against God was a picket against heaven, and it demanded everything except forgiveness. All sins could be forgiven in the OT, and atonement was available for all types and categories of sin except blasphemy against God and his Word.

WERE THE OT SACRIFICES PERSONALLY AND OBJECTIVELY EFFECTIVE?

The repeated statement of the law of Moses on the effects of the sacrifices offered for sin in the Levitical law is "and he shall be forgiven" (Lev 1:4; 4:20, 26, 31, 35; 5:10, 16). So effective and so all-embracing was this forgiveness that it availed for such sins as lying, theft, fraud, perjury, and debauchery (Lev 6:1–7). In David's case the list extended to adultery and complicity in murder (Pss 32 and 51). In fact, in connection with the Day of Atonement, what is implicit in these other lists is clearly stated: "*all* their sins" were atoned (Lev 16:21, 22; my emphasis). Thus, instead of limiting the efficacy of this forgiveness to ceremonial sins, all the sins of all the people who were truly repentant were included. It is important to note that the qualification of a proper heart attitude is clearly stated in Leviticus 16:29 and 31 where the people are asked to "afflict (*'ānâh*) their souls" (KJV). Accordingly, only those who had inwardly prepared their hearts were eligible to receive the gracious gift of God's forgiveness (cf. also 1 Sam 15:22).

Nevertheless, a major problem appears whenever the Christian introduces the argument of Hebrews 9–10 into this discussion. The writer of Hebrews states in no uncertain terms that:

> The law is only a shadow of the good things that are coming—not the realities themselves. For this reason it can never, by the same sacrifices repeated endlessly year after year, make perfect those who draw near to worship . . . because it impossible for the blood of bulls and goats to take away sins (Heb 10:1, 4).

This surely seems to diminish the high claims that we just finished attributing to the writer of Leviticus. In fact, Hebrews 9:9 adds that "the gifts and sacrifices being offered were not able to clear the conscience of the worshiper." What shall we say then about the forgiveness offered in the Torah? It would be too much to contend that the OT offer of forgiveness repeated so often in the

Levitical institution of the sacrifices was only symbolic and offered no actual cleansing from or removal of sin.

The only solution is to take both the OT and NT statements seriously. We conclude then, with Hobart Freeman,[28] that the OT sacrifices were *subjectively efficacious,* in that the sinner did receive full relief based on the clear declaration of God's appointed servant. But it is just as clear that the sacrifices of bulls and goats *were not in themselves* expiatory and efficacious. The most these sacrifices could do was to point to the need for a perfect, living substitute who would, in the timing of God, ransom and deliver all from the debt, guilt, and effects of their sin. Thus, the OT sacrifices were not *objectively* efficacious; but then neither did the OT ever claim that the blood of these bulls and goats was inherently effective.

Geoffrey Grogan would not solve the problem by using the distinction Freeman has used here; in fact, he believes that the OT sacrifices were ineffective both objectively and subjectively. He cites two reasons for the ineffectiveness of the sacrifices: (1) they had to be repeated, and (2) they were animal sacrifices and thus could not truly act as substitutes for humans. But when the natural question is put to Grogan, "Did they effect nothing then?" he answers that their true function was provisional, "imposed until the time of reformation" (Heb 9:9–10 RSV). In the meantime, the OT sacrifices typified the sacrifice that was to come in Christ, and thus they were a means of grace by which the sacrifice of Christ could be channeled even to OT worshippers.[29]

We believe that both Freeman and Grogan end up with the same position, though Freeman has the advantage in treating the fact that real forgiveness was effected in connection with a proper use of the sacrifices and with a declaration that their sins were gone and remembered against them no more.

The efficacy of the OT sacrifices, then, rested in the Word of God, who boldly announced that sacrifices done in this manner and with this heart attitude (Ps 50:8, 14; 51:16 [Heb 10:8]; Prov 15:8, 21:3; Isa 1:11–18; 66:3; Jer 7:21–23; Hos 6:6; Amos 5:21; Mic 6:6–8) would receive from God a genuine experience of full

---

[28] Hobart E. Freeman, "The Problem of Efficacy of Old Testament Sacrifices," *Bulletin of The Evangelical Theological Society* 5 (1962): 73–9; idem, *An Introduction to the Old Testament Prophets* (Chicago: Moody, 1968), 316–24.

[29] Geoffrey W. Grogan, "The Experience of Salvation in the Old and New Testaments," *Vox Evangelica* 5 (1967): 11.

forgiveness. Of course, everything depended on the perfect payment for this release, a payment that would occur sometime in the future. Therefore, not the blood of bulls and goats but the "blood" (i.e., the life rendered up in violent death) of a perfect sacrifice finally made possible all the forgiveness proleptically enjoyed in the OT and retrospectively appreciated in the NT. Only the lamb of God could have provided *objective efficacy,* even though the *subjective efficacy* that had preceded it was grounded on the authority and promised work of Christ.

Until the death of Christ happened, the sins of the OT saints were both forgiven and "passed over" (*parēsis,* Rom 3:25) in the merciful grace of God until the expiatory death of Christ provided what no animal ever could do and what no OT text ever claimed it could do.

During the OT period, sins were forgiven and remembered against men and women no more (Ps 103:3, 10–12)—in fact, removed as far from the OT confessor as the east is from the west! Thus, the OT saint experienced sins forgiven on the basis of God's Word and sins forgotten (i.e., "remembered against him no more," (Ezek 18:22, my translation) on the same basis.

WHAT WAS THE OT BELIEVER'S EXPERIENCE OF THE HOLY SPIRIT?

The OT believer's experience of the Holy Spirit has frequently been a neglected topic of theological discussion. All too many interpreters merely brush the topic aside with some brief traditional adage that says that the Holy Spirit temporarily came *upon* certain OT leaders, but he did not indwell or remain *with* believers until NT times.

What else may be said on this subject, such a quick prepositional treatment of the work of the Holy Spirit in the lives of OT believers is all too cursory and, in fact, inaccurate! The subject is indeed difficult, and not enough scholars have written on this theme,[30] at least on this theme as it relates to the experience of the OT believer.

---

[30]The best known recent work in the United States is by Leon J. Wood, *The Holy Spirit in the Old Testament* (Grand Rapids: Zondervan, 1976). But the most original discussion, albeit brief, is by Geoffrey Grogan, "The Experience of Salvation in the Old and New Testament," *Vox Evangelica* 5 (1967): 12–17. Grogan refers to J. C. J. Waite, *The Activity of the Holy Spirit Within the Old Testament Period* (London: London Bible College Annual Lecture, 1961). See also

True, most are familiar with the Spirit's presence and activity in creating the world (Gen 1:2; Job 26:13; Isa 32:15) and in sustaining the created order (Job 34:14; Ps 104:30). Again, most concede it is the Holy Spirit who gave wisdom, understanding, and basic skills to such OT men as Moses (Exod 18:22–23; Num 11:17), the seventy elders (Num 11:16–17), and the craftsman of the tabernacle, Bezaleel (Exod 31:2–11).

But where many interpreters disagree or display a poor grasp of the subject is at the experiential level. Here most conclude with the fact that the OT prophets were men who "had the Spirit" (Ezek 2:2; 3:24; Dan 4:8, 9, 18; 5:11, 14; Mic 3:8). Other than this Spirit of revelation given to the prophets, OT men and women would need to wait until the age of the Spirit anticipated by Jeremiah (31:31–34), Ezekiel (Ezek 11:19; 36:26–27; 39:29), and Joel (Joel 2:28–32) had come.

But a moment of careful reflection will reveal that something has been left out. If the Holy Spirit was not active in the individual lives of ordinary believers in the OT, would this mean that they were unregenerate? Since the Holy Spirit is the only One who can bring new life and effect subjectively the salvation that Christ would secure for them objectively, did this mean that OT believers did not possess faith—which is always said to be a gift of God (effected by the Holy Spirit) and not of works, lest any man or woman (e.g., lest Adam, Eve, Noah, Abraham, David, or Isaiah) should boast (Eph 2:8–9)?

There is no evidence, some will object, for such a high claim. Surely this is merely a theological inference based on NT theology! But is it? Did not Jesus himself expect better theology from Nicodemus, even though he was still in OT times, or at least in a pre-Cross situation? When Nicodemus made his discreet nocturnal inquiry about salvation, Jesus openly spoke about the need for a new birth by the work of the Holy Spirit. Nicodemus reacted by expressing surprise and intellectual confusion: he had not known of such requirements. That, in turn, provoked Jesus' rebuke: How can you claim to be a teacher in Israel and yet not know something as elementary as the need for being born again? (John 3:10). Presum-

Carl Armerding "The Holy Spirit in the Old Testament," *Bibliotheca Sacra* 92 (1935): 277–91; 433–41; M. R. Westall, "The Scope of the Term 'Spirit of God' in the Old Testament," *Indian Journal of Theology* 28 (1977): 29–43; and P. A. Nordell, "The Old Testament Doctrine of the Spirit of God," *The Old Testament Student* 4 (1885): 433–44.

ably our Lord held Nicodemus responsible for the teaching in Ezekiel 36:26–27. Likewise, Nicodemus was perhaps familiar with David's prayer: "Create in me a clean heart, O God, and put a new and right spirit within me" (Ps 51:10 RSV). Indeed, had not David worried that God would "cast [him] . . . away from [his] presence and take . . . [his] holy Spirit from [him]" (Ps 51:11 RSV)? Had not Israel as a nation also "grieved his holy Spirit" (Isa 63:10)?

It is possible, though it cannot be proven, that Paul is claiming in 2 Corinthians 4:13 that our faith is the product of "the same spirit of faith" (by which we Christians believe and therefore speak) that worked in the lives of OT saints. Paul had just quoted Psalm 116:10, "I believed; therefore I said. . . . " His claim, then, is this: the same Holy Spirit who authored the faith of the psalmist who believed—and who thereby was also enabled to speak—is the identical Holy Spirit who enabled me, Paul, and all NT Christians to believe and, therefore, likewise to speak.

However, there are even greater difficulties to our thesis that have not been faced as yet. What shall we say about those NT passages that appear to suggest that the Holy Spirit had not been given in the OT or even in the days of our Lord? His advent would, in fact, only take place at Pentecost. These NT texts are:

Matt 3:11 (and parallels)	"He will baptize you with the Holy Spirit and with fire" (versus John's baptism with water only).
John 1:33	"He who will baptize with the Holy Spirit."
John 7:37–39	"Up to that time the Spirit had not been given, since Jesus had not yet been glorified."
John 14:16–17	"The Father . . . will give you another counselor [who will] . . . live with you and will be [or, is] in you" (my translation).
John 14:26	"But . . . the Holy Spirit . . . will teach you all things and will remind you of everything I have said to you."
John 15:26	"When the Counselor comes, . . . the Spirit of truth . . . , he will testify about me."
John 16:7	"Unless I go away, the Counselor will not come to you."

John 16:13–15	"When . . . the Spirit of truth comes, he will guide you into all truth. . . . He will tell you what is yet to come."
John 20:22	"He breathed on them and said, 'Receive the Holy Spirit.'"
Acts 1:5	" . . . in a few days you will be baptized with the Holy Spirit."
Acts 11:15–16	"The Holy Spirit came on them as he had come on us . . . [as] the Lord had said . . . 'You will be baptized with the Holy Spirit.'"
Acts 15:8	"God . . . showed that he accepted them by giving the Holy Spirit to them, just as he did to us."

The evidence is almost overwhelming, and it is no wonder that for many the subject is closed. These verses seem to say all that needs to be said on the subject. However, there is room to question the absoluteness of these passages. First of all, we must delete from this list the references to the baptism of the Holy Spirit (Matt 3:11 with its parallels; John 1:33; Acts 1:5; 11:15–15; and 15:8). This was a unique work of the Holy Spirit by which he, for the first time, incorporated all believers into one new body, his church.

This interpretation is certain because the promise of John the Baptist and Jesus points forward to such a work, one that is just days away from happening in Acts 1:5 as the disciples tarried in the Upper Room. With the birthday of the church at Pentecost in Acts 2 and the apostolic interpretation in 1 Corinthians 12:13 pointing back to it, we have locked in the meaning of the "baptism of the Holy Spirit." "For we were all baptized by one Spirit into one body . . . and were all given the one Spirit to drink."

Likewise we must exclude those verses that specifically promise the apostles that they would be the ones through whom the Holy Spirit would reveal the NT canon (John 14:26; 15:26–27; 16:12–15). The apostles, not we NT believers, heard "everything" Jesus taught them (Jn 14:26) and had "been with [him] from the beginning" of his earthly pilgrimage (John 15:27). Almost every cult that attaches itself to the Christian faith has in one way or another abused the context and meaning of these three texts on Jesus' promise concerning the NT canon. It is tragic to continue to hear Evangelicals join in this parody by claiming that they too are the recipients of new truth from the Holy Spirit. Let these Christians prove that they walked with Jesus in Galilee and that they heard these words from Jesus very own lips, and then we will listen to their extravagant claims.

We are left with John 7:37–39, 14:16–17, and 16:7. Do these verses teach an absolutely new appearance of the Holy Spirit in the NT? We answer, "No." Not only has John 3:5–10 suggested otherwise, but so do three other passages: Matthew 10:20, Luke 11:13, and 12:12. When Jesus sent out the twelve, he assured them that "it will not be you speaking, but the Spirit of your Father speaking through you" (Matthew 10:20). This mission was clearly before his death and the advent of the church at Pentecost. Likewise, when Jesus taught his disciples how to pray, he concluded, "If you . . . know how to give good gifts to your children, how much more will your Father in heaven give the Holy Spirit to those who ask him!" (Luke 11:13). Finally, Jesus taught the crowd that those who believed on him should not fear the possible harassment that could come from interrogation about their reasons for believing in Jesus, "for the Holy Spirit [would] teach [them] at that time what [they] should say" (Luke 12:12).

The most interesting text in this group is John 14:17. "You know him, for he lives *with (para)* you and *will be* [or is] in you" (my emphasis). *Para* (Greek "with")

> does not denote a merely fluctuating relationship, for the same preposition is employed in [John] xiv.23 of the abiding of the Father and the Son [already] in them. It is doubtful that our Lord intended a contrast at this point. It is more likely that He desired to assure them that the One of whom He spoke was no stranger to them. He was going to indwell them in a new way, but this does not mean that He had not been present with them in a real sense already.[31]

A second observation can be made about the text in John 14:17. There is just as strong and just as early manuscript reading for the present tense "is in you" as there is for "will be in you." The two forms *estai* and *esti* were very easily confused, but, as B. F. Westcott concludes, " . . . the present tense appears to be less like a

---

[31]Grogan, "Experience," 13–14. See also Wood, *Holy Spirit*, 86, on the present perfect verb *menō* ("dwells"), who differs from John Walvoord (*The Church in Prophecy* [Grand Rapids: Zondervan, 1964], 37) on the distinction that Jesus makes between the Holy Spirit's being "near" Old Testament saints and being "within" New Testament saints.

correction."[32] Thus, the Holy Spirit already was "with" (*para*) the OT believer and was present (*esti*) in those who believed.

If the OT believer already possessed the Holy Spirit, why then was Pentecost necessary? When John added the comment in John 7:39, "The Spirit had not been given, since Jesus had not yet been glorified," we must observe with George Smeaton that:

> He does not mean that the Spirit did not yet exist—for all Scripture attests His eternal pre-existence; nor that His regenerating efficacy was still unknown—for countless millions had been regenerated by His power since the first promise in Eden; but that these operations of the Spirit had been but an anticipation of the atoning death of Christ rather than a giving.[33]

Smeaton went on to say that next to the Incarnation and the Atonement, Pentecost was the greatest event in all history. The necessity of Pentecost and the visible coming of the Holy Spirit was this:

> He must have a coming in state, in a solemn and visible manner, accompanied with visible effects as well as Christ had and whereof all the Jews should be, and were, witnesses.[34]

Concluded Smeaton, "Thus Pentecost was openly signalized as the day of the mission of the comforter."[35] It is this event that Joel pointed to and Peter witnessed in part when the Holy Spirit was poured out on "all flesh" (Joel 2:28).

Our summary of the experience of the OT believers' participation in the ministry of the Holy Spirit cannot be put any better than Geoffrey Grogan concluded:

> Hence we may say that the *full* N.T. experience of the Spirit as the Spirit of Christ from Pentecost onwards is at one with that of the true saints of the O.T. in that it was always a regenerating experience, bringing men to newness of life, but that there is an important difference. It is not simply that the Spirit now operates on the basis of the perfect character of Jesus. Presumably [the Spirit] had already done this in

---

[32] B. F. Westcott, *The Gospel According to St. John* (1881; reprint, Grand Rapids: Eerdmans, 1967), 206.

[33] George Smeaton, *The Doctrine of the Holy Spirit*, 2d ed. (Edinburgh: T. & T. Clark, 1889), 49.

[34] Ibid., 53, citing T. Goodwin, *Works* (Edinburgh, 1861), 6:8.

[35] Ibid., 54.

anticipation even in the OT. Rather it is that [the Spirit] operates on the basis of that character *as now revealed historically* and so held before the minds of those who now experienced His activity in their hearts. For example, men in OT days had the command of God to love Him and to love the neighbor. However, our Lord had said "a new commandment I give you, that you love one another . . . (John xiii.34). There was . . . a partial realisation of it [in the OT]. . . . Now, however, the standard has been perfectly revealed in [Christ]. . . . [36]

Just so, the Holy Spirit already regenerated and was "in" OT believers, but it was necessary that he come visibly and formally to validate all that had been proleptically experienced in the OT, just as Calvary was necessary to validate all that had been offered in the name of the coming sacrifice and atonement of Christ.

WHAT HOPE DID OT BELIEVERS HAVE OF LIFE BEYOND THE GRAVE?

Thomas Ridenhour states what all too frequently is taken as the final word on this subject of life after death in the OT: "There is no 'uniform and sure doctrine of the afterlife' offered in the Old Testament."[37] Only one passage in the OT is counted as a "clear and undisputed reference to the resurrection of the dead"[38]—Daniel 12:2. With this opinion Robert H. Pfeiffer concurred, "The doctrine of the resurrection is first stated as a dogma in Dan 12:2 . . . a doctrine unknown in the Old Testament before the third century."[39] Harris Birkeland adds Isaiah 26:19 to Daniel 12:2 as "the only passages where the existence of a belief in an eschatological resurrection is testified beyond doubt."[40] But Manfred O. Meitzen would remove even these two texts, for in his view "The Old

---

[36] Grogan, "Experience," 17.

[37] Thomas E. Ridenhour, "Immortality and Resurrection in the Old Testament," *Dialog* 15 (1976): 109, citing, in part, H. H. Rowley, *Faith of Israel* (London: SCM, 1970), 167.

[38] Rowley, ibid.

[39] Robert H. Pfeiffer, *Introduction to the Old Testament* (New York: Harper, 1948), 778, 479. See also John H. Otwell, "Immortality in the Old Testament," *Encounter* 22 (1961): 15, and Robert Martin-Achard, *From Death to Life*, trans. John Penny Smith (Edinburgh: Oliver and Boyd, 1960), 185.

[40] Harris Birkeland, "The Belief in the Resurrection of the Dead in the Old Testament," *Studia Theologica* 3 (1950): 77.

Testament teaches virtually nothing about resurrection or life after death."[41]

Why were the Hebrews so bankrupt in this area when all over the ancient Near East there existed a considerable amount of writing about life after death (e.g., the Gilgamesh Epic, the Descent of Ishtar into the Netherworld, the Book of the Dead, the Pyramid Texts)? Whole cultures reflected on this subject and provided for life in the next world. Indeed, the whole economy of the Egyptian state was geared to providing for the Pharaoh's life (and the lives of his loyal subjects and servants) in the next world—thus those massive pyramids. By the time Abraham arrived in Egypt, the pyramids of Gizeh would already have been five to seven hundred years old! Accordingly, it turns out that so-called primitive patriarchal men and women thought more on the question of life after death than does modern man. The people of that day lived with life and death—they heard the screams of women in labor and heard the death rattle of the aged. Modern urban dwellers seldom are forced into such life and death situations, for we insulate ourselves from both ends of the spectrum, using hospitals, wards, rest homes, and the like.

As far as the biblical evidence is concerned, even before the patriarchs, kings, or prophets reflected on the subject of an afterlife, Enoch was "taken" (Gen 5:24) to be with God, and the mortal was swallowed up by immortality. Indeed, he entered the very presence of God. If we accept the canonical evidence at face value, that one event should have settled forever the theoretical question.

By Abraham's time such a hope was so deeply embedded in the general ethos that there was no reason to explain it even to Abraham's servants, who no doubt knew that their master's mission was to sacrifice his only son on Mount Moriah. However, Abraham calmly announced to his attendants, "We will worship and then we will come back to you" (Gen 22:5). In case we missed how such a feat was possible after a human sacrifice, Hebrews 11:17–19 explains that Abraham believed "that God was able to raise [Isaac] up, even from the dead!" (my translation). Why should we think this to be too advanced a doctrine, if in the second millennium B.C. Gilgamesh Epic, Utnapishtim (the Babylonian Noah) believed that his friend Enkidu could be raised from the dead by an act of the gods?

---

[41]Manfred O. Meitzen, "Some Reflections on the Resurrection and Eternal Life," *Lutheran Quarterly* 24 (1972): 254.

If Job represents that same patriarchal ethos, then his discussions on this topic are also amazing. Job inquires, If a tree is cut down, is there hope for that tree? Yes, he concludes. Sometimes the cut-off trunk of the tree *will sprout,* or *shoot forth,* again (Job 14:7). However, "If a man dies, will he live again?" (14:14a). Yes, answers Job: "All the days of my hard service will I wait until my *sprouting, shooting forth* or *release* comes" (14:14b, my translation). Even the warmly debated Job 19:25–27 affirms[42] that there is hope beyond the grave. Common to all the varying translations is this minimal assurance: "I know that my redeemer lives; and that he will at last arise to vindicate me: and after my death and the decomposition of my skin I shall see God" (my translation).

No less certain were at least three psalmists. The Davidic Psalter affirmed: "You will not abandon me to the grave, nor will you let your Holy One see decay" (Ps 16:10). In the hymns of the sons of Korah, this conviction grows to a full declaration: "But God will redeem me from the grave, He will surely take me to himself" (Ps 49:15, my translation).

From Asaph's songs came the realization (just when the psalmist had almost concluded that good things happen to bad people and there was no sense in trying to live a godly, righteous life) that the final destiny of the wicked was different from the destiny of the righteous (Ps 73:17). The prospect of a personal and real fellowship with God beyond the grave struck this Psalmist again: "You guide me with your counsel, and afterward you will take me into glory" (Ps 73:24).

The grave was not the end. Instead, the eighth-century prophet exclaimed, "But your dead will live; their bodies will rise. You who dwell in the dust, wake up and shout for joy. . . ; the earth will give birth to her dead" (Isa 26:19).

If the OT case is that there is the hope of personal fellowship with God beyond the grave and after death, where does the negative attitude come from? Antoon Schoors points to three texts in Ecclesiastes (2:14–16; 3:19–21; and 9:1–3). Even though Schoors concedes that the Preacher recognizes that "the dust returns to the ground it came from, and the spirit returns to God who gave it" (Eccl 12:7), he is still certain that "According to Koheleth, life 'under the sun' is closed with death, which is final. He shares the opinion of his people that a dead person is only a shadow, which

---

[42]See Kaiser, *Old Testament Theology,* 181.

leads a completely inactive existence in Sheol. . . . Death is even more final than it is in other texts of the Old Testament."[43]

But Schoors, like many modern interpreters of Koheleth, insists on translating *miqreh* as "fate, accident" (Eccl 2:15; 3:19; 9:2) rather than that which "meets" men as an "event," "happening,"[44] or even an "outcome." Nowhere does Koheleth hint at anything like the power of a blind force that is found in paganism. This same word appears in 1 Samuel 6:9, where the pagan Philistines want to set up an experiment using the natural affection of a cow for her calf before they will pass off what was no doubt a case of the bubonic plague in each city the ark visits as a mere happenstance, or a chance occurrence (*miqreh*).

Even more serious is the persistent refusal of interpreters to reckon with the articles preceding "go upward" and "go down" in Ecclesiastes 3:21 and instead treat the verse as an interrogative. Therefore, it is usually translated as "Who knows if the spirit of man rises upward and if the spirit of the animal goes down into the earth?" But the text clearly has an article, not the sign of the interrogative, before the two participles. Hence the meaning is just the opposite of the so-called one "fate" for humanity and animals. It reads: "the spirit of man [is] the one going upward, but the spirit of the beast [is] the one going down to the earth." The only event that the righteous and wicked share is death.[45] But the argument of the writer of Ecclesiastes is that life must take on a qualitative difference now, for after death comes the judgment (Eccl 3:17; 11:9; 12:14). But how could such an idea count if when old men die they cease to exist? Since men will be judged, Koheleth urges full, happy, but moral participation as long as we have breath and strength in this life.

The God of the OT is not the God of the dead, but the God of the living: the God of Abraham, Isaac, and Jacob (Exod 6:3; cf. Luke 20:37–38). The prospect of life after death in the OT is not as fully developed as it is in the NT, but there can be no doubt about the fact that OT saints believed they would see God and enjoy his presence.

---

[43] Antoon Schoors, "Koheleth: A Perspective of Life After Death?" *Ephemerides Theologicae Lovanienses* 61 (1985): 302–3.

[44] See the most recent commentary, J. A. Loader, *Ecclesiastes: A Practical Commentary* (Grand Rapids: Eerdmans, 1986), 29, 44, 107–8.

[45] Walter C. Kaiser, Jr., *Ecclesiastes: Total Life* (Chicago: Moody, 1979), 69–72.

PART III

THE OLD TESTAMENT AND LIFE

Chapter 7

The Old Testament as
a Way of Life

Despite all the positive affirmations about the formal principle of the authority of the OT for the Christian, the material question eventually reduces itself to one of the following methodologies: (1) everything the NT does not *repeat* from the OT is passe for the Christian or (2) everything that the NT has not *changed* in principle still remains in force for the Christian. Which of these two approaches is correct?

IS THE AUTHORITY OF THE OT LIMITED ONLY TO WHAT THE NT REPEATS OR MODIFIES FROM THE OT?

These two approaches to the OT can be illustrated in citations from Luther and Calvin. On the one hand, Luther dismissed all attempts to base a current practice on OT revelation that the NT had not repeated:

> There is one answer that can be made to all attempts to cite passages from the Old Testament to support [monastic] vows. . . . "Do you Christians want to be Jews?" Prove your

case from the New Testament. The Old Testament has been
set aside through Christ and is no longer binding.[1]

To be sure, Luther was not always consistent with this hermeneutic,
for he could, on occasion, rest his whole case on the Mosaic Law
and Israelite practice, as in the case of parental agreement for
engagements.[2] Yet his general approach was decidedly to go with
the NT.

Luther's general policy is all the more evident in his famous
essay on this topic. "The Law," Luther intoned,

> is no longer binding on us because it was given only to the
> people of Israel. . . . Exodus 20[:2] . . . makes it clear that
> even the ten commandments do not apply to us. . . . The
> sectarian spirits want to saddle us with Moses and all the
> commandments. We will skip that. We will regard Moses as
> a teacher, but we will not regard him as our lawgiver—
> unless he agrees with both the New Testament and the
> natural law.[3]

On the other hand, Calvin refused to relegate the Mosaic Law
to the past. Instead, he pointed to Deuteronomy 32:46–47 and
warned:

> We are not to refer solely to one age David's statement that
> the life of a righteous man is a continual meditation upon the
> law [Ps 1:2], for it is just as applicable to every age, even to
> the end of the world.[4]

But what, we ask Calvin, has been abrogated in the Law? Did
not Paul free the Christian from the Mosaic Law? His response was
clear:

> What Paul says, as to the abrogation of the Law [Gal 3:10]
> evidently applies not to the Law itself, but merely to its
> power of constraining the conscience. For the Law not only
> teaches, but also imperiously demands. . . . We must be

---

[1] Martin Luther, "An Answer to Several Questions on Monastic Vows" (1526), in
Luther's Works, ed. Helmut T. Lehman (Philadelphia: Muhlenberg, 1960), 46:146.

[2] Martin Luther, "That Parents Should Neither Compel nor Hinder the Marriage
of their Children and That Children Should Not Become Engaged Without their
Parents' Consent" (1524), in *Luther's Works*, 45:390–92. I am indebted to David
Wright for both of these citations, "The Ethical Use of the Old Testament in Luther
and Calvin: A Comparison," *Scottish Journal of Theology* 36 (1983): 465.

[3] Martin Luther, "How Christians Should Regard Moses," in *Luther's Works*,
35:164–65.

[4] John Calvin, *Institutes of the Christian Religion*, ed. John T. McNeill, trans.
Ford Lewis Battles (Philadelphia: Westminster, 1960), 2.7.13.

freed from the fetters of the law, ... those of rigid and
austere exaction. ... Meanwhile, ... the law has lost none
of its authority, but must always receive from us the same
respect and obedience.[5]

Accordingly, the church has tended to divide into these two
main camps, even while it continued to affirm with Paul in
2 Timothy 3:15–17 that the OT is indeed most useful and profitable
for Christians. But why must this division of the church continue, if
the profitability of the OT is so clear?

At the heart of this reluctance to allow the OT to have its full
usefulness in the life of the contemporary Christian lie these
two unresolved issues: (1) the relationship of law to promise, or
covenant, within the OT itself (i.e., how does the Sinaitic Covenant
relate to the Abrahamic-Davidic-New Covenant?) and (2) the
problem of how one derives principles, "middle axioms," from
these specific commands of God that were originally addressed to a
people in another culture, another time, and another situation than
ours? Both of these issues are worthy of an extended discussion.
Hopefully, each one can be legitimately disarmed as a real
objection for any Christian's profitable use of the OT as a guide for
believing and living.

WHAT IS THE RELATIONSHIP
OF THE LAW TO OT PROMISE?

Many are willing, of course, to allow what the NT refers to as
the OT "promise" of God (i.e., the substance of the Abrahamic-
Davidic Covenant) to have a permanent role in the teaching
ministry of the modern church. The numerous references to the tripartite formula of the promise doctrine ("I will be your God, You
shall be my people, and I will dwell in the midst of you"), along
with the repeated appeal to label the same provisions as those given
to the ancients as being identical to our "gospel" (e.g., Gal 3:8),
plainly demonstrate that the promise-plan of God continues from
its OT statement (see below for our chapter on the promise). But
how that promise was to be fitted into the Mosaic/Sinaitic Covenant
has never been very clear.

In fact, so embarrassing has this issue proved to be that it
became popular at the turn of this century to deal with the law by
shifting it to the periphery of the canon. Thus, instead of viewing

---

[5] Ibid., 2.7.15.

the prophets as the interpreters of the law, as all the church and the Jewish community had rightfully interpreted the prophets' claims up to the latter part of the nineteenth century, it now became the better part of scholarly wisdom in source criticism to place the majority of the law *later* than the prophets and at the end of the OT canon.

There were other attempts to devalue the law and to view it as symptomatic of a decline from the blessings of promise in the covenants made with the patriarchs or David. For example, in 1940, Martin Noth[6] argued that the laws did not belong to the nation of Israel; they were, instead, to be connected to a tribal alliance in the exile where the law was made absolute after it had lost its real relevance and its basis in the life of the people. In 1944, J. Begrich, with a similar view, proposed that the original form of the biblical covenant with its obligations on the powerful party for the sake of the weaker party was now changed in its secondary development into a treaty that was now binding on *both* sides.[7]

This distinction between an unconditional, unilateral, promissory covenant and a conditional, bilateral covenant of law brought the matter to a clearer focus. Did the OT present two fundamentally different ways of viewing Israel's privilege and position under God? Did the one (the Abrahamic-Davidic promise) stress God's sure and immutable promises, which were beyond cancellation, while the other (the Sinaitic covenant) stressed human obligation and compliance on penalty of retribution? And is the theological collision course between these two covenants the great reason for the Christian's continued discomfort with the OT in general? Which, then, is true? Are the promises and benefits that God gave in the Abrahamic-Davidic-[Re]new[ed] Covenant of no effect unless men and women obey the Sinaitic legislation?

Various responses have been offered to these two alternatives. Gunneweg appears to represent those who surrender all hope of finding any resolution to this tension. He rather despondently concluded:

> If we keep within the bounds of the Old Testament, either description is possible, since both are given. There is

---

[6]Martin Noth, "The Laws in the Pentateuch" in *The Laws in the Pentateuch and Other Essays* (Philadelphia: Fortress, 1967), 1ff.

[7]J. Begrich, "*Berit,* Ein Beitrag zur Erfassung einer alttestamentlichen Denkform," ZAW 60 (1944), 1ff, as cited by Antonius H. J. Gunneweg, *Understanding the Old Testament* (Philadelphia: Westminster, 1978), 126.

no possibility of drawing a line from law to covenant or from covenant to law.[8]

To be sure, Gunneweg does note that this issue is bound up with another: is the rule of God with his people brought into being in *this* world and in our history, or is it *outside* of our world and history?[9] To appreciate what otherwise seems to be a rather oblique and irrelevant question, one must only recall that the Sinaitic covenant called for a national destruction—with the imposition of all the covenant curses and ejection from the land—for disobedience to the covenant, while the Davidic traditions called for a reinstatement of the Davidic throne and kingdom, even following the awful times of chastisement.[10] But Gunneweg saw no resolution for this question either ("There is no way out of this dilemma"),[11] for here the question was also whether the kingdom of God was of this world or not. So he let the question stand with all of its unresolved tensions.

A second way to meet this problem was to declare that the Abrahamic and Davidic covenants are themselves also conditional and therefore require the same obedience posited by the Sinaitic Covenant. This stance is found in Oswald T. Allis[12] and in Ronald Youngblood.[13] Allis rightly insisted on the fact that the Mosaic Covenant rested on the Abrahamic Covenant (Exod 2:24; 3:6; 6:8) and the condition noted in Exodus 19:5–6 ("if you will obey my voice," RSV) was no more a condition for the Sinaitic Covenant than Genesis 22:18 ("because you have obeyed me") and Genesis 26:5 (Abraham "kept my requirements, my commands, my decrees, and my laws") were for the Abrahamic Covenant.

But Allis went on to complain that:

> The claim that the Abrahamic covenant was "unconditional" has dangerous implications; for it suggests an

---

[8]Gunneweg, *Understanding the Old Testament*, 139.

[9]Ibid., 138–39.

[10]See John Bright, *Covenant and Promise: The Prophetic Understanding of the Future in Pre-Exilic Israel* (Philadelphia: Westminster, 1976), 83.

[11]Gunneweg, *Understanding the Old Testament*, 138–39.

[12]Oswald T. Allis, *God Spake by Moses* (Nutley, N.J.: Presbyterian and Reformed, 1958), 72.

[13]Ronald Youngblood, "The Abrahamic Covenant: Conditional or Unconditional?" in *The Living and Active Word of God: Studies in Honor of Samuel J. Schultz*, ed. Morris Inch and Ronald Youngblood (Winona Lake, Ind.: Eisenbrauns, 1983), 31–46.

> antithesis between *faith* and *obedience* which is not war-
> ranted in Scripture.[14]

Such an antithesis between faith and obedience and the playing off of the "if" statement in Exodus 19:6 is indeed unfair. Must both of these concessions lead to positing an unconditional covenant for Abraham? Did the text attach any stipulations to any of the patriarchal or Davidic promises? We cannot find any; therefore, while granting to Allis the legitimacy of his observations on obedience in both covenants, we cannot agree that that makes the Abrahamic covenant conditional.

Youngblood also declared the Abrahamic Covenant to be conditional and listed fifteen conditional passages (Gen 12:1; 12:7; 14:22–23; 15:9–10; 17:1–2; 17:3–4; 17:9–14; 17:23–27; 18:19; 22:2; 22:16–18; 26:4–5; Deut 28:15–68; Jer 4:1–2; Heb 11:8). The difficulty with this list is that almost one-third of them come from Genesis 17, which dealt with circumcision. But circumcision was granted a separate status and declared to be a separate covenant in Genesis 17:10. In fact, the *we'attâ* of verse 9 dramatically shifts the covenantal obligation from God to Abraham.[15] And even more disturbing is Youngblood's approval of George Shama's statement:

> The promise made to the seed of Abraham . . . was not
> unconditional, but clearly revokable . . . The promises made
> to the patriarch could be and ultimately have been annuled
> by national apostasy.[16]

Said Youngblood, " . . . his [Shama's] understanding of the relationship between the Abrahamic and Sinaitic covenants is surely on the right track."[17]

But we cannot agree. The alleged conditional elements in the Abrahamic (or even in the Davidic Covenant, such as 2 Sam 7:14, 15; 1 Kings 2:4; 8:25; 9:4–5; Ps 89:30–33; 132:11–12)[18] never threatened the constituent nature of these covenants, nor did they add any stipulations to them. It is true that there was a duty of

---

[14]Allis, *God Spake By Moses*, 72.

[15]Thomas E. McComiskey, *The Covenants of Promise: A Theology of the Old Testament Covenants* (Grand Rapids: Baker, 1985), 146–57.

[16]Youngblood, "The Abrahamic Covenant," 40, citing George Shama, "A False Claim to Palestine," *Christianity Today* 23 (October 6, 1978), 28–29.

[17]Ibid.

[18]Walter C. Kaiser, Jr., "The Blessing of David: The Charter for Humanity," in *The Law and the Prophets: OT studies in Honor of Oswald T. Allis,* ed. John H. Skilton (Nutley, N.J.: Presbyterian and Reformed, 1974), 306.

obedience, which was intimately tied up with promise as its only rightful *outcome* and *sequel,* but in no case could it be shown that the promising elements themselves were prior to the promise or were placed in jeopardy by human disobedience. Therefore, to go on to speak of the revocation and annulment of this promise to Abraham or David clearly runs in the face of both the OT and the NT evidence.

A third approach has recently been suggested by my colleague Thomas McComiskey. In his view,

> the people of God, from the time of Abraham on, are under two covenantal administrations: the promise-oath and the particular administrative covenant in force at the time. Thus, a bicovenantal structure governs the disposition of the inheritance for God's people.[19]

The administrative covenants, according to his definition, function in "terms of obedience"[20] and are the covenant of circumcision, the Mosaic Covenant, and the New Covenant.

The surprising feature here is to see the New Covenant classified as an administrative covenant. Even though McComiskey recognizes the strong promissory note in the New Covenant's constituent elements, he contends that the New Covenant does not fit his definition of a promissory covenant, since it involves a stipulation: there is a *torah* to be obeyed, even if its mode of administration is a work of grace in which the law would be written on the heart.[21]

The interplay between the administrative and promissory covenants, both of which are always simultaneously in operation at all times for McComiskey, is not worked out exactly in this otherwise interesting attempt to relate law and gospel. It is still strange that the New Covenant is here assigned on the side of law instead of gospel. This may reveal that the problem still has not been fully handled, since promise always precedes law even while it presumes law as having a confirmatory status (a fact that McComiskey acknowledges) and is a natural outworking of the grace of God in each believer's heart.

My own contribution owes much to Willis J. Beecher. He had opined:

---

[19]McComiskey, *The Covenants,* 172–73.
[20]Ibid., 144–45.
[21]Ibid., 165.

Ordinarily Yahaweh's [sic] promises to men are conditioned
on obedience. Even the promises of eternal blessing to
Israel are thus conditioned (e.g. Deut iv.40, xii.28). In some
passages it is perhaps fairly implied that the promise to
Abraham and Israel for the nations is conditioned on Israel's
obedience. However this may be, there are a few remarkable passages in which the promise is expressly declared to
be unconditional—not forfeited even by disobedience. In
Leviticus, for example . . . [after] a series of terrible . . .
punishments . . . in retribution for sin . . . [it says] . . . "I will
not reject them, neither will I abhor them, to destroy them
completely, and to break my covenant with them" (Lev
xxvi.44–45). . . . It is not difficult to solve the verbal paradox
involved in thus declaring this promise to be both conditional and unconditional. So far as its benefits accrue to any
particular person or generation in Israel, it is conditioned on
their obedience. But in its character as expressing God's
purpose of blessing for the human race, we should not
expect it to depend on the obedience or disobedience of a
few. . . . Israel may sin, and may suffer grievous punishment; but Israel shall not become extinct, like other sinning
peoples. The promise is for eternity, and Israel shall be
maintained in existence, that the promise may not fail.[22]

For Beecher, the explanation of the paradox that David's
promise also was sometimes conditioned on obedience and in other
places beyond recall was capable of easy harmony. He found the
promise irrevocable because, " . . . any member of the line of David
may by sin forfeit his own share in the promise, but he may not
forfeit that which belongs to his successors to eternity."[23]

Thus, there was an obligation to *transmit* the unconditional
promise to each Davidic generation, even though that was not in
itself a guarantee that each transmittor was also automatically a
participant in the benefits of that promise, for they came only by
faith and that faith was attested only by obedience.

We conclude, then, that "The 'breaking' or conditionality of
the Abrahamic/Davidic covenant can only refer to *personal* and
individual invalidation of the benefits of the covenant, but it cannot
affect the transmission of the promise to the lineal descendants."[24]
That is why both the OT text (Jer 31:32) and the NT (Heb 8:8)

---

[22]Willis J. Beecher, *The Prophets and the Promise* (1905; reprint, Grand Rapids:
Baker, 1963), 219–20.
[23]Beecher, *The Prophets*, 232 (see also 256–57). Cf. Walter C. Kaiser, Jr.,
Toward an Old Testament Theology (Grand Rapids: Zondervan, 1978), 92–94.
[24]Kaiser, *Old Testament Theology*, 157.

distinctly say, "[God] finds fault with *them*" (RSV, my emphasis). It does *not* say that he found fault with any of his covenants; it was the *people,* not the promises or the stipulations, that were and always have been the source of the problem.

Christians must stop hiding behind the stipulatory covenant of Sinai as their reason for disregarding the whole message of the OT. The tensions erected between promise and law are either of our own contrivance or have already been cared for by careful qualifications within the OT itself. Law is the natural companion of promise, when it is preceded by promise and is a way of life for all who are already in the promise.

HOW CAN CHRISTIANS DERIVE PRINCIPLES FROM THE SPECIFIC COMMANDS OF THE LAW?

If we agree in principle that the law of God is not basically antithetical to promise, how, then, does one go about accomplishing this in practice? Does this mean that, in order to save the Bible from what some might regard as "unfair exposure," we should content ourselves with uttering a few general and bland principles that would cover a multitude of otherwise unmanageable specific laws?

The issue of the high level of specificity of OT commands must be boldly faced, for much of OT law comes to us not as moral absolutes and in a book of moral, social, and legal abstractions. Instead, it is comes as a host of specific enactments distinctively relevant to particular times, persons, and places. It is the awkwardness of this obviously "dated" material that threatens to doom our whole discussion to failure.

But the problem of particularity and specificity were not meant to prejudice the universal usefulness of these portions of the Bible; rather, they were intended in many ways to reduce our labors by pointing directly to the concrete, real, personal, and practical application of the injunctions proffered. Since the text was given primarily for the common people, the message was relayed on a level where they would find it easiest to grasp. Had the truth been confined to abstract and theoretical axioms, the prerogative would have been confined to the elite and the scholarly.

Indeed, the Bible shares this problem of particularity in the formulation of law with several other aspects of OT study. For example, this same problem of particularity can be observed in the Bible's recording of historical events and narrative. Once again, this was not done in order to remove that text from any further usefulness or profitability to any subsequent users of this same text.

In fact, the OT illustrates the opposite procedure when it deliberately reuses earlier narrative materials and addresses them directly to "us" or by using "we". Thus, the prophet Hosea (Hos 12:3–6)[25] used the narratives from Jacob's life one thousand years earlier and boldly declared that in those past events (in the situations described from 1800 B.C. in Gen 25:26 and 32:24ff) God spoke to Hosea and his generation in 700 B.C.[26] This same phenomena can be seen in the NT as well (Matt 15:7; Mark 7:6; Acts 4:11; Rom 4:23–24; 15:4; 1 Cor 9:8–10; 10:11; Heb 6:18; 10:15; 12:15–17). We conclude, therefore, that the specificity or particularity of the OT in either its narratives or its laws must be no impediment to our general use or a hindrance in the formation of universal injunctions.

Even the specificity of the laws did not indicate that they were only applicable to one, and only one, particular situation. Instead, we find the same law being used for multiple applications. That is the way the *Westminster Larger Catechism* viewed the matter as well: "That one and the same thing in diverse respects, is required or forbidden in several commandments."[27]

Since there is a single underlying principle and since a particular law uniquely aimed at a particular situation could be repeated two or three times in the *Torah,* for quite different applications, it is clear that one and the same law had multiple equity or applications even while it retained a single meaning.

One illustration of the same law being used for several different applications is the prohibition on witchcraft (Exod 22:18). There it appears along with laws on adultery, but in Deuteronomy 18:10 the same prohibition is included with laws on submission to authority (since rebellion and witchcraft share some commonality

[25] Walter C. Kaiser, Jr., "Inner Biblical Exegesis as a Model for Bridging the 'Then' and 'Now' Gap: Hos 12:1–6," *Journal of the Evangelical Theological Society* 28:1 (March 1985): 33–46.

[26] This phenomena was first called to my attention by Patrick Fairbairn, "The Historical Element in God's Revelation," now conveniently reprinted in Walter C. Kaiser, Jr., *Classical Essays in Old Testament Interpretation* (Grand Rapids: Baker, 1972), 67–86.

[27] *Westminster Larger Catechism*, Question 99, Section 3, as cited by James B. Jordan, *The Law of the Covenant: An Exposition of Exodus 21–23* (Tyler, Tex.: Institute for Christian Economics, 1984), 18.

according to 1 Sam 15:23). Then in Leviticus 19:31 and 20:27 witchcraft is forbidden in the context of separating life and death.

What, then, could be more distinctive and restricted to the hoary antiquity of the past, some will interject, than witchcraft? Surely, to appeal to that text in the Christian era is a good illustration of methodological misdirection in using the OT.

However, this protest fails to account for the laws of God having multiple equity (i.e., multiple application). As James Jordan concluded: "The anti-witchcraft legislation has equity in the areas of adultery, rebellion, and blasphemy (as well as others)."[28] Thus, the context in which the law is found, as well as its undergirding moral and theological principle must set the range of applications. To restrict the usefulness of each specific case law or civil injunction would betray a wooden use of the text. This textual abuse would come closer to being called "letterism"; it would not be a patient listening to the literal meaning of that text as informed by the antecedent morality and theology embedded in earlier Scripture.

But to assert that these particularistic laws have a broader interpretive base that is rightfully incorporated within the single-truth-intention of the author is one thing; to demonstrate how is another thing.

The most common method of deriving contemporary relevance from particular laws of another time and culture is to seek out "middle axioms,"[29] or principles which underlie these specifics. However, this search for principles or axioms must not be imposed as a grid over Scripture; Scripture itself must supply them. Moreover, these principles must not be so general and so all-embracing that they give very little guidance in dealing with specific applications.

Such a high level of abstraction was introduced by William Temple[30] in the 1930s, but his approach yielded little more than a

---

28 Jordan, *The Law*, 18.

29 John Goldingay, *Approaches to Old Testament Interpretation* (Downers Grove: InterVarsity, 1981), 55, lists these scholars as those who look for "middle axioms": R. H. Preston, "Middle Axioms in Christian Social Ethics," *Crucible* 10 (1971): 9–15; idem, "From the Bible to The Modern World: A Problem for Ecumenical Ethics," *Bulletin of John Rylands Library* 59 (1976–77): 164–87; S. Paradise, "Visions of the Good Society and the Energy Debate," *Anglican Theological Review* 61 (1979): 106–17.

30 William Temple, *Christianity and the Social Order* (London: Penguin, 1942), a reference I owe to Michael Schluter and Roy Clements.

discussion on the dignity of man and the significance of social fellowship.

Surely this is too bland and too general a level of abstraction to be helpful when it comes to the specifics of such chapters of the OT as Leviticus 18 and 19. Should these laws on marriage (Lev 18:6–23), on prohibitions against cross-breeding of plants and animals (Lev 19:19), and prohibitions on wearing garments with mixed kinds of materials (Lev 19:19b) still be binding on Christians in the present day?

The chorus of loud "no's" can be expected from most of contemporary Christendom. We have all been taught that these laws belong to the purely ceremonial section of the law and that it is this portion of the code that has been abrogated by Christ. But even though the sacrifices, priestly regulations, and such central rites as the Day of Atonement formed the heart of what many regard as the ceremonial aspect of the law, there was more to the ceremonial law; it included tithes, gifts, dietary and hygiene regulations, holy days, festivals, teaching on property, land use and ownership, economic institutions such as the sabbatical year, the year of Jubilee, and other laws bearing on social, scientific, and moral development.

But how are we to "get at" these principles if it is conceded that most of these laws are in their practical and illustrative form rather than in their principial level of abstraction? In fact, some, like Ronald H. Preston, have warned us "We cannot move directly to particular fixed ethical conclusions from either the Bible or Natural law."[31] However, to follow this advice is to concede the whole project before testing the evidence.

Other objections can still be raised. How can we guarantee any uniformity of middle axioms from the same law if we grant that there are differences between interpreters? And how do we keep from being so general and vague, on the one hand, as to be of little practical help, so specific and detailed, on the other, as to substitute our pronouncements for biblical law and thereby drown out the biblical word? And how shall we decide between two or more conflicting norms? Which one takes priority over the other? And by virtue of what authority or touchstone?

In order to solve this problem, several hermeneutical procedures can be recommended. These may be listed as follows:

---

[31]Ronald H. Preston, *Religion and the Persistence of Marxism* (London: SCM, 1979), 8, as cited by Brian Griffiths, *Morality and the Market Place* (London: Hodder and Stoughton, 1982), 73.

1. "There seem to be four levels of generality and particularity in the Bible:"[32]
   a. First, the greatest commandment: You shall love the Lord your God with all your heart, soul, mind and strength (Deut 6:5; Matt 22:37);
   b. Second, "love your neighbor as yourself" (Lev 19:18; Matt 22:39);
   c. Third, the Ten Commandments, which carry out the previous two levels in ten parts; and
   d. Fourth, case laws that relate to one or more of the Ten Commandments.

2. We can translate the particularity, say of the case laws, to the generality of middle axioms or universal principles by observing the morality and theology that undergirds or informs each law. Such informing, or undergirding, theology and moral law can be found:
   a. by noting if a theological or moral *reason* is explicitly given either with the special case law or in the context of similar laws found in that section;
   b. by observing if direct *citations*, indirect *allusions*, or historical references are made to incidents or teachings that had occurred earlier in the Scriptures and prior to the time when this legislation was given;
   c. by comparing this text by *analogy* with a similar text where the same conditions and problems exist but where, because of the context, the informing theology, or clearer dependence on moral law and theology, the solution suggests itself more easily; and
   d. by using the principle of legitimate *inference* or implication to extend what is written into a series of parallel commands, where the moral or theological grounds for what is written and what is inferred remain the same.

Perhaps several illustrations will be helpful in demonstrating the interpretive steps set forth so far. Let us take the degrees of affinity (i.e., degree of relationship) prohibited in marriage. These are described in a source many regard as the ceremonial law, the holiness law of Leviticus 18. Observed S. H. Kellogg,

> It seems somewhat surprising that the question should have been raised, even theoretically, whether the Mosaic law, as

---

[32]Jordan, *The Law*, 21–23.

regards the degrees of affinity prohibited in marriage, is of permanent authority. The reasons for these prohibitions, wherever given, are as valid now as then; for the simple reason that they are grounded fundamentally in a matter of fact,—namely, the nature of the relation between husband and wife, whereby they become "one flesh," implied in such phraseology as we find in [Lev 18:] 16; and also the relation of blood between members of the same family, as seen in vv 10 etc.[33]

Thus, the specificity of prohibiting marriage to one's close kin is rooted in concern for the "one flesh" informing theology from earlier revelation (Gen 2:24) and regard for one's "neighbor."

Now that the theological ground and the permanent relevance of these injunctions have been brought to our attention, are we therefore limited to the specific applications that Leviticus 18 made? Are all the restrictions and every close relative with whom I am forbidden to marry stated exclusively in Leviticus 18?

No! this would be an undue restriction, since it would overlook the obligation that the interpreter has to use the method of theological inference and implication. For example, nowhere does Scripture expressly forbid a man to marry his own daughter, but by inference and implication this degree of affinity is likewise prohibited on the same grounds as undergirded the named affinities: the degree of relationship is the same. Thus, certain express prohibitions or permissions involve similar prohibitions or permissions where the theological and moral grounds are identical to those instances explicitly given in Scripture.

This last point was persuasively argued by George Bush.

> If *inferences* are not binding in the interpretation of the divine law, then we would ask for the *express* command which was violated by Nadab and Abihu in offering strange fire [Lev 10:1–3], and which cost them their lives. Any prohibition in set terms on that subject will be sought for in vain. So again, did not our Saviour tell the Sadducees that they *ought to have inferred* that the doctrine of the resurrection was true, from what God said to Moses at the bush?[34]

We agree. There are legitimate extensions of laws by inference.

---

[33] S. H. Kellogg, *The Book of Leviticus*, 3d ed. (1899; reprint, Minneapolis: Klock and Klock, 1978), 383.

[34] George Bush, *Notes, Critical and Practical, on the Book of Leviticus* (New York: Newman and Ivison, 1852), 183, his emphasis.

But what about asking new questions never faced before from an old law whose moral and theological rooting was not immediately transparent? For example, what are the moral limits of recombinant DNA (deoxyribonucleic acid) technology? Can Leviticus 19:19 ("Do not mate different kinds of animals. Do not plant your fields with two kinds of seed") and Genesis 1:11–12 ("Let the land produce vegetation: seed-bearing plants and trees . . . according to their various kinds") give us a nuanced response to the questions raised by DNA research?[35]

Nine prohibitions are grouped in Leviticus 19:19–30 under the general heading of "keep my statutes."[36] These prohibitions could be applied to us today by appeal to violations of natural law or by analogy with other prohibitions in this chapter—e.g., Lev 19:26, where the essence of sorcery according to Halevy, "is the making of 'forbidden mixtures', joining together things which God intended to remain separate, and thereby repudiating and intervening with the Divine plan."[37] Thus, for Leviticus 19:19 (on breeding and fertilization), it is clear that the informing theology and undergirding morality was to be found in the creative purpose (Gen 1:11–12).

But was this prohibition against cross-breeding and fertilization of plants and animals meant to be absolute with no exceptions? If that had been God's intention, wisely argued the Rabbis, why was Adam not born circumcised—especially since circumcision was so "dear to the Lord"? We are not, therefore, to remain entirely passive with no interference at all with nature. How much interference, then, shall we permit?

The fact that some DNA exchange occasionally occurs spontaneously (and hence "naturally") does nothing to legitimize *every* type of recombinant experimentation. Argued Freedman, "What was prohibited was not inter-species crossbreeding, but *men's causing* such reproduction . . . [where it was] intended to be harmful."[38] Accordingly, mixing of the species that was "therapeutically directed" (e.g., in manufacturing human insulin or in the

---

[35] My stimulation for this section came from the ground-breaking article by Benjamin Freedman, "Leviticus and DNA: A Very Old Look at a Very New Problem," *Journal of Religious Ethics* 8 (1980): 105–13.

[36] Walter C. Kaiser, Jr., *Toward Old Testament Ethics* (Grand Rapids: Zondervan, 1983), 122–23.

[37] Benjamin Freedman, "DNA," 109, quoting 'Aharon Halevy's Commandments 62 and 244).

[38] Freedman, "DNA," 111–12.

prevention of genetic disease)[39] could be encouraged, but not research motivated by pure curiosity. Freedman warns that the latter type will move the scientific community into the Tower of Babel syndrome: "Now nothing shall be withholden from [us] that [we] purpose to do"(Gen 11:6, my translation).

More and more our fast moving society is asking more and more difficult ethical questions of those who are working in religion and theology. If proper extensions of the law of God in all of its wholeness are not legitimately utilized, we shall find ourselves in as difficult straits as people were when the Wade-Roe decision suddenly broke over our heads and no one had any biblical directives to offer, since the NT says nothing explicitly about abortion.

OT law is not so esoteric or so culturally bound that it cannot aid contemporary Christians with their problems. At the heart of all law is the Lawgiver himself to whom we owe all our love and loyalty. The law, in its most basic goal, wants to help us to fulfill this objective: loving God. It also wants to help us in fulfilling the next objective: loving our neighbors as ourselves. In order to break this down into more manageable areas, these two objectives were spelled out in more detail in the Ten Commandments.

The scope and interpretation of the Ten Commandments may be graphically seen in Bishop Lancelot Andrewes' arrangement:[40]

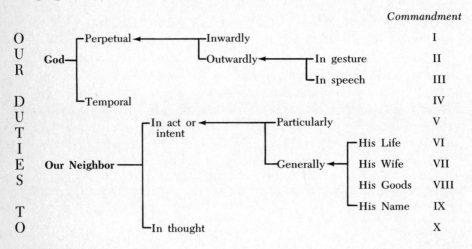

---

[39] Ibid.

[40] Lancelot Andrewes, "Pattern of Catechistical Doctrine," *Minor Works* (Oxford: 1846), 63ff.

The Ten Commandments were illustrated in the various case laws found in the Covenant Code (Exod 20:22–23:33), the Holiness Law (Lev 18–20), and the Law of Deuteronomy 5–25. The following table illustrates our point:

Command-ments	Jordan[41]	Kaufmann[42]	Kaiser[43]	Schultz[44]
1st	Exod 23:20–33 Deut 6–11	Deut 5:6–10 Deut 12:1–31	Deut 5–11	
2nd	Exod 25–Lev 10 Deut 12–13		Lev 20:1–8, 27 Deut 12:1–31	Deut 6–11
3rd	Lev 11–24 Deut 14	Deut 5:11 Deut 13:1–14:27	Deut 13:1–14:27	Deut 12–14
4th	Exod 21:1–11; 23:10–19 Lev 25 Deut 15:1–16:17	Deut 5:12–15 Deut 14:28–16:17	(Commandments 4–10) Exod 21:2–11 Exod 23:10–19 Lev 19:1–37 Lev 20:9–26 Deut 14:28–16:17	Deut 15–16:7
5th	Num 1–4 Deut 16:18–18:22	Deut 5:16 Deut 16:18–18:22	Deut 16:18–18:22	Deut 16:18–18:22
6th	Exod 21:12–36 Deut 19:1–22:8	Deut 5:17 Deut 19:1–22:8	Exod 21:12–17, 18–32 Deut 19:1–22:8	Deut 19:1–21:9
7th	Exod 22:16–31 Deut 22:9–23:14	Deut 5:18 Deut 22:19–23:19	Exod 22:16–31 Lev 18:1–30 Deut 22:9–23:19	Deut 21:10–23
8th	Exod 22:1–15 Deut 23:15–24:7	Deut 5:19 Deut 23:20–24:7	Exod 21:33–22:15 Deut 23:20–24:7	Deut 22
9th	Exod 23:1–9 Deut 24:8–25:4	Deut 5:20 Deut 24:8–25:4	Exod 23:1–9 Deut 24:8–25:4	Deut 23–25
10th	Deut 25:5–26:19	Deut 5:21 Deut 25:5–16	Deut 25:5–16	

[41] Jordan, *The Law*, 199–200.
[42] Stephen A. Kaufmann, "The Structure of the Deuteronomic Law," *MAARAV* 1 (1978–79): 105–58.
[43] Kaiser, *Toward Old Testament Ethics*, 81–137.
[44] W. Schultz, *Das Deuteronomium* (Berlin: G. Sclawitz, 1859), 13ff.

The laws of the OT, then, are rooted in the moral and theological principles of the Ten Commandments. The Ten Commandments are to the case laws of the OT what legal precedents are to trial lawyers and judges today, for just as these lawyers and judges extract the legal principle on which the whole case rests as the basis for applying it to a new situation, so the interpreter of Scripture must search for that legal principle, usually embodied in a text like the Ten Commandments, before applying this principle to a new and contemporary situation.

Nowhere is this appeal to the reason behind a case law (the *ratio decidendi*) clearer than in Paul's use of what, on *prima facie* grounds, appears to be a strange appeal to the prohibition on muzzling an ox (Deut 25:4). Paul argued that the laborer, in this case the preacher, was worthy of his hire (1 Cor 9:11–12).[45] Instead of plainly stating this and pointing to a text like Deuteronomy 24:14–15 ("Do not take advantage of a hired man . . . pay him his wages . . . "), Paul appealed to the text about oxen and commented that it was written "for us" (1 Cor 9:10).

The basis for commonality in the two situations, though widely separated in applications (from the case of allowing oxen to take a swipe of grain as they wearily tread out the grain to the case of allowing the preacher to receive an honorarium for his work) is to be found in Moses' concern that gentleness and gratitude be developed both in owners of hard-working oxen and in listeners to hard-working preachers. "It was the duties of *moral beings* [not oxen] to one another that God wished to impress" on mankind.[46] Deuteronomy 25 merely works out the implication of the second greatest commandment, especially as it relates to the ninth commandment in the matter of truth and verity in one's total being. One of the ways to develop such verity is serving others and thereby becoming more gentle and grateful to God.

There are enormous possibilities for abuse of such a system of interpretation that lays heavy emphasis on a ladder of abstraction, analogy, and the search for undergirding principle. For example, one might wrongly declare that two cases (an ancient situation and a modern situation) were similar just because the factual similarities appeared to be numerous, yet the underlying moral and theological

---

[45] See Walter C. Kaiser, Jr., "Applying the Principles of the Civil Law," *The Uses of the Old Testament in the New* (Chicago: Moody, 1985), 203–20.

[46] F. Godet, *Commentary on the First Epistle of St. Paul to the Corinthians*, trans. A. Cousin (Grand Rapids: Zondervan, 1957), 11.

differences between the two could be so great as to overrule any apparent analogies. Contrariwise, there may be situations where the factual correspondences between the ancient and modern situation are negligible, but the differences in the moral and theological underpinnings are small or even nonexistent.

Thus, interpreters must exercise great care when they use this method of analogy or where they move up or down the ladder of abstraction (i.e., going from the highly specific, which applies to a single situation either in the past or present, to the highly general). The term, "ladder of abstraction" may be defined as "a continuous sequence of categorizations from a low level of generality up to a high level of specificity."[47]

This raises the question about the various levels of generality and specificity. It also raises the issue about definitions of such terms as *principles* or *norms*. To take this second problem first, a principle is a general law or rule of conduct that is stated broadly enough so that it embraces the essential elements on which many institutions, personal relationships, or ways of conduct can be based. On the other hand, a norm (from the Latin: a carpenter's square, a rule) is a more specific term that measures individual or particular institutions, relationships, and ways of conducting one's life. Of course, there is some overlap between principle and norm, but for our purposes they may be distinguished at the point where we move from a specific situation in a particular time and space setting (a norm) to a discussion about multiple instances of that institution, conduct, or relationship.[48]

To illustrate our point, let us use 1 Corinthians 9:10–12 and draw a schema that shows the levels of specificity and generality that interpreters must deal with in getting at the underlying theology and morality. Then we may move back to supplying specific ethical answers in the contemporary culture.

Sometimes the interpreter begins in the middle of this dual ladder of abstraction and thus enters at the heart of the problem. But the difficulty for the interpreter in that case is to move either to the past or to the contemporary level of specificity. If the message remains on the general level, it will be remote, distant, abstract, and

---

[47]William Twining and David Miers, *How to Do Things With Rules* (London: Weidenfeld and Nicolson, 1976), 45, as pointed out to me by Michael Schluter and Roy Clements.

[48]I am indebted to Michael Schluter and Roy Clements for these distinctions and for prompting me to consider the whole "ladder of abstraction" model from the area of jurisprudence.

THE LADDER OF ABSTRACTION

Ancient Specific Situation	BC Specific Situation	Institutional & Personal Norm	General Principle	Theological and Moral Principle	NT Specific Situation	Modern Specific Situation
Feed those who work for you.	Oxen tread wheat (Deut 25:4).	Animals are gifts from God for the service of mankind. Be kind to those serving you.	Giving engenders gentleness and graciousness in humans.	"Love your neighbor" (and Ninth Commandment).	Paul could be paid for preaching (1 Cor 9:10–12).	Pay those who minister the word to you.

Level of Generality

Level of Specificity

Level of Specificity

unrelated to reality. It will be mainly descriptive, didactic, and principial preaching and teaching, but people will long for more detail and complain especially about the lack of good application.

But to begin at either end of the ladder—with the specifics of the OT case laws or the specifics of our present moral, ethical, or sociological predicaments—is to raise the difficult issue of identifying that underlying general principle so that we can move from the instruction of the biblical case law to its modern applications. The process is somewhat difficult, but it is, nonetheless, both possible and beneficial.

The law, therefore, is not antithetical to the promise of God, nor is its specificity a roadblock to the Christian's profitable use even of its case laws. All Scripture continues to be just as useful to modern Christians as Paul declared it to be for Timothy.

Chapter 8

The Old Testament as
an Object of Proclamation

"Do you understand what you are reading?" Philip asked
(Acts 8:30) the Ethiopian eunuch who was pondering the identity of
the Servant mentioned in Isaiah 52:13–53:12. And that is the key
question for teachers and preachers of the OT.

Even we moderns agree with the Ethiopian's response to
Philip's query, "How can I, unless someone explains it to me?"
(Acts 8:31). Hence, the role of the interpreter, whose main task is to
assist the reader in understanding the text—but especially the OT,
which most Christians feel is a totally different world from the one
to which they are accustomed.

With no less than 77 percent of the Bible located in the OT,
all who care about presenting a balanced menu of biblical truth will
include a healthy selection of OT blocks in their teaching schedule.
In fact, many pastors have taken ordination vows that include
references to the whole canon; therefore, the practical demonstration of such affirmations, if they are to be more than mere
shibboleths, is to reflect that same scope in one's preaching.

A second reason why Christians should teach and preach
from the OT can be found in the example of the NT's use of the OT.
Our Lord himself came using the vocabulary ("Repent, for the

kingdom of heaven is near," Matt 3:2) and the texts of the OT ("Today this Scripture [Isa 61:1–2] is fulfilled in your hearing" Luke 4:21).

Not only does the NT have some 300 explicit quotations from the OT, but there are hundreds more allusions—950 quotations and allusions according to Nestle's Greek Testament, 2,500 NT texts representing nearly 1,800 OT passages according to the United Bible Society's Greek text, 1,640 according to Wilhelm Dittmar, and 4,105 by E. Huhn's count.[1] Regardless of what the finally agreed criteria are and the resulting official numbers of quotations and allusions from the OT in the New, it surely has to be a most remarkable and impressive number. Our Lord and the apostles were more than just mildly affected by the Scriptures that they possessed at that time.

In the third place, the OT must be taught and proclaimed because it declares some truths or states certain doctrines or responsibilities more fully and dynamically than does the NT. For example, the doctrine of creation has its primary teaching passage in the OT, while the NT assumes it, alludes to it, and builds on it. Likewise, the OT prophetic texts and the law call for justice and care of the orphan, the widow, the poor, and the oppressed in language so eloquent that it was never equalled in the NT.

"But all of this," some will object, "is fine and good. But how are we to put into contemporary terms—and, beyond that, apply to altogether new settings and situations—something we have a hard enough time understanding as it now stands?" The church, in the past, has offered many answers to this question, but each must be carefully evaluated lest the end result be the same, or an even worse, neglect of the OT.

Origen, in the fourth chapter of his work *On the First Principles,* devised an answer by announcing a threefold meaning of the text. Since man has a body, soul, and spirit, so Scripture must also possess a tripartite package of meaning: the *body* is the literal meaning of the text, the *soul* is its moral meaning, and the *spirit* became its spiritual, or allegorical, meaning. The fact that a text had three kinds of meanings, even though such an affirmation would violate the rules of noncontradiction in the test for truth, did not stop him.

This threefold meaning became the classical fourfold mean-

---

[1] Consult Walter C. Kaiser, Jr., *Uses of the Old Testament in the New* (Chicago: Moody, 1985), 2, for full documentation and further discussion.

ing when the spiritual and the allegorical meanings were separated. Hence this Latin jingle became the reigning hermeneutic of the day:

> *littera gesta docet*
> *quid credas allegoria*
> *moralis quid agas*
> *quo tendas anagogia*

In English, this rubric announced (with some poetic license but loads of creativity in translation):

> The letter shows us what God and our fathers did;
> The allegory shows us where our faith is hid;
> The moral meaning gives us rules of daily life;
> The anagogy shows us where we end our strife.[2]

On this basis, "Jerusalem" could simultaneously have four different values:

> Literal: the physical city of Jerusalem
> Allegorical: the church
> Tropological: the human soul
> Anagogical: the heavenly Jerusalem (i.e., life hereafter)

But the method was syncretistic in that it attempted to combine a number of methods that were in vogue at the time. There was an element worth praising in the motivation for using this fourfold method of interpreting Scripture, and that was the search for a so-called "deeper" meaning.

This search for a "deeper" meaning had begun as early as 520 B.C., when Theogenes of Regium, it is said, felt so repulsed by the immoral conduct of the gods in Homer's poems that he diverted attention away from the literal meaning of the text and offered instead an allegorical interpretation.

In a similar manner, the Jews of Alexandria—in particular Philo—saw the allegorical method as a convenient means of "explaining away" features of the OT text that were troublesome for one reason or another. Already in the second century B.C., one Aristobulus declared that a "deeper" meaning was present in all those passages that used such anthropomorphic expressions as "the hand of God," "the eyes of the Lord," "the arm of the Lord," and the like. For example, Aristobulus announced that the idea of God

---

[2] Robert M. Grant, *A Short History of the Interpretation of the Bible* (New York: Macmillan, 1963), 119.

"standing" symbolized the steadfastness of the earth created by God. Thus, the prohibition of eating beasts of prey (Lev 11) taught that we should practice righteousness and never inflict violence on others.

It was Philo (20 B.C. to A.D. 40) who formalized the allegorical interpretation for the Jewish community at Alexandria. While he recognized that there was a *body* to the text and it did have a literal meaning, the *real* meaning of that text was to be found, not in its literal meaning, but in its *soul* hidden in the body. Just as man's soul passes through various stages in its relationship to God, so these stages are seen in the text everywhere.

These stages Philo handily illustrated in the life of Abraham. As a first step, Abraham had to leave Ur of the Chaldeans, a step that depicts our leaving the world of material things. Next, he had to leave his family, a fact that symbolizes leaving behind the world of sensory perceptions. Abraham's final step, as is ours, was to leave his father's house, thereby symbolizing the abandonment of the world of reasoning intellect.

All of this is so wonderful and "deep" we could wish that it were true or that the Holy Spirit had included it instead of what appears to us to be nothing but the "bare bones" account of Abraham. Is it any wonder that teachers and preachers who are desperate for a word from God should so quickly "latch on" to somewhat arcane but instantaneous "deep" teaching? Our instincts are correct: we ought to be able to derive something for our spiritual nourishment from the OT, if indeed it is a word for all times from our Lord. But have you not felt, after having made such arbitrary assignment of similar types of symbolically "deep" meanings, that they were devoid of authority, force, and any commanding power, since we could not be sure or point out for the priesthood of believers what it was in the OT text itself that signalled the presence of these values?

Parallel to the body analogy as the grounds for dividing the meaning of the text into three levels comes another line of argumentation: the doctrine of correspondences. This view confidently stated that for every earthly reality there was a corresponding heavenly archetype to which it pointed—pointed for those who by reason of spiritual insight were the more adept and ready to search for this "deeper" reality. But again, where did Scripture teach this doctrine? This comes closer to forms of emanations in Gnostic theology, where there was a ladder, or gradation, of beings from man all the way up to God. This, too, we will have to reject as another ploy "to get spiritual quick."

A more contemporary variation of the same search, but one that had its roots as far back as the Qumran community, is the *pesher* method of interpreting Scripture. Concluding that political conditions had made the use of "ordinary" language dangerous, the text was cast in a type of cryptic code, or a "mystery" (*rāz*) that could only be deciphered by the elect.

Now the element of truth in this thesis is that at the time of Jeremiah, when the Babylonians were closing in on Jerusalem, Jeremiah did use the famous Jewish literary device known as *Atbash*. This well-known coding device writes one half of the Hebrew alphabet on a line and then writes the other half underneath the first line, only starting at the end of the top line thereby matching the two middle letters of the alphabet with each other and the first and last letters of the alphabet; in English we would have called this device "azmen" (to parallel the Hebrew *atbash*), for a becomes z (or vice versa) and m becomes n (or vice versa). What you spell out then is not the word you intend, but the one whose letters match it when you use the code. Thus Jeremiah recorded (Jer 51:1), "I will stir up the spirit of a destroyer against Babylon and the people of *Leb Kamai*." Now *Leb Kamai* is "Chaldea," or "Babylon," in this system. In like manner, Jeremiah 51:41 has "How *Sheshach* will be captured, the boast of the whole earth seized!" *Sheshach* is nothing but a cryptogram for Babylon.

But does this phenomenon of the text—best illustrated, not in Jeremiah, but in apocalyptic literature—give us enough of a precedent to claim that all of the words of the prophets (and many of the words of Jesus and his disciples) contain "secrets" (*rāzîm*), or "hidden meanings," that could be detected only by a revealing exegesis (*pesher*)? Is that what Paul was claiming when he wrote in Ephesians 3:2–3 how "God has assigned the gift of his grace to me for your benefit. It was by a revelation [=*pesher*?] that his secret [=*rāz*?] was made known to me" (my translation)?

I think it is not. The words are Aramaic, not Greek; hence Paul did not use these words, nor did he mean that he had received in addition to the literal meaning an esoteric, hidden sense that lay below the surface of the text.

The *pesher* method, like the allegorical method, was just one more attempt to gain some spiritual value or a deeper meaning from the text than many would find in the literal or historical context the OT. In actual practice, this appears to be little more than a

sophisticated form of allegorizing, or spiritualizing, of the OT—
with this one exception: it tended to equate present or future
personages, nations, movements, and events with past personages,
nations, movements, and events in the OT.[3]

However, if none of these shortcuts has produced the desired
dimensions of spiritual guidance from the OT, what will? This, of
course, is not the place to treat what I have previously devoted an
entire book to.[4]

What we would propose instead is a preliminary indication of
the manner in which each of four major representative genra could
be approached so that the gap between the historical truth intention
of the author and the practical and spiritual needs of the contemporary generation might be bridged. We should caution, however, that
this "merging of horizons," to use Hans Georg Gadamer's patented
phrase, is not one in which the reader/listener frame of reference
should become normative and usurp the role that belongs uniquely
to the author. Rather, what we intend to affirm is that the exegetical
process is not complete until the meaning, as determined by the
author's use of his own words, has been directly related to the
contemporary audience's need for relevance and "merging practical
address."

HOW CAN CHRISTIANS TEACH OR PREACH FROM THE LEGAL PORTIONS OF THE OT?

Granted that the law has not been nullified in all its forms,
but rather established by faith (Rom 3:31), how may the believer
find it "profitable," as Paul declared it was (2 Tim 3:16–17)?

First, we must understand that *Torah* does not connote
rigidity, inflexibility, and a penchant for the pedantic minutia. Its
basic meaning is "instruction, direction," probably reflecting the
verb "to shoot [an arrow]" or "to point [out a direction]." Christians
may expect to receive guidance for their lives in some of the most
basic and mundane questions one could ask. Thus, it would be
more accurate to speak, not about "law," but about "instruction" or
the "guidance" offered in the first five books of the OT.

But in the second place, the problem of OT particularity (i.e.,

---

[3] See our further discussion of *pesher* in Kaiser, *Uses of the Old Testament*, 6, 9,
14, 44–45, 227.

[4] Walter C. Kaiser, Jr., *Toward an Exegetical Theology* (Grand Rapids: Baker,
1981).

the fact that this "instruction" seems to be bound to a particular culture in a particular time and addressed to a particular person or group of persons) was not meant to prejudice its universal usefulness. On the contrary, it was meant to help us in identifying with that text by taking it out of the realm of the abstract and placing it in the real world of concrete illustration and personal attachment. On this view, the civil laws or instructions of the "Covenant Code" (found in Exodus 21–23) are, as we have argued above, merely illustrations of the universal, all-embracing principles already announced in the decalogue of Exodus 20. Likewise all of Deuteronomy 12–26 is a structured composition whose topical units are so arranged that they merely illustrate and further elucidate the same ten commandments repeated in Deuteronomy 5, following the same order and principles set down there.[5]

What is needed for teaching or preaching the "instruction of God" is an ability to cut through the particular and contextualized form in which the laws are currently framed to that which is abiding, principial, and permanent in those laws. This must not be done, however, by reviving the allegorical (*pesher*) or some modern variation of the same in order to get behind the literal, historical meaning to an alleged "deeper" or spiritual meaning.

Instead, by following first the grammar, syntax, and author's intention, and then adding the "antecedent Scripture," which acts as the "informing theology"[6] of these passages, one is able to be led to internally derived principles, universals, and abiding truths that operate trans-culturally and across temporal barriers.

Nor are we left without models as to how we should do this, for James took a piece of text from such an unlikely place (as far as many Christians are concerned) as the Holiness Law of Leviticus 19:12–18 and developed from it a series of paraeneses in his epistle. Surely there are few books in the NT or OT that can be said to be more practical than the book of James, yet he developed the "royal law of love" by teaching us what Leviticus 19:12–18 was all about.[7]

---

[5] Walter C. Kaiser, Jr., *Toward Old Testament Ethics* (Grand Rapids: Zondervan, 1983), 127–37; also Stephen Kaufman, "The Structure of Deuteronomic Law," *MAARV* 1 (1978–79): 105–58. Also, on the use of law for practical teaching, see Kaiser, *Uses of the Old Testament*, 197–224.

[6] For an explanation of these terms and procedures, see Kaiser, *Toward an Exegetical Theology*, 131–40.

[7] The first to announce this thesis was Luke T. Johnson, "The Use of Leviticus 19

In like manner, Paul took a fairly remote and somewhat antiquated illustration from Deuteronomy 25:4 about not muzzling an ox that tramps out the grain and penetrated to its contextual and informing theology base (1 Cor 9:8–10).

Paul asked, "Is it [only] about oxen that God is concerned? Is not [God] speaking simply (*pantōs*) for our sakes?" "Yes," Paul answered, "it was written for our sakes" (my translation).

Many cannot fathom how Paul can avoid having the charge of allegorizing placed on his doorstep, in light of what he has done here. But we have defended Paul against that charge by contending that what the apostle has done is to note that this was from a series of injunctions in Deuteronomy 24–25 that were aimed at inculcating a gentle spirit in those who should be growing in their sensitivities to the needs about them. In fact, only by catering to these needs could they themselves grow. Likewise, Paul did not need to be paid; he was more concerned about what could happen in the lives of those who might pay him for ministering to them. Thus, the principle in both Testaments was the same.[8]

There is no need to archaize ourselves or our teaching in order to proclaim "the instruction" of God with the same truth intention of the author who gave us the law. We need only to assume that there is something constant, universal, and representative of the character and will of God *indicated in the text itself*. These signals of principle must not be foisted on the text from the outside; otherwise we shall have returned to the theory that there are various levels of meaning, most of which are hidden somewhere in the depths of the law.

As we noted in chapter 7, there is a "Ladder of Abstraction" by which we can move from the specific/particular to the general/universal and back again to the specific/particular. But the signals for these exegetical moves must be "read out" from the text and not introduced *ab extra*.

HOW CAN CHRISTIANS TEACH OR PREACH FROM THE NARRATIVE PORTIONS OF THE OT?

OT narratives are great fun to preach, but how is one to avoid "plain storytelling" on the one hand or "thin moralizing" on the

---

in the Letter of James," *Journal of Biblical Literature* 101 (1982): 391–401; also Kaiser, *Uses of the Old Testament*, 221–24.

[8]For further development of this passage, see Kaiser, *Uses of the Old Testament*, 203–20.

other? Obviously, there is more that needs to be done than merely repeating the story, even if it is told in contemporary language. We need to know what in the text gives us a command, a summons to action, a challenge to think or act in a certain way. How can we move from the purely descriptive to the prescriptive in teaching?

The practice of giving "moralisms" loosely associated with narrative texts will hardly meet the need of the hour. A. H. DeGraaft vigorously denounced such moralizing, which he defined as "the reduction of the radical, all-embracing, fundamental religious directives of the Word of God to culturally conditioned, human categories of good and bad.[9]

But what do such man-centered observations about our concepts of good or bad have to do with the mighty, authoritative Word of God? Extracting lessons, examples, or morals from Scripture, be it "by hook or by crook," is hardly a proper way to treat the abiding Word of God. Instead of standing under the authority of the text and asking what its own intent is, the moralizer charges ahead and attributes a series of dreary (but fortunately, in most cases, harmless) homilies as a fast route to edifying one's listeners.

It is easy to extend this harangue against moralistic preaching on OT narrative texts, but Carl G. Kromminga's question must be pressed: "What distinguishes such 'moralizing' from the acceptable and even necessary 'ethical application' of the text in preaching?"[10]

After surveying a number of authors who passionately denounced moralizing of narrative texts, Kromminga[11] found the following four common methodological characteristics:

1. Although "surface lessons" were not denied (e.g., Samuel-like obedience, Saul-like disobedience), these "lessons" were not allowed to become the main thrust of the texts in these authors' examples of preaching.

2. The main ethical thrusts of the narrative were derived from those significant themes that were larger than the given passage and that ran through the passages, both from prior and later revelation.

---

[9] A. H. DeGraaft and C. G. Seerveld, *Understanding the Scripture: How to Read and How Not to Read the Bible* (Toronto: Association for the Advancement of Christian Scholarship, 1968), 21.

[10] Carl G. Kromminga, "Remember Lot's Wife: Preaching Old Testament Narrative Texts," *Calvin Theological Journal* 18 (1983): 33.

[11] Ibid., 37.

3. The larger literary and canonical contexts of the passage were used to identify and to trace the themes that give it its unique significance.

4. The intention of the biblical writer functioned as the most important method for discovering how the narrative was to be understood.

The most important gain discovered here is that each narrative belongs to a larger web of continuing themes of revelation. The exegete may not exploit any narrative text in isolation and thereby force it to yield up some known moral or spiritual truth. This avoidance of the author's intention, as discovered by the larger context, the informing or antecedent theology, leads to a religious individualism or spiritual Lone Rangerism. Its costs, in terms of loss of understanding, are much too high.

Few have chronicled the important debate on this issue among the clergy in pre-World War II Holland better than Sidney Greidanus.[12] For those advocates who espoused "exemplary" preaching (in which people in the OT narrative were used as examples), all forms of preaching the line of redemptive history from these narratives were too "objective" and stultifying, resulting, in their view, in little more than a biblical-theological lecture. Moreover, application of the narrative was almost totally lacking among many of those who were preaching the line of salvation-history in the Dutch church of that era. Therefore, they felt it was necessary to supplement this factual salvation-history line with the interjection of the exemplary element, thus balancing off the objective, straightforward doctrinal discussions with the subjective.

But could this side-by-side approach be the answer? Such a division of the doctrinal and practical would lead to a bifurcation of the truth of God just when the teacher should be illustrating the unity of God's progressive revelation.

If this loose pairing of methods did not work, can the "then-ness" of the text be overcome by using a sacramental view of preaching to come to a "now" view? This method, called a "representation"[13] of the truth, would view the act of preaching of Scripture each Sunday to be very similar to the Roman Catholic

---

[12]Sidney Greidanus, *Sola Scriptura: Problems and Principles in Preaching Historical Texts* (Toronto: Wedge, 1970).

[13]Martin Noth, "The 'Re-presentation' of the Old Testament in Proclamation," in *Essays on Old Testament Interpretation*, ed. Claus Westermann, trans. James Luther Mays (Richmond: Knox, 1963), 76–88.

theology of the mass, wherein Christ is again sacrificed during each celebration of the sacrament.

Now it is true that God and his activity are always present, and his past acts are the bases for issuing exhortations and promises in the present (e.g., Deut 5:3; 6:20–25; 26:16–19; Ps 95:7). But the problem with this approach, as C. Trimp[14] points out, is the opposite of the problem of concentrating on the historical, mundane details; this approach transcends history in a Docetic-like stance that rejects all historical connections by isolating the Word into some new "Word-event" of preaching.

The problem of the "then" and the "now" of narrative texts can only be bridged by seriously heeding the following principles: First, it is extremely important that a proper unit of narrative text be identified. To rearrange the text in some kind of imposed chronological order by transplanting and relocating portions of the narrative is to blunder badly right from the start.[15] The text must be left in its own context and heard in the organic unity it forms with its immediate context, section context, book context, and the entire context of the Bible.

Second, the *arrangement* of the material in the text and the way it relates to its immediate and more distant contexts is extremely important. The word *text* comes from *texere* ("to weave"). Therefore, the skillful exegete will discern how the unit was woven together both in its internal and external parts and relationships. This is more important than attempting to supply dates, give historical information, or any other similar venture that the text does not record. We must exegete, instead, on the basis that all we need to get at the main teaching of the text can be found right within the text itself.

Third, one must ask what details were selected for inclusion. This principle of *selection* is the next most determinative feature for interpreting narrative. Close analysis and reflection on what these details share in common, how they compare to one another, and the way they line up with the stated or implied purpose for which the narrative appears at this point in the book will all be most helpful. While prose texts state in direct and plain terms what they are about, narrative texts prefer to use an indirect means of laying out

---

[14]C. Trimp, "The Relevance of Preaching (in the Light of the Reformation's 'Sola Scriptura' Principle)," trans. Stephen Voorwinde, *Westminster Theological Journal* 16 (1973–74): 6–9.

[15]Greidanus, *Sola Scriptura*, 221–22.

their message. That is why arrangement and selection become so crucial in leading the meaning out of the text.

Fourth, each narrative has a special device for indicating when the high moment, or its focal point, has arrived. A frequent device is to put a key speech in the mouth of one of the leading characters. Thus, *quotations* are very helpful. For example, the quotation, which in this case concludes the section of 1 Kings 17 (v. 24), of the widow of Zarephath, unlocks what the four episodes in that chapter are all about: "Now I know that you are a man of God and the word of the LORD from your mouth is the truth (or is dependable)." Accordingly, this set of episodes is "woven" around the theme that what God says is dependable in each of these (and all similar) settings of life.

Another device is to use repetition, so that a key prop, an unusual word, or a frequently occurring verb or noun begins linking together separate episodes or the same episode. Thus, Robert Alter[16] suggested a way to explain the account of Tamar and Judah in Genesis 38—a narrative that many had given up on, concluding that it was nothing more than an intrusion into the record of Joseph's life (Gen 37–50). Two verbal clues—the word for young goat (a "kid") and the verb "to recognize"—apparently linked the account of the selling of Joseph (Gen 37:31, 33) and the account of Tamar and Judah (Gen 38:17, 25, 26). Many such structuring devices are available to the narrator: the *Leitwort* that explores the semantic range of the root word, wordplay, synonymity, antonymity, the recurrence of an image, quality, action, or object that becomes a motif or theme, and the like.

Narrative-text preaching offers a wonderful field for the proclaimer. If the distinctive notions of the narrative form are carefully kept in mind, the gap between the "then" and the "now" begins to dissolve as the text's own organizing principles and its own transcendent values are found embedded in the very fabric of the carefully woven piece of text.[17]

HOW CAN CHRISTIANS TEACH OR PREACH FROM THE WISDOM PORTIONS OF THE OT?

In many ways, all that has been said about the approach to law would hold true for wisdom. That is because wisdom is merely

---

[16] Robert Alter, *The Art of Biblical Narrative* (New York: Basic, 1981), 3–22.

[17] For further discussion of "The Use of Narrative in Expository Preaching," see Kaiser, *Toward an Exegetical Theology*, 197–210.

an expansion of law, only placed in more aphoristic, short epigram-matic statements. One might call this type of teaching "bumper-sticker theology," for it tries to get the most teaching across in the briefest, most memorable, and most ear and eye attention-getting manner possible.

Wisdom literature is found in its largest gathered corpus in Proverbs, Ecclesiastes, Job, and Psalms 1, 32, 34, 37, 49, 111, 112, 127, 128, and 133. The distinctive marks of the wisdom style in the Psalms are (1) alphabetic structure such as acrostic psalms, (2) numerical sayings (e.g., "three, yea four"), (3) "blessed" say-ings, (4) "better" sayings, (5) comparisons or admonitions, (6) address of a father to his "son," (7) use of wisdom vocabulary or turn of phrases, and (8) the employment of similes, rhetorical questions, proverbs, and instructions like, "listen to me."[18] But wisdom forms are found scattered throughout the prophetic corpus as well.

What marks wisdom off as distinctive is that it typically addresses the mundane, everyday affairs of life. Thus, for all who have felt that religion is too impractical and is not really down to where life is being lived in the real world of hard knocks, wisdom is the answer. This is not to say that wisdom is secular and humanistic in the sense that man has become the measure of all things. But it does mean that it refuses to exempt any area of life as being too removed from the concerns of faith to be reached by the message of God.

Wisdom also is typically very personal in that it is more frequently addressed to the individual. Its concerns are for the outcome of the person in his/her life instead of the hope of the whole nation of Israel.

Its teaching tends to be bright with hope and joy—including that much maligned and badly understood book, Ecclesiastes.[19] One must not expect that such an apocopated literary form as the proverb will include everything that could be said on a subject, any more than we expect the same from our contemporary proverbs. Some proverbs do appear to counter one another, but that is

---

[18]For discussions on style, see Roland E. Murphy, "Psalms," *Jerome Biblical Commentary*, ed. Raymond E. Brown, Joseph A. Fitzmyer, and Roland E. Murphy (Englewood Cliffs: Prentice-Hall, 1968), 574; idem, "The Classification of Wisdom Psalms," *Vetus Testamentum Supplement* 9 (1963): 156–67; Sigmund Mowinckel, "Psalms and Wisdom," *Vetus Testamentum Supplement* 3 (1955) 204–24.

[19]See my semi-popular exposition, Walter C. Kaiser, Jr., *Ecclesiastes: Total Life* (Chicago: Moody, 1979).

because they have only part of the subject in mind and are not meant to be a comprehensive discussion of all the aspects of the truth involved.

We don't choose between proverbs, considering one to be true and the other false; instead, we wisely try to apply the relevant proverb to the proper situation. Thus,

"Look before you leap"
and
"He who hesitates is lost";

or:

"Out of sight, out of mind"
and
"Absence makes the heart grow fonder";

Again:

"Happy is the wooing that is not long in doing"
and
"Marry in haste, repent at leisure."

Likewise the biblical proverb has the same features:

"Do not answer a fool according to his folly,
or you will be like him yourself";

but:

"Answer a fool according to his folly,
or he will be wise in his own eyes" (Prov 26:4–5).

The important thing to remember is that it is not a matter of indifference (adiaphora) which rule one adopts, so long as it meets some imagined need or alleged higher principle. Rather, it is that some circumstances require different standards in order to maintain a consistency of policy and practice. Therefore, many moral principles set forth in this proverbial format prescribe what takes place in the greatest number of instances[20] without absolutizing or universalizing their application to every situation.

How should the teacher proceed who wishes to use wisdom materials of the Bible? Certainly, the wisdom psalms or Ecclesiastes can be used in the larger units or blocks of material beyond the single proverb or "bumper-sticker slogan." There a whole

---

[20]For a fuller list of guidelines, see Kaiser, *Toward Old Testament Ethics*, 64–67; or idem, *Uses of the Old Testament*, 198–201.

psalm or a whole chapter or section of a chapter from Ecclesiastes or Job would be the teaching unit for proclamation.

In Proverbs the matter is somewhat more difficult. Certainly the more philosophical parts of Proverbs, chapters 1–9, are fairly easy to segment based on the introductory rubric "My son". There also are unified chapters, such as chapter 16, which belong together and have a common theme.

Similar principles can be applied elsewhere to detect the organizing theme that drew the various proverbs into association and to determine how far that pattern extended. Having established (1) the unit and (2) the organizing principle, (3) the next step involves a search for that aspect of the moral law that stands behind the individual proverb, imparting to it its informing theology. It is indicated to be such by some clue in the text: it may be quoted, alluded to, or further amplified through shared vocabulary or implied contextuality. Only this third step can fully save the interpreter from falling into the allegorizing or spiritualizing trap.

HOW CAN CHRISTIANS TEACH OR PREACH FROM THE PROPHETIC PORTIONS OF THE OT?

The sixteen writing prophets exhibit at least three major types of material: (1) biographical material on the lives of the prophets themselves (Isa 6, Jer 1, Ezek 1–3, Amos 7:10–17), (2) hymns, prayers, and laments that the prophets addressed to God (e.g., Jeremiah's "confessions" sprinkled generously throughout Jer 11–20; Jonah 2; Amos 4:13; 5:8–9; 9:5–6), and (3) prophetic speeches. The bulk of the material is found in this third category, for that is where the prophets claimed to be acting as God's spokespersons.

The biographical material should be handled much as one would teach or preach from narrative passages. The second category often involves poetic forms and carries an additional requirement that the interpreter distinguish between that which is purely descriptive of how the prophet felt or personally reacted to certain announcements or facts and that which is prescriptive and carries the authority of God.

The prophets, in the main, were bold to speak about both the individual's need and the ills and injustices of the society in their day. However, this did not mean that the prophets, as many contemporary social reformers do, appealed primarily to the structures and institutions of their society as their hope for change.

The revolution the prophets of the OT proposed began in the changed hearts and lives of individuals, who in turn affected society. That which would effect this revolution was nothing less than the mighty, proclaimed Word of God. While they hated every form of oppression, injustice, and unrighteousness, these ills were merely symptomatic of deeper spiritual problems that only the Word of God could heal. However, even granting a positive response to this spiritual message, the effectiveness of that Word was not finished until it worked for changes in society as well. But, first things first.

In many ways, the prophets also were preachers of the law. Witness the programmatic statements found in Leviticus 26 and Deuteronomy 28 that laid down the alternative prospect of either blessing or judgment in accordance with the response of faith or lack thereof. There are literally scores, yes hundreds, of citations and allusions in the prophets to these two passages alone. Once again, Torah is seen to be a foundational building block for prophetic teaching as well.

Elsewhere I have discussed various inadequate approaches to prophetic texts,[21] such as (1) prophetic typological preaching, (2) prophetic action preaching, (3) prophetic motto preaching, and (4) prophetic parable preaching. Each of these methods tends to decide in advance what needs to be said based on other canons of thought and then deposits that message-freight on top of these unsuspecting prophetic texts.

Prophetic preaching and teaching must be controlled by the single truth intention of the author. To say other, less, or more than the prophet said as part of the meaning package would be, at best, to confuse meaning with significance, or at worst, to substitute our thoughts for the writer's messages. The theology that the prophets themselves state as the motivating force that lies behind their message is this: "Turn," "turn back" to God, or, simply put, "repent." That is how Zechariah, next to the last of this long line of prophets, analyzed the heart of his predecessors' messages (Zech 1:4), "The former prophets cried out, 'Thus says the Lord of hosts, Return from your evil ways and from your evil deeds'"(RSV).

And so they pleaded with their generation as we must plead

---

[21]Walter C. Kaiser, Jr., "The Use of Prophecy in Expository Preaching," *Toward an Exegetical Theology*, 186–93. See also G. Gerald Harrop, *Elijah Speaks Today! The Long Road into Naboth's Vineyard* (Nashville: Abingdon, 1975), 59–86.

with ours. The conditional aspect of prophecy has already been "principlized" in Jeremiah 18:7–10.

> Whenever I announce that a nation or a kingdom will be uprooted, torn down and destroyed, if that nation that I spoke against will repent of its evil, then I will relent and not bring on it the evil I had intended to bring. And whenever I announce that a nation or kingdom will be built up and established, if it does evil in my sight and does not obey me, then I will relent and not do to it as I had intended to do (my translation).

Armed with these stated principles from the prophets, the prophetic speeches could be treated much as one would treat a didactic passage, with the one caution that most of the prophetic speeches are also in poetic form and require additional steps as outlined in most hermeneutical textbooks.[22]

The OT can and must be preached once again in the Christian community. We will be the substantial losers if we persist in our mono-Testament, condensed canon approach. The profitability of the OT, so boldly declared by the apostle Paul to Timothy, must be reestablished in our times. There are few pleasures that can compare to that of the proclaimer who honestly tackles an OT text and discovers the power of the principles and the relevance of the applications to the needs of modernity in that Testament. We urge that a whole new galaxy of teachers join this burgeoning group of surprised, but delighted, proclaimers.

---

[22]See my chapter "The Use of Poetry in Expository Preaching," in *Toward an Exegetical Theology*, 211–31; and now also add Robert Alter, *The Art of Biblical Poetry* (New York: Basic, 1985).

Chapter 9

Conclusion: The Old Testament as the Christian's Scripture

The church is far from being finished with the OT; in fact, in many ways we have barely begun to enter into the richness of its message and mission.

The case we have attempted to set forth in the preceding chapters is this: the OT is still extremely relevant to the precise questions, the needs, and the great issues that are being raised in our day. It would be the height of folly for the Christian church to pass off the OT as a passé document when in so many ways it is now dramatically evident to all that we would have been better positioned in the modern debate and in the contemporary challenges if we have been more aware of its contents.

By now the lesson from history is all too clear: neglect the OT, and the individual Christian and the church will suffer irreparable damage. And so we have! Not more than a dozen years ago, the church stood helplessly to one side when the Wade-Roe decision on abortion broke in the United States of America. Since a large of number of Evangelicals had been taught that we believers in the NT era were finished with the law and it had no role whatsoever in our lives, is it any wonder, then, that we had no opinion at first on the question as to whether abortion was right or wrong in God's sight? It took the church more than five years finally to come to its senses and say, "Wait a minute; something is wrong here."

In the meantime, in order to make up for the hiatus of instruction on all sorts of practical questions about how to deal with everyday problems such as "youth conflicts" and the like, Evangelicals flocked by the thousands in every major metropolitan area to special seminars as an open testimony to their hunger for true biblical instruction on matters that were dealt with in the OT law. To be sure, most of these seminars on youth problems, marriage enrichment, and management techniques drew heavily from the wisdom books of the OT (especially Proverbs, Ecclesiastes, and Song of Solomon). But what few realized, and what still remains as one of the best kept secrets to this very day, is that these same wisdom books have as their fountainhead the Mosaic Law. One need only take a marginal reference Bible and notice how frequently the text of Proverbs, for example, directly quotes or alludes to the books of Exodus, Numbers, and Deuteronomy in its more popularized "bumper-sticker" way of theologizing.

Just these few examples should be enough to warn the contemporary teacher and pastor. We must overcome our inherited prejudice against the OT, especially the law of God. We must immediately move to balance the spiritual diet of God's people. Few today would espouse a junk food nutritional plan as a regular pattern of eating, but how many Christians prefer to eat only the "deserts" found in the NT? In order to address this imbalance, the following sections are intended as some foundational suggestions that will "prime the pump" on ways in which we can begin to use the OT in a more balanced and holistic teaching ministry.

WHAT IS THE CHALLENGE OF THE OT TO SOCIETY?

The fabric of society, insofar as it is made up of individuals who are made in the image of God, or is composed of human institutions that have their origins and rightful functions in the Word of God, remains a matter of great concern to a holy God.

The OT insists on holiness and justice in every relationship in life. Without truthfulness and integrity in oaths, contracts, finances, and covenants, life itself becomes intolerable. The needs of society do not stop where my nose ends, limited to such personal topics as the sanctity of sex, the need for truthfulness, and the sanctity of life; I must, in addition, be actively concerned over

185

questions of racism, nuclear holocausts, and the needs of the Third World.

Hardening one's heart or shutting up one's hand against a brother who is poor is a sin not only against those deprived of my aid but even more startlingly against God himself (Deut 15:7–11). To show contempt for the poor, or even worse still, to actively oppress the poor, is likewise to show contempt for the Maker and to oppress him (Prov 14:21, 31).[1]

International, national, or urban isolationism are all unacceptable Christian responses to complex modern problems. The exploitation of the oppressed, whether it is done by multi-national corporate giants in the developing countries or by wealthier and brighter individuals, is equally reprehensible in the sight of God.

This does not mean that we should teach the misdirected doctrine of liberation. Like the prophets of old, we should seek a change in the hearts of the leaders of these multi-national corporate giants and in the hearts of individuals as our method of changing institutions and society itself. Christian revolutions do not arm themselves with the weapons of this world but espouse even mightier weapons, ones that effectively and more lastingly pull down strong-holds and vested emplacements by appealing to spiritual weapons not readily available to the rulers and corporate magnates of this age.

WHAT IS THE CHALLENGE OF THE OT TO SCHOLARSHIP?

Methods are not ends in themselves; they are means to the goal of understanding the OT and, thereby, to understanding ourselves and our times. But OT scholarship has indeed been stirred to its depth by several waves of revolutionary approaches to the OT. Next to the problem of law and gospel, few things have made pastors and teachers more wary of venturing into the troubled waters of the OT than the unprecedented confusion of approaches, conclusions, and counter-claims of the scholars themselves. Ever since Astruc's famous "clue" in 1753 about using the divine names as telltale signs of possible marks of originally separate sources, the

---

[1] See my discussion and the beginnings of a huge bibliography on this subject in Walter C. Kaiser, Jr., *Toward Old Testament Ethics* (Grand Rapids: Zondervan, 1983), 158–63, 159n.14.

discipline has been in a "stew," commanding precious little agreement amongst the competing schools of thought.

Now, once again, the pendulum appears to be swinging away from a search for what may, or may not, have stood "behind' the text to an open concern for what is in the document itself. If ever there was a time when Evangelicals could enter the dialogue and contribute to some chastened forms of critical discussion, it is now.

Genuine liberality on the part of non-Evangelical scholars rarely has been exhibited in the journals and reviews. Instead of patiently listening to the evidence Evangelicals ʾwish to present and appreciating what contributions one could agree with, the tendency has been to condemn the whole work because no agreement could be reached on primary presuppositions. Meanwhile, Evangelicals have continued to cite (with several areas of appreciation) numerous contributions made by liberal theologians, in spite of their disagreement over presuppositions. So it is high time that the question be asked: who should be labeled as "closed-minded purveyors of the tradition," and who are the new "liberals" of the day who will espouse truth, or any part of it, no matter where it is found or who speaks it?

But all of this aside, there is much yet to be done in the OT. Aside from the historical-critical issues about sources and what is or is not historical, there remain enormous tasks. We still look for the OT counterparts to Westcott and Hort, who will tackle the question of textual criticism and give us a new critical edition to the Hebrew text. The present editions of Kittel, even the Stuttgart edition, hardly fill this need, for there are too many conjectured readings and, given the options on hand, very little discussion of the reasons for making varying text decisions. There are whole new fields of study, such as the sociology of religion, as well as the need for a revival of fields of study long ago abandoned, like OT ethics, that await the work of newer scholars. Time fails us to mention the needs for new scholarly works in cognate languages, archaeology, historical geography, religion of Israel, biblical theology, and exegetical methodology (with its interfacing with homiletics and hermeneutics).

WHAT IS THE CHALLENGE OF THE OT
TO THE CHURCH?

Without a proper understanding of her OT roots, the church cannot locate her identity, her task, her mission, or her relationship to Israel and the world. Even if we assume, as this writer does, that, in many ways, the church began anew at Pentecost, this is not to say that there were no OT intimations of the church or that there were no continuities with the OT.

The continuity term for the church in both Testaments is "the people of God." Even though we may distinguish a number of *aspects* of that one people, such as Israel or the church, yet as "people of God" all believers of all ages belong to *one* body. There are our continuities as well as a modified statement of our discontinuities.

The continuity term for the program of the church is the promise-plan of God. Some would have thought that we would have said the "kingdom of God," for that indeed is one of the largest parts of that plan. The point is, as I have already argued in my fourth chapter, that the announcement of the kingdom and its anointed King, Jesus the Messiah, rests on the basis of the divine promise and is itself even larger in its provisions and specifications than the themes of the kingdom and its King.

To be sure, Christ and his kingdom are central, but we need to know what is the all-embracing and the total plan of God that gathers up all its diverse parts. We must answer with the OT and NT writers: the promise-plan of God.

But this single, all-embracing promise-plan was itself made up of a vast multitude of parts. Again, we may speak of a number of *aspects* of that plan, even though the plan is *one*. Accordingly, the church had its roots in the OT. That is why Peter could preach that what had been revealed (aorist tense, i.e., at a set point in the past) in the OT was not only for the OT saints, but, declares Peter, the OT prophets spoke concerning "us," the NT church (1 Peter 1:12). Now there is a staggering thought for the exegete and theologian!

Consequently, we must resist the practical or theoretical temptation to say that the OT was Israel's mail addressed exclusively to them and of little or no relevance to the church. That attitude runs directly counter to the claims of the text and the fact that there is one God, one people, one body, one faith, and one hope. Nowhere does Scripture aid and abet those who wish to bifurcate or divide the peoples and the programs of God. A plurality of aspects in the one people and one plan? Yes! But a division in the plan or the body of believers? No!

WHAT IS THE CHALLENGE OF THE OT FOR MISSIONS?

For many, the heart of the missionary call is to be located in the "Great Commission" given in Matthew 28:18–20 or Mark 16:15–20. It all began there, concludes the average theologian and layperson.

On the contrary, missions and the challenge to call every individual in every nation to faith in God's anointed One has much earlier rootage. Already in Genesis 3:15 there were hints that God's method of rescuing an entrapped humanity would be from a male descendant of the woman. But if the pre-patriarchal texts merely hint at this fact, certainly Genesis 12:3 makes it a statement of fact.

That some promised male descendant was to be God's means of bringing "blessing" to all the families of the earth, Abraham was told in Genesis 12:3. In fact, a list of what was at that time some seventy nations, or families, of the earth had just been given in Genesis 10 in anticipation of this promise in Genesis 12:3. It was as if the mission field of the Gentiles had to be listed before the provision of God's medium of providing relief could be inscripturated in detail. But mark it well, the divine plan from earliest times envisaged the necessity of bringing all the nations of the earth to the same decision that Abraham also had to make. Only by so believing in that promised man of promise could we be said to be "Abraham's seed" or "belong to Christ" and thus "heirs according to the promise" (Gal 3:29).

The plainest OT statement of the gospel to which the nations of the earth were invited to respond was the promise that "All peoples on earth will be blessed through you" (Gen 12:3). Paul exclaimed in Galatians 3:8, "The Scripture [=OT] foresaw that God would justify the Gentiles by faith, and announced *the gospel* in advance to Abraham: 'All nations will be blessed through you'" (my emphasis).

Israel's task as part of that "seed," then, was to be "a light to the nations" (Isa 42:6 and 49:6 RSV), indeed, "a kingdom of priests" (Exod 19:5–6). Generally she failed in this mission more miserably than in any other task given to her, but the call, as is also true of us, was never anything less than this.

That is why the Psalmist urges "Praise the Lord, all you nations; extol him, all you peoples" (Ps 117:1). And the desire of the author of Psalm 67, twice repeated, is this: "May all the peoples praise you" (Ps 67:3, 5); promise theology, indeed, motivated Israel to enter into this task with an all-consuming zeal: "God will bless

189

us, and [so that] all the ends of the earth will fear him" (Ps 67:7). Missions remain a vital part of the OT challenge. Thus, if we are to understand the OT holistically, we dare not omit the call for an internationalization of the gospel. Missions are a real part of the OT.

Our conclusion, then, is that the OT must cease being a problem for the Christian. It is instead the Christian's most basic premise and deeply valued revelation from God. The difference between a strong, virile Christian faith and a gutless, mediocre, reductionistic Christianity is too striking to be left without a decision from the church in the last third of the twentieth century. The OT can and must be understood if it is properly to be appropriated in our day and age. Instead of concluding that the OT is THE Christian problem, may it instead become THE Christian challenge to understand it so that it might be appropriately related to each nuanced issue raised in our day.

Bibliography

1. The OT as the Christian Problem

Ackroyd, P. R. "The Old Testament in the Christian Church." *Theology* 66 (1963): 46–52.

————. "The Place of the Old Testament in the Church's Teaching and Worship." *Expository Times* 74 (1963): 164–67.

Alonso-Schokel, L. "The Old Testament, a Christian Book." *Biblica* 44 (1963): 210–16.

Amsler, S. *L'ancien Testament dans l'Eglise.* Neuchâtel, 1960.

Anderson, Bernhard W. "Introduction: The Old Testament as a Christian Problem." In *The Old Testament and Christian Faith*, ed. Bernhard W. Anderson. New York: Harper and Row, 1963.

Atkinson, B. F. C. *The Christian's Use of the Old Testament.* London: InterVarsity, 1952.

Auray, Paul. *L'ancien Testament et les chrétiens.* Paris: Les Éditions du Cerf, 1951.

Baker, D. L. *Two Testaments: One Bible.* Downers Grove: InterVarsity, 1976.

Barker, Kenneth L. "False Dichotomies Between the Testaments." *Journal of the Evangelical Theological Society* 25 (1982): 3–16.

Barr, James. *Old and New in Interpretation: A Study of the Two Testaments.* London: SCM, 1966.

Barry, G. R. "The Old Testament: A Liability or an Asset?" *Colgate Rochester Divinity School Bulletin* (1930): 8–22.

Baumgärtel, Friederich. *Verheissung: Zur Frage des evangelischen Verständnisses des Alten Testaments.* Gütersloh: C. Bertelsmann, 1952.

Bennett, W. H. *The Value of the Old Testament for the Religion of Today.* London: 1914.

Bentzen, A. "The Old Testament and the New Covenant." *Hervormde Teologiese Studies* 7 (1950): 1–15.

Betz, Otto. "The Problem of Variety and Unity in the New Testament." *Horizons in Biblical Theology* 2 (1980): 3–14.

Bewer, J. A. "The Christian Minister and the Old Testament." *Journal of Religion* 10 (1930): 16–21.

———. "The Authority of the Old Testament." *Journal of Religion* 16 (1936): 1–9.

Blackman, E. C. *Marcion and His Influence*. London: SPCK, 1948.

Boisset, J., et al. *Le Probleme Biblique dans le Protestantisme*. Paris: Presses Universitaires de France, 1955.

Bowden, John. *What About the Old Testament?* London: SCM, 1969.

Box, G. H. "The Value and Significance of the Old Testament in Relation to the New." In *The People and The Book*, ed. A. S. Peake. Cambridge: Clarendon, 1925.

Boyer, P. J. "The Value of the Old Testament: A German Estimate." *The Interpreter* 1 (1905): 258–63.

Bright, John. *The Authority of the Old Testament*. Nashville: Abingdon, 1967.

Bruce, F. F. *The Christian Approach to the Old Testament*. London: Inter-Varsity, 1955.

Brunner, Emil. "The Significance of the Old Testament for Our Faith." In *The Old Testament and Christian Faith*, ed. Bernhard W. Anderson, 243–64. New York: Harper and Row, 1963.

Bultmann, Rudolf. "The Significance of the Old Testament for the Christian Faith." In *The Old Testament and Christian Faith*, ed. Bernhard W. Anderson, 8–35. New York: Harper and Row, 1963.

Burney, C. F. *The Gospel in the Old Testament*. Edinburgh, 1921.

Cate, Robert L. *Old Testament Roots for Christian Faith*, 11–25. Nashville: Broadman, 1982.

Cazelles, H. "The Unity of the Bible and the People of God." *Scripture* 18 (1966): 1–10.

Congar, Y. M. J. "The Old Testament as a Witness to Christ." In *The Revelation of God*, 8–15. New York: Herder and Herder, 1968.

Childs, Brevard. "The Old Testament as Scripture of the Church." *Concordia Theological Monthly* 43 (1972): 709–22.

Coppens, J. *Vom christlichen Verstandnis des Alten Testaments*. Louvain: Publications Universitaires de Louvain, 1952.

Dentan, Robert C. "The Unity of the Old Testament." *Interpretation* 5 (1951): 153–73.

Dillenberger, J. "Revelational Discernment and the Problem of the Two Testaments." In *The Old Testament and Christian Faith*, ed. Bernhard W. Anderson, 159–75. New York: Harper and Row, 1963.

Driver, S. R. "The Moral and Devotional Value of the Old Testament." *Expository Times* 4 (1892): 110–13.

———. "The Permanent Religious Value of the Old Testament." *The Interpreter* 1 (1905): 10–21.

Duesberg, H. "He Opened Their Minds to Understand the Scriptures." *Concilium* 10 (1967): 56–61.

Fensham, F. C. "The Covenant as Giving Expression to the Relationship Between Old Testament and New Testament." *Tyndale Bulletin* 22 (1971): 82–94.

Filson, Floyd V. "The Unity of the Old and New Testaments: A Bibliographical Survey." *Interpretation* 5 (1951): 134–52.

Bibliography

――――. "The Unity Between the Testaments." In *The Interpreter's One-Volume Commentary on the Bible*, ed. Charles M. Laymon, 989–93. Nashville: Abingdon, 1972.

Goldingay, John. "'That You May Know that Yahweh is God': A Study in the Relationship Between Theology and Historical Truth in the Old Testament." *Tyndale Bulletin* 23 (1972): 58–93.

――――. "The Old Testament and Christian Faith: Jesus and the Old Testament in Matthew 1–5." *Themelios* 8 (1982): 4–10; 9 (1983): 5–12.

――――. "Diversity and Unity in Old Testament Theology." *Vetus Testamentum* 34 (1984): 153–68.

Grant, Robert. "The Place of the Old Testament in Early Christianity." *Interpretation* 5 (1951): 194–97.

Grelot, P. *Sens crétien de l'Ancien Testament: Esquisse d'un traite dogmatique.* Tournai: Deschlée and Cie, 1962.

Gunneweg, A. H. J. *Understanding the Old Testament.* Trans. John Bowden. Philadelphia: Westminster, 1978.

Hall, Basil. "The Old Testament in the History of the Church." *The London Quarterly and Holborn Review* 190 (1965): 30–36.

Hansen, Paul D. *The Diversity of Scripture.* Philadelphia: Westminster, 1982.

Hasel, Gerhard. "The Relationship Between the Testaments." In *Old Testament Theology: Basic Issues in the Current Debate.* 3d ed., ed. Gerhard Hasel, 145–67. Grand Rapids: Eerdmans, 1984.

Hebert, A. G. *The Authority of the Old Testament.* London: Faber and Faber, 1947.

Higgins, A. J. B. *The Christian Significance of the Old Testament.* London: 1949.

Hultgren, Arland J. "The Old Testament and the New." *Word and World* 3 (1983): 215–83.

Jasper, F. N. "Relation of the Old Testament to the New." *Expository Times* 78 (1967–68): 228–32; 267–70.

Kirkpatrick, A. F. "The Use of the Old Testament in the Christian Church." In *The Divine Library of the Old Testament*, 112–43. London: Macmillan, 1906.

Kraeling, Emil. *The Old Testament Since the Reformation.* New York: Harper, 1955.

Larcher, A. D. *L'Actualité chrétienne de l'Ancien Testament.* Paris: Les Editions du Cerf, 1962.

Lofthouse, W. F. "The Old Testament and Christianity." In *Record and Revelation*, ed. H. Wheeler Robinson, 458–80. Oxford: Clarendon, 1938.

Lohfink, N. *The Christian Meaning of the Old Testament.* London: Burns and Oates, 1969.

Lys, Daniel. *The Meaning of the Old Testament: An Essay in Hermeneutics.* Nashville: Abingdon, 1967.

McCausland, S. Vernon. "The Unity of the Scriptures." *Journal of Biblical Literature* 73 (1954): 1–10.

McDermet, William W., III. "The 'Old' Testament as Revelation for Contemporary People." *Encounter* 44 (1983): 291–99.

McKenzie, John L. "The Significance of the Old Testament for Christian Faith in Roman Catholicism." In *The Old Testament and Christian Faith*, ed. Bernhard W. Anderson, 102–14. New York: Harper and Row, 1963.

———. "The Values of the Old Testament." In *How Does the Christian Confront the Old Testament? Concilium 30*, ed. Pierre Benoit, Roland E. Murphy, and Bastiaan van Iersel, 5–32. New York: Paulist, 1967.

Manson, T. W. "The Old Testament in the Teaching of Jesus." *Bulletin of the John Rylands Library* 34 (1952): 312–32.

Mellor, E. B. "The Old Testament for Jews and Christians Today." In *The Making of the Old Testament*, ed. E. B. Mellor, 167–201. Cambridge: Cambridge University Press, 1972.

Mercer, J. E. "Is the Old Testament a Suitable Basis for Moral Instruction?" *Hibbert Journal* 7 (1909): 333–45.

Michaeli, F. *How to Understand the Old Testament*. London, 1961.

Mirtow, P. *Jesus and the Religion of the Old Testament*. London, 1957.

Mowinckel, Sigmund. *The Old Testament as Word of God*. Nashville: Abingdon, 1959.

Mozley, J. B. *Ruling Ideas in Early Ages and Their Relation to Old Testament Faith*. London, 1889.

Murphy, J. Roland E. "The Relationship Between the Testaments." *Catholic Biblical Quarterly* 26 (1964): 349–59.

———. "Christian Understanding of the Old Testament." *Theology Digest* 18 (1970): 321–32.

Nineham, S. E. (ed). *The Church's Use of the Bible*. London, 1963.

Orr, James. "The Old Testament Question in the Early Church." *The Expositor*. Fifth Series. (1895): 346–61.

O'Doherty, E. "The Unity of the Bible." *The Bible Today*. 1 (1962): 53–57.

Peake, A. S. "The Permanent Value of the Old Testament." In *The Nature of Scripture*, 137–98. London, 1922.

Porteous, N. W. "The Limits of Old Testament Interpretation." In *Proclamation and Presence: Old Testament Essays in Honor of G. Henton Davies*, ed. J. I. Durham and J. R. Porter, 3–17. London, 1950.

Reid, W. Stanford. "The New Testament Belief in an Old Testament Church." *Evangelical Quarterly* 24–25 (1952–53): 194–205.

Richardson, Alan. "Is the Old Testament Propaedeutic to Christian Faith?" In *The Old Testament and Christian Faith*, ed. Bernhard W. Anderson, 36–48. New York: Harper and Row, 1963.

Robinson, T. H. "Epilogue: The Old Testament and the Modern World." In *The Old Testament and Modern Study*, ed. H. H. Rowley, 345–71. London: Oxford University Press, 1967.

Rowley, H. H. "The Gospel in the Old Testament." In *The Enduring Gospel*, ed. R. Gregor Smith, 19–35. London: 1950.

———. *The Unity of the Bible*. London, 1953.

Ruler, A. A. van. *The Christian Church and the Old Testament*. Trans. Geoffrey W. Bromiley. Grand Rapids: Eerdmans, 1966.

Runia, Klaus. "The Interpretation of the Old Testament by the New Testament." *Theological Students' Fellowship Bulletin* 49 (1967): 9–18.

Rylaarsdam, J. C. "Jewish-Christian Relationships: The Two Covenants and the Dilemma of Christology." *Journal of Ecumenical Studies* 9 (1972): 249–68.

Saphir, Adolph. *Christ and the Scriptures*. London: Hodder and Stroughton, 1867.

Smart, James D. *The Interpretation of Scripture*, 65–92. Philadelphia: Westminster, 1962.

Smith, W. R. "The Attitude of Christians to the Old Testament." *The Expositor*, 2d ser., 7 (1884): 241–51.

Sparks, H. F. D. *The Old Testament in the Christian Church*. London, 1944.

Stamm, J. J. "Jesus Christ and the Old Testament: A Review of A. A. van Ruler's Book." In *Essays on Old Testament Hermeneutics*, ed. Claus Westermann, 200–210. Richmond: Knox, 1960.

Sundberg, A. C. *The Old Testament of the Early Church*. Cambridge: Harvard University Press, 1964.

_____. "The Old Testament of the Early Church." *Harvard Theological Review* 51 (1958): 205–26.

_____. "The 'Old Testament': A Christian Canon?" *Catholic Biblical Quarterly* 30 (1968): 143–55.

Tollinton, R. B. "The Two Elements in Marcion's Dualism." *Journal of Theological Studies* 17 (1916): 263–70.

Verhoef, Peter A. "The Relationship Between the Old and New Testament." In *New Perspectives on the Old Testament*, ed. J. Barton Payne, 280–303. Waco: Word, 1970.

Vischer, Wilhelm. "The Significance of the Old Testament for the Christian Life." *Proceedings of the Fourth Calvinistic Congress Held in Edinburgh 6th to 11th July 1938*, 237–60. Edinburgh: T. & T. Clark, 1938.

_____. "Everywhere the Scripture Is About Christ Alone." In *The Old Testament and Christian Faith*, ed. Bernhard W. Anderson, 90–101. New York: Harper and Row, 1963.

Waltke, Bruce K. "Is It Right to Read the New Testament Into the Old?" *Christianity Today* 27 (1983): 77.

Wiles, M. F. "The Old Testament in Controversy with the Jews." *Scottish Journal of Theology* 8 (1955): 113–26.

Wolf, H. W. "The Old Testament in Controversy: Interpretive Principles and Illustration." *Interpretation* 12 (1956): 281–91.

Woods, J. *The Old Testament in the Church*. London, 1949.

Wright, George Ernest. "Interpreting the Old Testament." *Theology Today* 3 (1946): 176–91.

_____. "The Problem of Archaizing Ourselves." *Interpretation* 3 (1949): 450–56.

Zyl, A. H. van. "The Relation Between the Old Testament and the New Testament." *Hermeneutica* (1970): 9–22.

2. The Old Testament as Part of the Canon

Anderson, G. N. "Canonical and Non-Canonical." In *The Cambridge History of the Bible. Vol. I: From the Beginning to Jerome*, ed. Peter R. Ackroyd and C. F. Evans, 113–59. Cambridge: Cambridge University Press, 1970.

Baldwin, Joyce G. "Is There Pseudonymity in the Old Testament?" *Themelios* 4 (1978): 6–12.

Brueggemann, W. "Canon and Dialectic." In *God and His Temple*, ed. L. E. Frizzell, 20–29. South Orange, N.J.: Institute of Judaeo-Christian Studies, 1981.

Toward Rediscovering the Old Testament

Buhl, F. *Canon and Text of the Old Testament.* Trans. J. McPherson. Edinburgh, 1892.

Campenhausen, Hans von. *The Formation of the Christian Bible.* Philadelphia: Fortress, 1977.

Childs, Brevard S. "The Hebrew Scriptures and the Hebrew Bible." In *Introduction to the Old Testament As Scripture,* 659–761. Philadelphia: Fortress, 1979.

Christie, W. M. "The Jamnia Period in Jewish History." *Journal of Theological Studies,* n.s. 1 (1950): 135–54.

Dunbar, David G. "The Biblical Canon." In *Hermeneutics, Authority, and Canon,* ed. D. A. Carson and John D. Woodbridge, 299–360. Grand Rapids: Zondervan, 1986.

Dunn, James D. G. "Levels of Canonical Authority." *Bible Translator* 4 (1982): 13–60.

Eybers, Ian H. *Historical Evidence on the Canon of the Old Testament With Special Reference to the Qumran Sect.* Ann Arbor: University Microfilms, 1966.

Filson, F. V. *Which Books Belong in the Bible? A Study of the Canon.* Philadelphia: Westminster, 1957.

Gaussen, L. *The Canon of the Holy Scriptures.* Boston: American Tract Society, 1862.

Harris, R. Laird. *Inspiration and Canonicity of the Bible.* Grand Rapids: Zondervan, 1957.

Hebert, A. G. "The Completion of the Canon and the Old Testament in the New." In *The Authority of the Old Testament,* 165–225. London: Faber and Faber, 1978.

Katz, P. "The Old Testament Canon in Palestine and Alexandria." *Zeitschrift für die neutestamentliche Wissenschaft* 47 (1956): 191–217.

Kline, Meredith G. "Canon and Covenant: Part I." *Westminster Theological Journal* 32 (1969–70): 49–67.

———. "Canon and Covenant: Part II." *Westminster Theological Journal* 32 (1969–70): 179–200.

Leiman, Sid Z. *The Canonization of the Hebrew Scriptures: The Talmudic and Midrashic Evidence.* Hamden, Conn.: Archon, 1976.

Lewis, Jack P. "What Do We Mean By Jabneh?" *Journal of Bible and Religion* 32 (1964): 125–32.

Lightstone, Jack N. "The Formation of the Biblical Canon in Judaism of Late Antiquity: Prolegomena to a General Reassessment." *Studies in Religion* 8 (1979): 135–42.

Mandel, Hugo. "The Nature of the Great Synagogue." *Harvard Theological Review* 60 (1967): 69–91.

Newman, R. C. "The Council of Jamnia and the Old Testament Canon." *Westminster Theological Journal* 38 (1975–76): 319–49.

Ridderbos, N. H. "Canon of the Old Testament." In *The New Bible Dictionary,* ed. J. D. Douglas, 186–94. Grand Rapids: Eerdmans, 1962.

Roberts, B. J. "The Old Testament Canon: A Suggestion." *Bulletin of John Rylands Library* 46 (1963): 164–78.

196

Bibliography

Ryle, Herbert E. *The Canon of the Old Testament*. 2d ed. London: Macmillan, 1885.

Sheppard, Gerald T. "Canonization: Hearing the Voice of the Same God Through Historically Dissimilar Traditions." *Interpretation* 36 (1982): 21–33.

Stevenson, Dwight E. "How a Writing Becomes Scripture." *Lexington Theological Quarterly* 17 (1982): 59–66.

Sundberg, A. C. "The Old Testament: A Christian Canon?" *Catholic Biblical Quarterly* 30 (1968): 143–55.

_____. "The Old Testament of the Early Church." *Harvard Theological Review* 51 (1958): 205–26.

_____. *The Old Testament of the Early Church*. Cambridge: Harvard University Press, 1964.

Swanson, Theodore N. *The Closing of the Collection of Holy Scripture: A Study of the History of the Canonization of the Old Testament*. Ann Arbor: University Microfilms, 1970.

Thieme, R. B. *Canonicity*. Houston: The Author, 1973.

3. The Old Testament as an Object of Criticism

Armerding, Carl E. *The Old Testament and Criticism*. Grand Rapids: Eerdmans, 1983.

Baker, David W. "The Old Testament and Criticism." *Journal of Theological Studies* 48 (1984): 13–20.

Barton, John. *Reading the Old Testament: Method in Biblical Study*. Philadelphia: Westminster, 1984.

Best, E. "The Literal Meaning of Scripture, The Historical-Critical Method and the Interpretation of Scripture." *Proceedings of the Irish Biblical Association*. 5 (1981): 14–35.

Blenkinsopp, Joseph. "The Documentary Hypothesis in Trouble." *Bible Review* 1 (1985): 22–32.

Bromiley, G. W. "History and Truth: A Study of the Axiom of Lessing." *Evangelical Quarterly* 18 (1946): 191–98.

Brown, Colin, ed. *History, Criticism and Faith*. 2d ed. Downers Grove: Inter-Varsity, 1977.

Clements, Ronald E. "History and Theology in Biblical Narrative." *Horizons in Biblical Theology* 4 (1982): 45–60.

Ebeling, G. "The Significance of the Critical Historical Method for Church and Theology in Protestantism." In *Word and Faith*, 17–61. London, 1963.

Edwards, O. C. "Historical-Critical Method's Failure of Nerve and a Prescription for a Tonic." *Anglican Theological Review* 59 (1977): 115–34.

Gilkey, L. B. "Cosmology, Ontology and the Travail of Biblical Language." *Journal of Religion* 41 (1961): 194–205.

Johnson, Alan F. "The Historical-Critical Method: Egyptian Gold or Pagan Precipice?" *Journal of the Evangelical Theological Society* 26 (1983): 3–15.

Kaufman, Stephen A. "The Temple Scroll and Higher Criticism." *Hebrew Union College Annual* 53 (1982): 24–43.

Kelly, George A. *The New Biblical Theorists: Raymond E. Brown and Beyond.* Ann Arbor: Servant, 1983.

Kikawada, Isaac M. and Arthur Quinn. *Before Abraham Was: The Unity of Genesis 1–11.* Nashville: Abingdon, 1985.

Klaaren, Eugene M. "A Critical Appreciation of Hans Frei's *Eclipse of Biblical Narrative." Union Theological Seminary* 37 (1983): 283–97.

Kugel, James. "On the Bible and Literary Criticism." *Proof Texts: A Journal of Jewish Life and History* 1 (1981): 217–36.

Long, Valentine. "Higher Criticism Has Gone Bankrupt." *Homiletical and Pastoral Review* 83 (1982–83): 50–57.

Maier, Gerhard. *The End of the Historical-Critical Method.* Trans. Edwin W. Leverenz and Rudolph F. Norden. St. Louis: Concordia, 1977.

Nations, Archie L. "Historical Criticism and the Current Methodological Crisis." *Scottish Journal of Theology* 36 (1983): 59–71.

Peters, Ted. "The Use of Analogy in the Historical Method." *Catholic Biblical Quarterly* 35 (1973): 475–82.

Purunak, H. van Dyke. "Some Axioms for Literary Architecture." *Semitics* 8 (1982): 1–16.

Ramsey, George W. *The Quest for the Historical Israel.* Atlanta: Knox, 1981.

Steinmetz, David C. "The Superiority of Pre-Critical Exegesis." *Theology Today* 37 (1980): 27–38.

Stuhlmacher, Peter. *Historical Criticism and Theological Interpretation of Scripture.* Trans. Roy A. Harrisville. Philadelphia: Fortress, 1977.

Vicary, D. K. "Liberalism, Biblical Criticism, and Biblical Theology." *Anglican Theological Review* 34 (1950): 114–21.

Wenham, Gordon. "History and the Old Testament." In *History, Criticism and Faith*, ed. Colin Brown, 13–78. Downers Grove: InterVarsity, 1977.

West, Cornel. "On Frei's Eclipse of Biblical Narrative." *Union Seminary Quarterly Review* 37 (1983): 299–302.

White, Leland J. "Historical and Literary Criticism: A Theological Response." *Biblical Theology Bulletin* 13 (1983): 32–34.

Wink, Walter. *The Bible in Human Transformation: Toward a New Paradigm for Biblical Study.* Philadelphia: Fortress, 1973.

4. The Old Testament as the Promise-Plan of God

Beecher, Willis J. *The Prophets and The Promise.* Grand Rapids: Baker, 1976.

Blythin, Islwyn. "The Patriarchs and the Promise." *Scottish Journal of Theology.* 21 (1968): 56–73.

Bright, John. *Covenant and Promise: the Future in the Preaching of the Pre-Exilic Prophets.* Philadelphia: Westminster, 1976.

Clines, David J. A. *The Theme of the Pentateuch*, 31–60. Sheffield, England: University of Sheffield, 1978.

Fensham, F. Charles. "Covenant, Promise and Expectation in the Bible." *Theologische Zeitschrift* 5 (1967): 305–22.

Funderburk, G. B. "Promise." In *The Zondervan Pictorial Encyclopedia of the Bible*, ed. Merrill C. Tenney, 5 vols., 4:872–74. Grand Rapids: Zondervan, 1975.

Bibliography

Hoffman, E. "Promise." In *The New International Dictionary of New Testament Theology*, ed. Colin Brown, 3 vols., 3:68–74. Grand Rapids: Zondervan, 1979.

Kaiser, Walter C., Jr. *Toward an Old Testament Theology*. Grand Rapids: Zondervan, 1978.

McCurley, Foster, R., Jr. "The Christian and the Old Testament Promise." *Lutheran Quarterly* 22 (1970): 401–10.

Premsager, P. V. "Theology of Promise in the Patriarchal Narratives." *Indian Journal of Theology* 23 (1974): 112–22.

Ramlot, Marie-Léon and Jean Giblet. "Promises." In *Dictionary of Biblical Theology*, ed. Xavier Leon-Dufour, trans. P. Joseph Cahill, 411–13. New York: Desclee, 1967.

Schniewind, Julius, and Friedrich, Gerhard. "Epangellō, epangelia." In *Theological Dictionary of the New Testament*, ed. Gerhard Kittel and Gerhard Friedrich, 2:576–86. Grand Rapids: Eerdmans, 1964.

Smith, Wilbur M. "Promise." In *Evangelical Dictionary of Theology*, ed. Walter A. Elwell, 885–86. Grand Rapids: Baker, 1984.

Westermann, Claus. "The Way of Promise Through the Old Testament." In *The Old Testament and Christian Faith*, ed. Bernhard W. Anderson, 200–224. New York: Harper and Row, 1963.

5. The Old Testament as a Messianic Primer

Baron, David. *Rays of Messiah's Glory: Christ in the Old Testament*. 1886. Reprint. Grand Rapids: Zondervan, n.d.

Bartling, Victor A. "Christ's Use of the Old Testament With Special Reference to the Pentateuch." *Concordia Theological Monthly* 36 (1965): 567–76.

Becker, Joachim. *Messianic Expectation in the Old Testament*. Trans. David E. Green. Philadelphia: Fortess, 1980.

____. "Das historische Bild der messianischen Erwartung im Alten Testament." In *Testimonium veritati*, ed. Hans Wolter. *Frankfurter theologische Studien* 7 (1971): 125–41.

Borland, James A. *Christ in the Old Testament*. Chicago: Moody, 1978.

Briggs, Charles Augustus. *Messianic Prophecy*. New York: Scribner, 1889.

Brown, John. *The Sufferings and Glories of the Messiah*. Byron Center, Mich.: Sovereign Grace, 1970.

Caquot, André. "Peut-on parlez de messianisme dans l'oeuvre du Chroniste?" *Revue de theologie et de philosophie* 99 (1966): 110–20.

Cooper, David L. *Messiah: His First Coming Scheduled*. Los Angeles: Biblical Research Society, 1939.

Coppens, Joseph. *Le messianisme royal*. Lectio divina 54. Paris: Editions du Cerf, 1968.

____. "La relève du messianisme royal." *Ephemerides theologicae Louvanienses* 47 (1971): 117–43.

Duesberg, Hilaire. "He Opened Their Minds to Understand the Scriptures." In *How Does the Christian Confront the Old Testament?* ed. Pierre Benoit, Roland E. Murphy, and Bastiaan van Iersel, 111–21. New York: Paulist, 1967.

Dexinger, Ferdinand. "Die Entwicklung des jüdisch-christlichen Messianismus." *Bibel and Liturgie* 47 (1974): 5–31, 239–66.

Ellison, H. L. *The Centrality of the Messianic Idea for the Old Testament.* London: Tyndale, 1957.

Fischer, John. *The Olive Tree Connection.* Downers Grove: InterVarsity, 1983.

Fohrer, Georg. "Das Alte Testament und das Thema 'Christologie'." *Evangelische Theologie* 30 (1970): 281–98.

France, R. T. *Jesus and the Old Testament.* London: Tyndale, 1971.

Fruchtenbaum, Arnold G. "Messianism." In *Hebrew Christianity: Its Theology, History, and Philosophy.* Washington, D.C.: Canon, n.d. (52–58).

Gray, G. B. "The References to the 'King' in the Psalter in their Bearing on the Questions of Date and Messianic Belief." *Jewish Quarterly Review* 7 (1895): 658–86.

Grech, Prosper. "The Old Testament as a Christological Source in the Apostolic Age." *Biblical Theology Bulletin* 5 (1975): 127–45.

Grelot, Pierre. "Le Messie dans les apocryphes de l'Ancien Testament." In *La venue du Messie,* ed. É. Massaux et al. *Recherches bibliques* 6 (1962): 19–50.

Gorgulho, Luiz Bertrando. "Ruth et la 'Fille de Sion,' mère du Messie." *Revue Thomiste* 63 (1963): 501–14.

Hagner, Donald A. *The Jewish Proclamation of Jesus.* Grand Rapids: Zondervan, 1984.

Hebert, A. G. *The Throne of David.* London: Faber and Faber, 1941.

Hengstenberg, E. W. *Christology of the Old Testament.* Abr. T. K. Arnold. 1847. Reprint. Grand Rapids: Kregel, 1970.

Hummel, Horace D. "Christological Interpretation of the Old Testament." *Dialog* 2 (1963): 108–17.

Kac, Arthur W. *The Messianic Hope: Divine Solution for the Human Problem.* Grand Rapids: Baker, 1975.

Kaiser, Walter C., Jr. "Messianic Prophecies in the Old Testament." In *Dreams, Visions and Oracles: The Layman's Guide to Biblical Prophecy,* ed. Carl Armerding and W. Ward Gasque, 75–88. Grand Rapids: Baker, 1977.

Kellermann, Ulrich. *Messias and Gesetz. Biblische Studien.* Neukirchen: Neukirken Verlag, 1971.

King, Nicholas. "Expectation: Jesus in the Old Testament." *Way* 21 (1981): 14–21.

Knierim, Rolf. "Die Messianologie des ersten Buchen Samuel." *Evangelische Theologie* 30 (1970): 113–33.

Lapide, Pinchas. *The Resurrection of Jesus: A Jewish Perspective.* Minneapolis: Augsburg, 1983.

LaSor, William S. "The Messiah: An Evangelical Christian View." In *Evangelicals and Jews in Conversation: On Scripture, Theology and History,* ed. Marc H. Tanenbaum, Marvin R. Wilson, and A. James Rudin, 76–97. Grand Rapids: Baker, 1978.

Levey, Samson H. *The Messiah: An Aramaic Interpretation: The Messianic Exegesis of the Targum.* Cincinnati: Hebrew Union College, 1974.

MacKay, W. M. "Messiah in the Psalms." *Evangelical Quarterly* 11 (1939): 153–64.

Mackenzie, Roderick A. F. "The Messianism of Deuteronomy." *Catholic Biblical Quarterly* 19 (1957): 299–305.

Manson, T. W. "The Old Testament in the Teaching of Jesus." *Bulletin of John Rylands Library* 34 (1951–52): 312–32.

Martin, Ralph A. "The Earliest Messianic Interpretation of Genesis 3:15." *Journal of Biblical Literature* 84 (1965): 425–27.

Mowinckel, Sigmund. *He that Cometh.* Trans. G. W. Anderson. Oxford: Blackwell, 1956.

Murray, John. "Christ and the Scriptures." *Christianity Today* (May 13, 1957): 15–17.

Neusner, Jacob. *Messiah in Context: Israel's History and Destiny in Formative Judaism.* Philadelphia: Fortress, 1984.

Nichols, Aidan. "Imagination and Revelation: The Face of Christ in the Old Testament." *Way* 21 (1981): 270–71.

Patai, Raphael. *The Messiah Texts.* New York: Avon, 1979.

Preus, James S. "Old Testament *Promissio* and Luther's New Hermeneutic." *Harvard Theological Review* 60 (1967): 145–61.

Ringgren, Helmer. *The Messiah in the Old Testament.* Chicago: Allenson, 1956.

Rivkin, Ellis. "The Meaning of Messiah in Jewish Thought." In *Evangelicals and Jews in Conversation: On Scripture, Theology, and History,* ed. H. Tanenbaum, Marvin R. Wilson, and A. James Rudin, 54–75. Grand Rapids: Baker, 1978.

Schoenfield, Hugh J. *The History of Jewish Christianity: From the First to the Twentieth Century.* London: Duckworth, 1936.

Siebeneck, Robert T. "The Messianism of Aggeus and Proto-Zacharias." *Catholic Biblical Quarterly* 19 (1957): 312–38.

Talmon, Shmarjahu. "Typen der Messiaserwartung um die Zeitenwende." In *Probleme biblischer Theologie,* 571–88. Germany: Chr. Kaiser Verlang München, 1971.

Thomson, J. G. S. S. "Christ and the Old Testament." *Expository Times* 67 (1955): 18–20.

Tournay, Raymond. "Les affinités du Ps XLV avec le Cantique des Cantiques et leurs interprétation messianique." In Congress Volume, *Supplements to Vetus Testamentum* 9 (1962): 168–212.

Welch, A. C. *The Preparation For Christ in the Old Testament.* Edinburgh: 1933.

Zerafa, O. P. "Christological Interpretation of the Old Testament." *Angelicum* 41 (1964): 51–62.

_____. "Priestly Messianism in the Old Testament." *Angelicum* 42 (1965): 315–45.

6. *The Old Testament as the Plan of Salvation*

Abba, Raymond. "The Origin and Significance of Hebrew Sacrifice." *Biblical Theology Bulletin* 7 (1977): 123–38.

Armerding, Carl. "The Holy Spirit in the Old Testament." *Bibliotheca Sacra* 92 (1935): 277–91; 433–41.

Barre, M. L. "A Note on Job XIX.25." *Vetus Testamentum* 29 (1979): 107–10.

Birkeland, Harris. "Belief in the Resurrection of the Dead in the Old Testament." *Studia Theologica* 3 (1950): 60–78.

Blumenthal, David R. "A Play on Words in the Nineteenth Chapter of Job." *Vetus Testamentum* 16 (1966): 497–501.

Dahood, Mitchell. "Death, Resurrection and Immortality." In *The Anchor Bible: Psalms III (101–150)*, xli-lii. Garden City: Doubleday, 1970.

Davis, John D. "The Future Life in Hebrew Thought." *Princeton Theological Review* 6 (1908): 246–68.

Denton, D. R. "The Biblical Basis of Hope." *Themelios* 5 (1980): 19–27.

Erlandsson, Seth. "Faith in the Old and New Testaments: Harmony or Disagreement?" *Concordia Theological Quarterly* 47 (1983): 1–14.

Freeman, Hobart E. "The Problem of Efficacy of the Old Sacrifices." *Bulletin of the Evangelical Theological Society* 5 (1962): 73–79.

Grogan, Geoffrey W. "The Experience of Salvation in the Old and New Testaments." *Vox Evangelica* 5 (1967): 4–26.

Harris, R. Laird. "The Meaning of Sheol as Shown By Parallels in Poetic Texts." *Bulletin of the Evangelical Theological Society* 4 (1961): 129–35.

Heick, Otto W. "If a Man Die, Will He Live Again?" *Lutheran Quarterly* 17 (1965): 99–110.

Heras, Henry. "Standard of Job's Immortality." *Catholic Biblical Quarterly* 11 (1949): 263–79.

Honsey, Rudolph E. "An Exegetical Paper on Job 19:23–27." *Wisconsin Lutheran Quarterly* 67 (1970): 172–84.

Hummel, Horace D. "Justification in the Old Testament." *Concordia Journal* 9 (1983): 9–17.

Irwin, William A. "Job's Redeemer." *Journal of Biblical Literature* 81 (1962): 217–29.

John, E. C. "The Old Testament Understanding of Death." *Indian Journal of Theology* 23 (1974): 123–28.

Kuyper, Lester J. "Righteousness and Salvation." *Scottish Journal of Theology* 30 (1977): 233–52.

Kuzhivelil, Matthew V. "Reconciliation in the Old Testament." *Biblebhashyan* 9 (1983): 168–78.

Lewis, Arthur H. "The New Birth Under the Old Covenant." *Evangelical Quarterly* 56 (1984): 35–44.

Logan, Norman A. "The Old Testament and a Future Life." *Scottish Journal of Theology* 6 (1953): 164–72.

Meek, Theophile J. "Job XIX.25–27." *Vetus Testamentum* 6 (1956): 100–103.

Meitzen, Manfred O. "Some Reflections on the Resurrection and Eternal Life." *Lutheran Quarterly* 24 (1972): 254–60.

Orr, James. "Immortality in the Old Testament." In *Classical Evangelical Essays in Old Testament Interpretation*, ed. Walter C. Kaiser, Jr., 253–65. Grand Rapids: Baker, 1972.

Otwell, John. "Immortality in the Old Testament." *Encounter* 22 (1961): 15–27.

Reist, Irwin. "Old Testament Basis for Resurrection Faith." *Evangelical Quarterly* 43 (1971): 6–24.

Ridenhour, Thomas E. "Immortality and Resurrection in the Old Testament." *Dialogue* 15 (1976): 104–9.

Rowley, Harold H. "Future Life in the Thought of the Old Testament." *Congregational Quarterly* 33 (1955): 116–32.

Bibliography

Sawyer, John F. A. "Hebrew Words for the Resurrection of the Dead." *Vetus Testamentum* 23 (1973): 218–34.

Schep, J. A. *The Nature of the Resurrection Body*, 17–63. Grand Rapids: Eerdmans, 1964.

Schoors, Antoon. "Koheleth: A Perspective on Life After Death?" *Ephemrides Theologicae Louvanienses* 61 (1985): 295–303.

Smick, Elmer. "Bearing of New Philological Data on the Subjects of Resurrection and Immortality in the Old Testament." *Westminster Theological Journal* 31 (1968): 12–21.

Westall, M. R. "The Scope of the Term 'Spirit of God' in the Old Testament." *Indian Journal of Theology* 26 (1977): 29–43.

Wood, Leon J. *The Holy Spirit in the Old Testament*. Grand Rapids: Zondervan, 1976.

Zink, James K. "Salvation in the Old Testament: A Central Theme." *Encounter* 25 (1964): 405–14.

7. The Old Testament as a Way of Life

Bahnsen, Greg L. *Theonomy in Christian Ethics*. Phillipsburg: Presbyterian and Reformed, 1984.

Barton, John. "Understanding Old Testament Ethics." *Journal for the Study of the Old Testament* 9 (1978): 44–64.

_____. "Approaches to Ethics in the Old Testament." In *Beginning Old Testament Study*, ed. John Rogerson, 113–30. Philadelphia: Westminster, 1982.

Bosman, H. L. "Taking Stock of Old Testament Ethics." *Old Testament Essays* 1 (1983): 97–104.

Freedman, Benjamin. "Leviticus and DNA: A Very Old Look at a Very New Problem." *Journal of Religious Ethics* 8 (1980): 105–13.

Harris, R. Laird, "Theonomy in Christian Ethics: A Review of Greg L. Bahnsen's Book." *Covenant Seminary Review* 5 (1979): 1ff.

Hayes, John H. "Restitution, Forgiveness and the Victim in Old Testament Law." *Trinity University Studies in Religion* 11 (1982): 1–21.

Kaiser, Walter C., Jr., *Toward Old Testament Ethics*. Grand Rapids: Zondervan, 1983.

Kline, Meredith G. "Comments on an Old-New Error." *Westminster Theological Journal* 41 (1978): 172–89.

Lightner, Robert P. "Theonomy and Dispensationalism." *Bibliotheca Sacra* 143 (1986): 26–36.

_____. "Nondispensational Responses to Theonomy." *Bibliotheca Sacra* 143 (1986): 134–45.

_____. "A Dispensational Response to Theonomy." *Bibliotheca Sacra* 143 (1986): 228–45.

McKeating, H. "Sanctions Against Adultery in Ancient Israelite Society with Some Reflections on Methodology in the Study of Old Testament Ethics." *Journal for the Study of Old Testament*. 11 (1979): 57–72.

Vellanickal, Matthew. "Norm of Morality According to the Scripture." *Biblebhashyam* 7 (1981): 121–46.

Wright, David. "The Ethical Use of the Old Testament in Luther and Calvin: A Comparison." *Scottish Journal of Theology* 36 (1983): 463–85.

8. *The Old Testament as an Object of Proclamation*

Achtemeier, Elizabeth. *The Old Testament and The Proclamation of the Gospel.* Philadelphia: Westminster, 1973.

———. "The Relevance of the Old Testament for Christian Preaching." In *A Light Unto My Path*, ed. Howard N. Bream, Ralph D. Heim, and Carey A. Moore, 3–24. Philadelphia: Temple University, 1974.

Bjornard, R. B. "Christian Preaching From the Old Testament." *Review and Expositor* 56 (1959): 8–19.

Bock, Darrell L. "Evangelicals and the Use of the Old Testament in the New." *Bibliotheca Sacra* 142 (1985): 209–23, 306–19.

Clowney, Edmund P. *Preaching and Biblical Theology.* Grand Rapids: Eerdmans, 1961.

Davidson, A. B. "The Uses of the Old Testament for Edification." *Expositor*, 6th ser., 1 (1900): 1–18.

DeGraff, A. H. and C. G. Seerveld. *Understanding the Scriptures: How to Read and How Not to Read the Bible.* Toronto: Association for the Advancement of Christian Scholarship, 1968.

Dreyfus, F. "L'actualisation à l'interieur de la Bible." *Revue Biblique* 83 (1976): 161–202.

Ford, D. W. Cleverly. *New Preaching From the Old Testament.* London: Mowbrays, 1976.

Fretheim, Terence. "The Old Testament in Christian Proclamation." *Word and World* 3 (1983): 223–30.

Gowan, Donald E. *Reclaiming the Old Testament for the Christian Pulpit.* Atlanta: Knox, 1980.

Graesser, Carl, Jr. "Preaching from the Old Testament." *Concordia Theological Monthly* 38 (1967): 525–34.

Greidanus, Sidney. *Sola Scriptura: Problems and Principles in Preaching Historical Texts.* Toronto: Wedge, 1970.

Johnson, Elliott E. "Dual Authorship and the Single Intended Meaning of Scripture." *Bibliotheca Sacra* 143 (1986): 218–27.

Juel, Donald H. "The Old Testament in Christian Proclamation—A New Testament Perspective." *Word and World* 3 (1983): 231–37.

Kromminga, Carl G. "Remember Lot's Wife: Preaching Old Testament Narrative Texts." *Calvin Theological Journal* 18 (1983): 32–46.

McCurley, F. R., Jr. *Proclaiming the Promise: Christian Preaching from the Old Testament.* Nashville: Abingdon, 1967.

McDermet, William W. III. "The Old Testament as Revelation For Contemporary People." *Encounter* 44 (1983): 291–99.

Marcus, R. A. "Presuppositions of the Typological Approach to Scripture." *Church Quarterly Review* 158 (1957): 442–50.

Mayer, H. T. "The Old Testament in the Pulpit." *Concordia Theological Monthly* 35 (1964): 603–8.

Bibliography

Read, D. H. C. "The Old Testament and Modern Preaching." *Union Seminary Quarterly Review* 12 (1957): 11–15.

Schneiders, Sandra M. "From Exegesis to Hermeneutics: The Problem of the Contemporary Meaning of Scripture." *Horizons* 8 (1981): 23–39.

Seerveld, C. G. *Balaam's Apocalyptic Prophecies: A Study in Reading Scripture.* Toronto: Wedge, 1980.

Smith, George Adam. "Modern Criticism and the Preaching of the Old Testament." *Expository Times* 90 (1979): 100–104.

Tison, Everett. "Homiletical Resources: Interpretation of Old Testament Readings for Easter." *Quarterly Review* 4 (1984): 55–90.

Toombs, L. E. *The Old Testament in Christian Preaching.* Philadelphia: Westminster, 1961.

———. "The Old Testament in the Christian Pulpit." *Hartford Quarterly* 8 (1968): 7–14.

———. "The Problematic Preaching From the Old Testament." *Interpretation* 23 (1969): 302–14.

Wolf, Hans Walter. *The Old Testament and Christian Preaching.* Philadelphia: Fortress, 1986.

Scripture Index

OLD TESTAMENT

Scripture Index

209

APOCRYPHA

NEW TESTAMENT

Author Index

213

Author Index

Subject Index

Allegorization, 19, 24, 170, 174
Amoraim, 42
Antecedent Scripture(s), 25, 26, 48, 104, 128, 157. *See also* Informing theology
Argumentation, method of, 68
Atbash, 174
Atonement, 26
Authorial intention, 77
Authority of the OT, 10, 15, 22
  formal question, 10, 14, 17, 22, 147
  material question, 10, 14, 17, 22, 147

Baba Bathra, 41, 42, 43, 108
Baraitha, 42
Ben Sirach, 43, 46
Bible. *See* Inspiration of Scripture; Revelation, divine; Scripture
Blessing, 24, 26, 49, 91–92, 93–94, 98, 114, 115, 117, 118, 124, 128, 150, 154, 182, 189–90

Cainites, 19–20, 22
Canonicity, 9
  canon within a canon, 24, 58
  of the OT, 10, 35–46
Catholicity, 17
Center of OT theology, 83–88
Christoexclusivism, 18
Church and Israel, 17
Continuity between the Testaments, 95–100, 188
Covenant, 85, 90–91, 94, 95, 120, 150
  Abrahamic, 51, 57, 149–55
  administrative, 153
  conditionality of, 50–51, 150–55
  Davidic, 51, 57, 149–55

everlasting, 49, 56, 119
Mosaic, 93, 149–55
New, 25, 35, 50, 51, 56, 57, 96, 159–55
Noahic, 51
of the New Heavens and the New Earth, 51
unconditionality of, 50–51, 150–55
Covenant Code, 163, 173
Covenant theology, 121
Criticism, biblical, 60
  anatomy of, 68–72
  assumptions of, 60
  definition of, 60
Criticism, historical, 60–67
Culture, theology of, 18
Cumulative fulfillment, 98

Day of Atonement, 133
Demiruge, 19, 21, 23
Didache, 41
Discontinuity between the Testaments, 95–100, 188
Discrepancies in Scripture, 69
Doctrine of correspondence, 170

Ebionites, 20–21, 22
Eisegesis, 58, 88, 174, 176
Epistemological question, the, 86–87
Exegesis, 48, 53, 88, 96, 100, 103, 125, 172, 174, 176, 177. *See also* Pesher exegesis

Faith in the OT, object of, 11, 122–28
Forgiveness, 11, 133–35

Gemarah, 42
Generality, levels of, 159

217

218